*England is a small island.*
*The world is infinitesimal.*
*But London is illimitable.*

Ford Madox Ford
*The Soul of London*

# Waterstone's Guide to London Writing

*Edited by Nick Rennison*

WATERSTONE'S GUIDES SERIES EDITOR
*Nick Rennison*

# Contents

# Introduction

This guide attempts the impossible. Ford Madox Ford wrote in his book *The Soul of London*, 'London is illimitable.' If this is true of the city itself, it is equally true of the writing that it has inspired. Yet the guide had to set limits. To limit the guide to what is in print and readily available was not a choice. Too many great London books, from Gerald Kersh's *Fowler's End* to Michael Moorcock's *Mother London* are currently out of print. To limit the guide to books of this century was an option. But what sort of guide to London writing excludes Pepys and Dickens? In the end the limits imposed were, perhaps necessarily, somewhat arbitrary. After all the idea of London writing is itself somewhat arbitrary. Not all fiction set in London is, by virtue of its setting alone, to be defined as 'London' fiction. How 'London' fiction *is* to be defined is a matter for endless but enjoyable debate. It may be an elusive concept but there is something about the way novels as different as *Mrs Dalloway* and *White Chappell, Scarlet Tracings, Hawksmoor* and *New Grub Street* treat the city and urban life that makes it one worth pursuing. *The Waterstone's Guide to London Writing* has had limits imposed by its length. There are only so many writers you can highlight in 200 pages. It has limits imposed by genre. It was decided that it would include fiction, poetry, drama and memoirs but not, for instance, any of the rich tradition of topographical and architectural writing on the city. Finally it had limits imposed by the Waterstone's booksellers who have, largely, written it. Their particular interests and enthusiasms inform every page of the guide. Comprehensiveness in a guide to London writing is an impossible goal. Another guide could have been produced, with 200 pages devoted to an entirely different choice of writers. However, if this guide leads people who might not otherwise have read them to novelists like Gerald Kersh and Iain Sinclair, Patrick Hamilton and Henry Green, if it persuades people that Mayhew and Maclaren-Ross, Boswell and Frank Norman are worth further investigation, if (who knows?) it convinces some enlightened publisher to issue a new selection from William Hickey's Memoirs or a new edition of Maureen Duffy's London tryptych of novels, it will have done its job.

*We would like to thank the National Museum of Photography, Film and Television for their help with photographs of 20th Century London.*

# London before the Great Fire

Wenceslaus Hollar's
1647 panorama of
London, courtesy of
the Guildhall Library,
Corporation of London

*A scattered town, spotted as thick with gardens as a common meadow is with daisies. Hovels stood cheek by jowl with stately monasteries, and the fortified mansions in the narrow City lanes were surrounded by citizens' stalls and shops. Westminster Palace, out in the suburbs among fields and marshes, was joined to the City walls by that long, straggling street of bishops' and nobles' palaces, called the Strand. The Tower and the Savoy were still royal residences. In all the West-end beyond Charing Cross, and in all the north of London beyond Clerkenwell and Holborn, cows and horses grazed, milkmaids sang and ploughmen whistled. There was danger in St. John's Wood and Tyburn Fields, and robbers on Hampstead Heath. The heron could be found in Marylebone pastures, and moorhens in the brooks round Paddington.*

Description of London in the reigns of Edward IV and Richard II taken from *Old and New London* by Walter Thornbury.

*Then to the Chepe I began me drawne,*
*Where mutch people I saw for to stande;*
*One offered me velvet, sylke, and lawne,*
*And other he taketh me by the hande,*
*"Here is Parys thred, the finest in the Lande"*

John Lydgate – London Likpenny

# From Courtly Grace to City Verse

*Poet and critic Neil Powell traces the slow emergence of a distinctly urban poetry in the sixteenth and seventeenth centuries*

English literature in the sixteenth and seventeenth centuries is punctuated by two cataclysmic historical transitions: the replacement of the Tudor dynasty by the Stuart at the start of the seventeenth century and the triptych of Revolution, Interregnum and Restoration which occurred in the middle of it. If the first of these seems, at least from our late twentieth century vantage point, to have had a surprisingly muted effect on the character of English poetry, that is doubtless because the careers of several major writers – Shakespeare, Jonson and Donne, for instance – run fluently across it. By contrast, the Restoration produces a much more decisive shift of literary texture and tone.

The earlier part of this period includes a creditable number of London poets, among them some of the greatest in the language, though rather less in the way of London poetry. The earliest, John Skelton (c.1460–1529) is usually remembered as the rector of Diss in rural Norfolk but in 1512 he was appointed King's Orator and he died at Westminster. Other Tudor poets enjoyed notably turbulent careers at the court of Henry VIII. Sir Thomas More (1477–1535), author of *Utopia* and poetry in both Latin and English, who rose from Under-Sheriff of London in 1510 to Lord Chancellor in 1529, and Henry Howard, Earl of Surrey (c.1517–1547), translator of Virgil and best-connected of courtiers, would both be executed on Tower Hill; while the finest lyric poet of the early part of the sixteenth century, Sir Thomas Wyatt (c.1503–1542), just managed to keep his head, despite an alleged affair with Anne Boleyn, and ended up as Commander of the Fleet. Even the conspicuously rustic George Gascoigne (c.1534–1577), who wryly chronicled his misfortunes in the wonderful *Gascoigne's Woodmanship*, spent much time in London as law student, member of Parliament and courtier.

So too with those somewhat later writers who are mostly thought of as the great 'Elizabethan' poets, although several of them were Jacobeans too. Sir Walter Ralegh (c.1552–1618), a favourite in Elizabeth's court, would fall catastrophically from grace under her successor; Edmund Spenser (1552–1599), author of *The Faerie Queen*, was a Londoner by birth who spent most of his diplomatic career in Ireland; Sir Philip Sidney (1554–1586), another of Elizabeth's favoured courtiers, died at Arnhem from a wound sustained while fighting the Spanish, while his friend and contemporary Fulke Greville (1554–1628) lived on to become James I's Chancellor of the Exchequer; Christopher Marlowe (1564–1593) and William Shakespeare (1564–1616) both wrote non-dramatic poetry as well as plays; Thomas Campion (1567–1620), the age's greatest song-writer, studied law at Gray's Inn before taking a degree in medicine, which he practiced in the capital; John Donne

(1572–1631), though from a London catholic family, eventually became Dean of St.Paul's; and Ben Jonson (1572–1637), born in Westminster, was appointed 'King's Poet' – effectively Poet Laureate – in 1616. So all of these had London lives, often linked to high offices of church and state: the most concise summary of the English renaissance poet's characteristically dual allegiance to court and literature is Greville's self-composed epitaph – 'servant to Queen Elizabeth, Councillor to King James, and friend to Sir Philip Sidney.'

The reader might very reasonably expect such writers to have produced poems which capture the atmosphere of a capital city in eventful times. They seldom did, however, for two main reasons. One, of course, is the nature of sixteenth century London itself, still a comparatively small place of under 200,000 inhabitants, in which the life of the court could be substantially insulated from the life of the streets – partly, indeed, because the principal thoroughfare linking Westminster and St. James's Palace on the west to the walled and gated City of London on the east was not the Strand but the River Thames, a point memorably illustrated in the film version of Robert Bolt's *A Man for All Seasons*. And, secondly, there is the behaviour of English poetry itself: the steady replacement of a rugged, essentially medieval style by Petrarchan formality (and, with it, abstraction and rhetoric) before the two converge in the major writers at the turn of the century. Consequently, even London-based poets were more inclined to inhabit imaginary worlds peopled by mythical figures, exemplary lovers, nymphs and shepherds or (increasingly) to develop theological and metaphysical arguments in their work than to describe the vigorous, crowded lives of the urban populace. When such low life appears in the literature of the period, it is usually to be found in plays such as Thomas Dekker's *The Shoemaker's Holiday* or in popular broadside ballads.

There is certainly a distinct poetry of the court (as opposed to courtly poetry) and it is often voiced by those who most memorably quarrelled with it, in lines such as Gascoigne's recollection of 'The crafty courtiers with their guileful looks' or Ralegh's even more embittered:

*Say to the court, it glows*
*And shines like rotten wood;*
*Say to the church it shows*
*What's good, and doth no good...*

But as soon as more literary poetry begins to treat London beyond the court at all realistically, it is likely to be swiftly deflected towards idealisation, as it is in Spenser's lovely 'Prothalamion', written to celebrate the marriages of the Earl of Worcester's daughters, Elizabeth and Katherine Somerset, in 1596. Spenser tells us that he 'walked forth':

*Along the shore of silver streaming Thames,*
*Whose rutty bank, the which his river hems,*
*Was painted all with variable flowers,*
*And all the meads adorned with dainty gems,*
*Fit to deck maidens' bowers,*
*And crown their paramours,*
*Against the bridal day, which is not long:*
  *Sweet Thames, run softly till I end my song.*

This is charming but it is notable that the strikingly down-to-earth 'rutty bank' at once gives way to the more generalised 'variable flowers' and 'dainty gems'; after another couple of lines, Spenser will have 'chanced to espy' nothing less than a 'flock of nymphs'. When, later in the poem, 'At length they all to merry London came,/ To merry London, my most kindly nurse', the repeated epithet is almost defiantly conventional, as if to insist that further description is not the poet's proper business. Similarly, in Donne's **Twicknam Garden**, the place is significant for its association (Twickenham Park was the home of Lucy, Duchess of Bedford) rather than for its appearance: he whimsically proposes his own transformation into a mandrake or a stone fountain, but of what is in the garden already he says nothing at all. Nevertheless, we might suspect that Donne – whose work so often combines apparently irreconcilable opposites – would be the poet likeliest to introduce a note of abrasive reality, as he does in the first of his 'Satires'. Here at last we get a sense of a teeming London street, with its 'fine silken painted fool', its 'prentices' and 'school-boys' performing 'elephant or ape', 'wise politic horse' and 'many-coloured peacock'.

It was Samuel Johnson who coined the term 'metaphysical' to describe the work of Donne and his seventeenth century successors, and it is certainly true that most of the period's finest poets – such as George Herbert (1593–1633), John Milton (1608–1674), Richard Crashaw (1612–1649), Abraham Cowley (1618–1667), Henry Vaughan (1622–1695) and Thomas Traherne (c.1637–1674) – are notably driven by devotional and philosophical concerns. However, this is not so straightforwardly the case with one other poet, Andrew Marvell (1621–1678), who is customarily grouped with them. Marvell, in fact, is among other things an outstanding poet of place, as his great poem **Upon Appleton House** amply demonstrates, but although he was a Member of Parliament for twenty years he did not write about the capital. For that we may turn to Robert Herrick (1591–1674), the son of a London goldsmith who, in **His Return to London**, vigorously celebrates the city of his birth, 'blest place of my nativity', with all its rich diversity: 'O Place! O People! Manners! framed to please/All nations, customs, kindreds, language!' 'His Tears to Thamasis' is still more eloquent, and it is touchingly specific:

*I send, I send her my supremest kiss*
*To thee, my silver-footed Thamasis.*
*No more shall I reiterate thy Strand,*
*Whereon so many stately structures stand;*
*Nor in the summer's sweeter evenings go*
*To bathe in thee (as thousand others do).*
*No more shall I along thy crystal glide,*
*In barge (with boughs and rushes beautified)*
*With soft-smooth virgins (for our chaste disport)*
*To Richmond, Kingston, and to Hampton Court.*
*Never again shall I with finny oar*
*Put from, or draw unto thy faithful shore;*
*And landing safely here, or safely landing there,*
*Make way to my beloved Westminster;*
*Or to the golden Cheapside, where the earth*
*Of Julia Herrick gave to me my birth.*

The sure-footed, life-relishing physicality of these lines marks a transition to the quite new tone of Restoration verse, which was to be typified by bawdy, boozy poets like Charles Cotton (1630–1687) and John Wilmot, Earl of Rochester (1647–1680). It was a time of re-birth: not only was there the re-establishment of the monarchy in 1660 but there was also the rebuilding, as significant symbolically as physically, of London itself, after the disastrous fire of 1666. The anonymous ballad-writer of **London Mourning in Ashes** (a 'Lamentable Narrative lively expressing the Ruine of that Royal City by fire which began in Pudding-lane on September the second 1666, at one of the clock in the morning being Sunday, and continuing until Thursday night following...') provides a racily galloping account of that devastation's progress:

*It swallow'd Fishstreet hil, and straight*
*    it lick'd up Lombard-street*
*Down Canon-street in blazing State*
*    it flew with flaming feet;*
*Down to the Thames*
*    Whose shrinking streams,*
*    began to ebb away;*
*As thinking that,*
*The power of Fate*
*    had brought the latter day.*

The balladeer, somewhat in the manner of a tabloid journalist, seems to relish every dreadful detail before eventually arriving at his pious moral: 'If this do not reform our lives, / A worse thing will succeed... ' But John Dryden (1631–1700), the greatest English poet of the late seventeenth century, brings a more convincing note of gravitas to his account of London's rebirth, near the end of his *Annus Mirabilis:*

> *Already labouring with a mighty fate,*
> *She shakes the Rubbish from her mounting Brow,*
> *And seems to have renew'd her Charters date,*
> *Which Heav'n will to the death of time allow.*
>
> *More great than human now, and more August,*
> *New deified she from her Fires does rise:*
> *Her widening Streets on new Foundations trust,*
> *And, opening, into larger parts she flies.*

In these lines of Dryden's, London seems for the first time to feel like a great modern city, ready to accommodate not only the enormous expansion of life and commerce but also the changed literary forms – the extended verse satire and, of course, the novel – which were to flourish in the century to come.

**New Oxford Book of Sixteenth Century Verse (ed. Jones)**
Oxford UP pbk £12.99 0192829718
**New Oxford Book of Seventeenth Century Verse (ed. Fowler)**
Oxford UP pbk £11.99 0192829963

## FRANCIS BEAUMONT
**The Knight of the Burning Pestle**
A & C Black pbk £4.99 0713629401

*The Knight of the Burning Pestle* is one of the most interesting and inventive plays of its period. Originally assumed to be the work of Beaumont (c. 1584–1616) and his frequent collaborator John Fletcher it is now most often assigned to Beaumont alone. It takes the form of a play-within-a-play and, amidst its satiric exaggeration and farce, provides valuable insights into both the dramatic practices of the time and the habits and tastes of the merchant classes in Jacobean London. A performance of a play called 'The London Merchant' is interrupted by a grocer and his wife in the audience who demand that the drama be modified so that a role can be found for their apprentice Ralph. The play begins to include scenes, written by the grocer himself, in which Ralph, the 'grocer errant', enters upon a series of quixotic and ludicrous adventures. Meanwhile another plot, that of a merchant's apprentice winning and wooing his master's daughter, is unfolding around Ralph, the knight of the burning pestle. We tend to assume that it is only our post-modern selves who can play elaborate games with notions of fiction and reality. *The Knight of the Burning Pestle* shows entertainingly that the Jacobeans had their own methods of doing so.

# GEOFFREY CHAUCER (c.1343–1400)

Chaucer was a native of London. He was born, the son of a vintner, in the parish of St. Martin Vintry, one of the churches destroyed in the Great Fire and not rebuilt. By marrying John of Gaunt's sister-in-law – the marriage, in all likelihood, took place in the Savoy Palace – he allied himself to one of the most powerful men in the kingdom and enjoyed Gaunt's patronage for the rest of his life. He travelled widely in Europe and was thus brought into contact with French literature and with the work of leading Italian writers such as Petrarch and Boccaccio, work which he was to recast and re-shape into distinctively English forms. Between 1374 and 1385 he leased rooms above Aldgate, one of the ancient gateways to the City and it was here that, almost certainly, he wrote works such as *The House of Fame* and *Troilus and Criseyde. The Canterbury Tales,* unfinished in the form he originally planned it, belongs to the last years of his life. The tales that we have range from a dark morality about the love of filthy lucre to a lewd fabliau in which two clerks take their revenge on a cheating miller by sleeping with his wife and daughter, from a tale of classical chivalry to a story of a husband cruelly testing his wife's obedience. Sense of place is not of any great interest to Chaucer in the tales but the pilgrims who tell them set out on their journey from a recognisable London landmark of the period.

> *In Southwerk at the Tabard as I lay*
> *Ready to wende on my pilgrimage*
> *To Caunterbury with ful devout corage*
> *At night was come in-to that hostelrye*
> *Wel nyne and twenty in a companye,*
> *Of sondry folk, by aventure y-falle*
> *In felawship, and pilgrims were they alle*
> *That toward Canterbury wolden ryde:*
> *The chambres and the stables weren wyde,*
> *And well we weren esed atte beste.*

The Tabard survived as an inn, under different names, until the nineteenth century. Talbot Yard, just off Borough High Street, now covers the site. After Chaucer died, in 1400, he was the first literary figure to be buried in Westminster Abbey and his grave became the nucleus of what is now Poets' Corner. That Chaucer was proud of his native city is clear from his writings – 'the citye of London that is to me so dere and sweete, in which I was forth growen; and more kindly love have I to that place than to any other in yerth.'

**The Riverside Chaucer**
Oxford UP pbk £13.99 0192821091

## THOMAS DEKKER (c.1570–1632)

Dekker probably came from a family of Dutch origin but he was born in London, lived most of his life there and his writings give a vivid picture of the manners and mores of the late Elizabethan / Jacobean city. As a playwright Dekker collaborated with nearly all the major figures in the theatre of the time (with the exception of Shakespeare) and his best-known play is *The Shoemaker's Holiday* (first published 1600). This story of an aristocrat who disguises himself as a shoemaker in order to pursue his courtship of the daughter of the lord mayor is set largely in real areas of the city such as Cornhill and Old Ford and in real taverns such as the Boar's Head, an Eastcheap hostelry also mentioned by Shakespeare. The vigorous, colloquial language it uses is as near as we can get to the everyday language of London at the time. Dekker was also a pamphleteer and proto-journalist. *The Wonderfull Yeare* (1603) describes the city during the plague of that year; *The Gull's Horn Book* (1609) is an amiable satire in which Dekker takes the reader on a trip through taverns, playhouses and the rowdy gathering place that was the old St.Paul's.

**The Shoemaker's Holiday**
A & C Black pbk £4.99
0713632887

## BEN JONSON (1572–1637)

Jonson was probably born in Westminster and is supposed, as a young man, to have worked for his stepfather as a bricklayer. Before turning to the stage he is thought to have served as a soldier and he was certainly a belligerent and quarrelsome man, only narrowly escaping execution for the killing of a fellow actor in a duel in 1598. The previous year he was imprisoned for his part in writing a satire, now lost, called *The Isle of Dogs*, which contained 'seditious and slanderous matter'. It was not to be the last time he suffered imprisonment (*Eastward Hoe* contained jibes at the Scots which the Scots King James I took offence at) but Jonson, through his plays and, more especially, through his work as a writer of court masques, moved inexorably towards respectability and the position he held for many years as the undisputed grandee of literary London. He presided over a circle of younger writers which met at taverns in the city such as the Mermaid in Bread Street. In 1628 he succeeded Middleton as City Chronologer but his last years were clouded by illness which probably left him bedridden.

Although his tragedies *Sejanus* and *Catiline* are set in Ancient Rome and his best-known comedy, *Volpone*, in Venice, many of Jonson's other works portray the city in which he spent most of his life. Three should be highlighted. *Eastward Hoe,* written in collaboration with Chapman and Marston and first printed in 1605, is typical of a number of plays of the time in putting on stage the lives of London tradesmen. It also prefigures Hogarth in contrasting the careers of two apprentices, Golding and Quicksilver, one (Golding) an industrious soul destined for civic success and the other a ne'er-do-well who robs his master and runs aground on the Isle of Dogs while trying to escape. The plot of *The Alchemist* (performed in 1610, first printed in 1612) is set in motion when Lovewit leaves his house in Blackfriars to escape the plague, thus allowing his dishonest servant Face to use it as a centre for the frauds he perpetrates in alliance with Subtle, a fake alchemist and astrologer. As well as reflecting contemporary obsessions with alchemy and the magic arts, the play introduces the audience to a succession of city 'types' – Sir Epicure Mammon, the pleasure-seeking knight, the Puritans Ananias and Tribulation Wholesome and the lawyer's clerk, Dapper. *Bartholomew Fair*, first printed in 1631 but performed much earlier in 1614, shares with Dekker's *The Shoemaker's Holiday* the distinction of being the play which most vividly portrays the street life of the time. Bartholomew began as a cloth fair but, by Jonson's time, the three days in August had become as much an excuse for travelling players, dwarfs, wrestlers, fire-eaters and other entertainers to divert the crowds as they were a trade fair. Almost as much a sequence of sketches as it is a plotted drama, Jonson's *Bartholomew Fair* is a vigorous presentation of the earthy pleasures of the event and the people, from the fanatical Zeal-of-the-Land Busy to the rich but half-witted Bartholomew Cokes, from Ursula the pig-woman to the disguised Justice Overdo, who attend it.

**Eastward Hoe**
A & C Black pbk £5.99
0713639830

**Five Plays**
Oxford UP pbk £5.99
0192817825

## JOHN LYDGATE

**London Lickpenny**

Once confidently attributed to John Lydgate (c. 1370–1449), a prolific poet of the early fifteenth century, *London Lickpenny*, a satirical poem which is extant in two different versions in two different metrical forms, is now often assumed to be the work of an anonymous and slightly older contemporary. Whoever wrote it – Lydgate or A. N. Other – it is of interest because it is one of the few works of medieval literature which gives much detail about the street life of the city in the period. It is also interesting to note that it embodies a theme that recurs time and again in London writing in the centuries to come. A countryman comes to the wicked city in search of justice but finds that corruption and bribery are the order of the day. The city is imagined as physically exciting but morally decadent.

## PHILIP MASSINGER (1583–1640)

Massinger was born in the West Country and studied at Oxford. During the first decade of the seventeenth century he settled in London and he became one of the most productive dramatists of the Jacobean and Caroline theatres, working for one company (the King's Men) for more than three decades. Like most of the playwrights of the period he wrote much of his work in collaboration and he wrote in a number of genres. His play *The City Madam* (performed in 1632 but not published until 1659) is one of the latest and darkest examples of what is termed 'city' or 'citizen' comedy, dramas in which the setting is contemporary London and the characters its everyday citizens. Its story of a successful merchant and his plan both to curb the vanity of his wife and daughters and to test the genuineness of his brother's reformation from prodigal to penitent is improbable enough. However, in its incidental details, the play does give a convincing portrait of Charles I's London and its inhabitants, from the wealthy mercantile classes to the brothels and prostitutes of the underworld.

**The City Madam** is not available in a current edition.

## THOMAS MIDDLETON (1580–1627)

Born in London, the son of a master bricklayer, Middleton probably spent time at Oxford and at Gray's Inn and was certainly writing plays by 1603 when he is mentioned in the diary of theatre-owner Philip Henslowe. He was a prolific writer in a number of genres, both on his own and in collaboration with others, and from about 1613 was also producing pageants and masques for special occasions in the city. For the last seven years of his life he held an official position as City Chronologer. Best known today for his tragi-comedy *The Changeling*, he wrote a number of the best of what are known as 'city comedies'. These deal satirically with the everyday life of the growing middle classes in the London of the time. Often as elaborately plotted as a farce and peopled by characters with emblematic names (Sir Walter Whorehound, Pecunius Lucre, Penitent Brothel), these comedies reflect Jacobean unease with the ways in which mercantile values were replacing more traditional notions of good citizenry and civic virtue. *A Mad World, My Masters*, in which a grandson attempts to cheat a wealthy grandfather, *The Roaring Girl*, based very loosely on the story of a real life thief known as Moll Cutpurse, and *Michaelmas Term* are all by Middleton. His best play in the genre, and one that is occasionally revived, is *A Chaste Maid in Cheapside* in which Sir Walter Whorehound pretends that his mistress is his niece and attempts to persuade the rich goldsmith, Yellowhammer, that she should marry the goldsmith's son.

**Five Plays**
Penguin pbk £8.99 0140432191

**A Chaste Maid in Cheapside**
A & C Black pbk £5.99 0713630841

# Shakespeare's London

*Pauline Kiernan, Leverhulme Research Fellow at the new Globe on Bankside, traces the geography of the city Shakespeare would have known.*

Renaissance London ended at Clerkenwell. The West End was meadowland, and the suburbs to the north and the south, in Middlesex and Surrey, were the marginalised, 'the liberties' which were beyond the boundaries of the City and the jurisdiction of its fat cats.

Shakespeare's London begins and ends with the 'silver streaming Thames' which was the metropolis's main highway, its economic and commercial lifeblood, its sewer – and its main water supply. Stand on Bankside today and look out across the river on a day in summer or winter, and you are likely to see no more than a couple of sightseeing water buses, a barge carrying paper waste downstream, and a dinky little motor boat emblazoned with the logo of a London advertising agency. If you had stood on the same spot four hundred years ago, you would have seen two thousand 'taxis', called wherries, carrying the three or four thousand people that crossed the river every day to hear a play at the Globe, the Rose and the Swan; to watch half a dozen mastiffs let loose on a bear tied to a stake in the middle of a similar amphitheatre for the same price it cost to watch the less grisly spectacle of Hamlet's duel with Laertes (one penny to stand in the yard, twopence to sit in the galleries); or to pay more for a prostitute in one of the hundreds of stews (brothels) licensed by the Bishop of Winchester that edged the riverbank, particularly in Rose Alley and Maiden Lane (now Park Street) where Richard Burbage would have been playing Hamlet, and William Shakespeare, King Hamlet's ghost, next door.

A traveller from Europe in 1599 noted more than a hundred vessels moored in the harbour. 'Never', he wrote, 'did I see so many large ships in one port in all my life.' You could see the royal barge upstream at Westminster in winter, downstream in Greenwich in summer, and, if it was around the time of the Christmas Royal Command performances, you might be able to spot the costume and prop boats taking the lighting equipment, scenery, costumes, props and all the tack and wire needed to set up a performance by Shakespeare's company before the Queen. You could see tall three-masted merchant ships unloading their cargoes at the crowded docks, wharves and warehouses – at Hay Wharf, Timberhithe, Fish Wharf, Salt Wharf, Vintry Wharf – that had sailed from an ever-expanding world of Europe, Africa, the Indies and America.

The events in Shakespeare's plays are mostly set in foreign countries, but it is the experience of living in Elizabethan and Jacobean London, where the public theatre nourished a cultural and social phenomenon unsurpassed in Europe, that provides the inspiration for his Venice, his Vienna and his ancient Rome. When Bassanio asks incredulously if the merchant Antonio's cargo ships have all been lost, he could be standing in London's Elizabethan 'stock exchange' talking to a London merchant:

> *But is it true, Salerio?*
> *Hath all his ventures failed? What, not one hit?*
> *From Tripolis, from Mexico and England,*
> *From Lisbon, Barbary, and India...?*
> (The Merchant of Venice, 3.2)

The Royal Exchange, built at Cornhill by Sir Thomas Gresham in 1566–7 on the model of the Bourse at Antwerp and one of the few large-scale Renaissance buildings in the City of London, was an imposing symbol of a rapidly growing mercantile city, with its spacious courtyard and cosmopolitan hubbub. Playwright Thomas Dekker, a contemporary of Shakespeare, said that, when walking in the Exchange 'at every turn, a man is put in mind of Babel, there is such a confusion of languages.' If Shakespeare's 'Venice' seems authentic, with its multicultural melting-pot and the workings of its law and commerce, London provided him with a useful model.

What news on the Rialto? is a recurring question in *The Merchant of Venice*. London's 'Rialto' was the Royal Exchange and probably also the imposing St.Paul's Cathedral which stood on the site of the present one, directly opposite the Globe across the river. At noon and at six every evening, the great bell summoned the English and foreign merchants in their thousands to worship at the altar of Mammon, the lawyers doing deals and meeting clients, the punters picking up prostitutes, and the pickpockets picking pockets. An arched cloister lined with shops on two levels created an extraordinary bazaar. All this, while in another part of the cathedral, divine services were being sung by the choir. But in the nave, called Paul's Walk or Duke Humphrey's Walk, the place was a babel of commercial activity and wheeler-dealing. The marble tombs of the nobility, even the baptismal font were used as counters for paying out money. And you could pick up your groceries on the way out – beer, bread, fruit and fish could all be bought at the cathedral. St. Paul's was also used as a short cut to Fleet Street by delivery men, although, by Shakespeare's time, they no longer led their horses and mules down the aisle. So many people passed through it every day, instead of using Carter Lane, that Paul's Walk became the place to post up small ads. Anyone who was out of work or wanted a change of job posted up an ad so that a prospective employer could write his or her name and address beneath. The west door of the cathedral was plastered with serving men's supplications. The original for Launcelot Gobbo in *The Merchant of Venice,* for example or for the Dromio twins in **The Comedy of Errors** might have advertised here but not, I think, those for the upwardly mobile Malvolio or Lear's Fool. The west door would also have advertised the services of language teachers. London's citizens wanted to know as much as possible about the trading nations of the world and teachers of Turkish, Polish, Dutch, Russian and Arabic as well as French were in demand.

But perhaps the most compelling reason for hanging out in Paul's Walk was to find out the latest news. The place was open by seven in the morning and the middle aisle was the meeting-place for every newsmonger in London. Outside, in the churchyard, was the centre of the publishing trade. Stationers lived in the streets around the cathedral close and set up their stalls and shops there: you could buy a quarto *Merchant of Venice,* or **Othello**, or **Hamlet**, or choose from a plethora of 'How To' manuals in cookery, gardening, accounts, how to play the cittern without a teacher, even how to be a courtier.

In the mid 1590's Shakespeare lived north of the river in the parish of St.Helen's, near the site of the present Bank of England. From his lodgings he would have walked through the city gate to the first purpose-built playhouse, The Theatre, which stood outside the city walls at Shoreditch, in fields just outside Bishopsgate, believed to be just to the east of present-day Curtain Street. James Burbage (father of Shakespeare's fellow Globe actor, Richard) chose to build his theatre outside the jurisdiction of the city authorities, a wise move at a time when the puritanical City money men were doing everything in their power to stop the 'evils' of playing and play-going. On the journey from home to work, Shakespeare would have had to walk through the appalling squalor of the town ditch and the chained inmates of Bedlam who gave entertainment and amusement to London sightseers.

Back on our vantage point on the south side of the river, London Bridge would be on the right, the sight that all Elizabethan and Jacobean tourists came to see. It would be crowded with people and traffic jams. Built on twenty arches, it carried a road once wide enough to allow wagons to pass freely in both directions. It was the only bridge across the Thames and the only direct access to the city from the south. To the east, the Tower of London, the building that is most frequently alluded to in Shakespeare's plays, which housed political prisoners (many of whom would climb Tower Hill to have their heads chopped off, stuck on pikes and displayed on London Bridge) as well as the royal zoo – lions, a tiger and lynx, an eagle, a porcupine and an excessively aged wolf. Prisoners taken to the wooden scaffold did not meet with so grisly an end as the poor Catholics taken to Tyburn to be hanged, drawn (disembowelled) and quartered. In Queen Mary's time, Protestants were taken to Smithfield, London's meat market, to be burned.

Shakespeare's London cannot begin to be imagined without feeling it on the senses. It was bursting at the seams. In 1550, fourteen years before he was born, the population was 120,000. By 1600, the year in which *The Merchant of Venice* and *A Midsummer Night's Dream* were first printed, it was 200,000. The assaults on the senses of smell and hearing were many and vicious. Elizabethan London had a hundred and fourteen churches with their belfries ringing out day and night to mark the hours – Shakespeare's plays are full of allusions to jangling bells. One Londoner complained: 'In every street carts and coaches make such a thundering as if the world ran on wheels.' The rattle of traffic, the roar of hawkers, the tormented sounds of dogs being slain or mutilated in the nearby bearpits – actors on stage at the Globe and the Rose would have welcomed the jet engines and honking geese that today's new Globe players contend with.

And the smell. The Thames itself a fetid sewer, the streets and thoroughfares used as loos, the belching, the putrid smoke from factories (the hazelnuts found at the sites of the Rose and the Globe were waste products from a nearby soap factory), everything conspired to make the battle against bubonic plague an impossible one. In 1593, the year of Shakespeare's erotic Ovidian poem, *Venus and Adonis*, there were eleven thousand deaths from the violent epidemic that closed the theatres and all public gatherings in London. References to body odour abound in the drama of the early modern period:

*You common cry of curs whose breath I hate*
*As reek of the rotten fens, whose loves I prize*

*As the dead carcasses of unburied men*
*That do corrupt my air.*

(Coriolanus 3.3)

The groundlings, the playgoers who stood in the yard at the Globe and other open playhouses, were often referred to by the playwrights as 'penny stinkards'.

Southwark, with its five prisons, its numberless brothels, its bear-pits and its theatres crowding round the river's edge, was nothing like the gracious region of space and splendour that stretched along the north bank of the river from the Inns of Court to Charing Cross where the highest of the nobility lived in huge mansions with gardens that stretched down to beautiful water-gates where their noble barges sat in waiting to carry them to Whitehall or Westminster. The botanist and surgeon John Gerarde (1545–1612) kept a garden for medical herbs in Holborn and gathered wild flowers on the banks of Piccadilly. Meanwhile, across the river in the Liberty of the Clink, in the suburban gardens of Southwark altogether different activities were taking place. In Brutus's orchard in ancient Rome, a wife called Portia, on stage at the Globe, would refer to the stews next door:

*Dwell I but in the suburbs*
*Of your good pleasure? If it be no more,*
*Portia is Brutus' harlot, not his wife.*

(Julius Caesar 2.1)

Pauline Kiernan taught English Literature at University College, Oxford for ten years and is the Leverhulme Research fellow appointed to record and study actor use of the new Globe on Bankside. She has published **Shakespeare's Theory of Drama** (Cambridge UP pbk £13.95 0521633583) and is the author of the forthcoming **Staging Shakespeare at the New Globe** (Macmillan pbk £12.99 0333662733).

## JOHN STOW (1525–1605)

Stow is often cited as London's first historian and, although others had written about the city before him, he was the first to make use of public records and his own private researches. As it says on the inscription on his tomb in St Andrew Undershaft, 'He exercised the most careful accuracy in searching ancient monuments, English annals and records of the City of London. He wrote excellently and deserved well of both his own and subsequent ages.' Stow worked as a tailor for many years but, from the late fifteen fifties onwards, he collected and annotated a mass of books and manuscripts. *A Survey of London* appeared in 1598 and its account of the city, arranged according to the city's wards, is a treasure trove of information about the Tudor and medieval London that was swept away in the Fire. Stow died in 1605 and was buried in St Andrew Undershaft. The effigy in the church was erected by his wife and each year, on the anniversary of his death, the Lord Mayor replaces the quill pen in its hand.

**A Survey of London**
Sutton Publishing pbk £9.99 0750908270

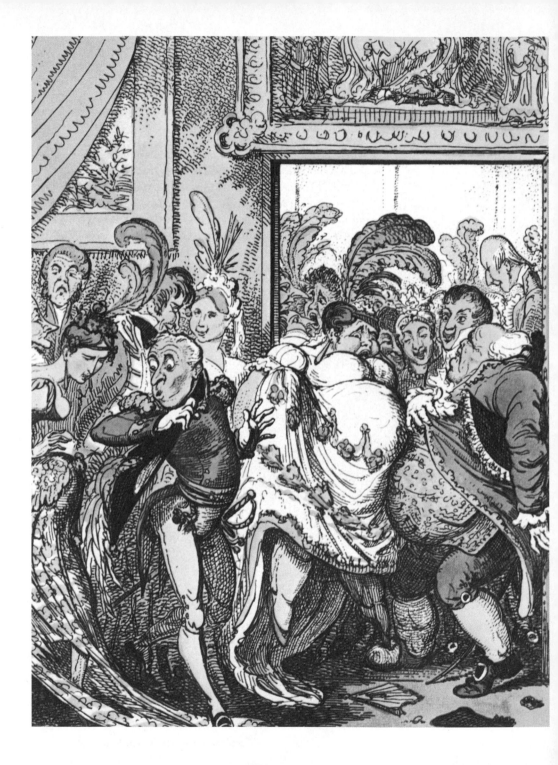

# From Restoration London to Regency London

The images in this chapter are from *Graphic Works of George Cruikshank* published by Dover Publications, Inc.

## JOSEPH ADDISON (1672–1719) and SIR RICHARD STEELE (1672–1729)

One of the great social innovations of late seventeenth and early eighteenth century London was the coffee-house. The first was opened in 1652 in St. Michael's Alley, Cornhill and by the end of the last decade of the eighteenth century there were nearly five hundred in the capital. In the same period as the coffee-houses grew so dramatically in number, there also developed a demand for a new image of polite behaviour, one removed from the perceived corruptions of the court, more suited to the needs of an increasingly mercantile and middle-class city. Few writers represented coffee-house society and reflected the needs for a new code of urban behaviour better than Addison and Steele. Indeed Addison was instrumental in the establishment of Button's, a coffee-house which rapidly became the great resort for the wits and writers of the day. The essays that the two wrote, for *The Tatler* and *The Spectator*, in the years between 1709 and 1714, both reflected the city that they saw around them and embodied a particular vision of what manners and morals should be. They were exceptionally popular with the growing middle-class readership and remain interesting historical documents.

**Selections from The Spectator and The Tatler**
Penguin pbk £8.99 0140432981

# WILLIAM BLAKE (1757–1827)

*Film-maker and writer Sean Martin on London's greatest mystic.*

Blake was born in Soho in 1757, and died in a house off the Strand in 1827; in his seventy years he lived outside London for only three. London for him was the Eternal City that became, in his writing and his life, the means by which the soul could come to realise its divine nature. Eternity, for Blake, like Traherne before him, was present in every street; every corner and back alley was an entrance to heaven.

A combination of poor judgment in business affairs and a certain amount of bad luck kept Blake in relative obscurity during his lifetime. His forthright views alienated his contemporaries at the Royal Academy and it was only in the last few years of his life, when he was living in Fountain Court (today the staff entrance of the Savoy Hotel), that he gathered about him a group of younger painters – including Samuel Palmer – who revered him. (Such was Palmer's devotion to Blake that he used to kiss the door-handle every time he called at the older man's door.) For most people, if he was known at all, it was either as a commercial engraver or as a madman who saw angels.

From infancy Blake had the ability to see agents of the divine mingling with his fellow Londoners and he retained this capacity throughout his life. He saw angels walking among haymakers in the fields. God appeared to him, at the age of four, in an upstairs window at his first home, a hosier's shop on the corner of Marshall and Broad Streets. Once his mother beat him for claiming that he had seen the prophet Ezekiel sitting under a tree. To escape the confines of the shop and his parents' lack of sympathy, Blake became a relentless walker, going beyond his immediate neighbourhood in what is now the West End and getting to know most of the London of his day.

> *I wander thro' each charter'd street,*
> *Near where the charter'd Thames does flow,*
> *And mark in every face I meet*
> *Marks of weakness, marks of woe.*

His familiarity with this geography, his love of the Bible, and the political turbulence of the period (wars and riots were to affect London for almost all of Blake's life) were the defining factors in both his poetry and his graphic work, lending to them both an apocalyptic and furious beauty.

Although 'isolated' by his lack of commercial success and the disdain of many of his peers, Blake laboured incessantly at his poetry and painting. He found an image to represent his relationship to the city in which he lived, one that may have had its origins in one of his many walks: an old man (London) 'blind and age-bent begging thro' the streets' is led by a child (Blake), the old man weeping tears that run down his beard...

*The corner of Broad Street weeps; Poland Street languishes*
*To Great Queen Street & Lincoln's Inn, all is distress & woe*

Blake saw it as his duty to provide an antidote to the 'distress & woe' he saw all about him. In his attempt to free himself from 'the mind forg'd manacles', the created institutions of society and the material reality which imprison the soul, he began to create a poetic mythology that often referred to the streets he saw every day. London becomes the battleground between the soul striving for Eternity and Satan, trying to pen it in time and matter.

The one area that Blake mentions more than any other is Lambeth, where he and his wife lived from 1790 to 1800 in a cottage on Hercules Road. It was here that he did some of his greatest work. Lambeth became for him 'Jerusalem's inner court', that contained 'a Grain of Sand... that Satan cannot find... tis translucent and has many angles', the grain of sand from which the fallen universe would be redeemed through the establishment of heaven on earth. 'From Lambeth/We began our foundations.' Lambeth, with its nearby workhouse and new steam-driven mill on Blackfriars Road also provided Blake with daily reminders of the unredeemed state of human nature, the darkness which was to be fought at all costs, a darkness from which the child would lead the old man to safety.

*And did the Countenance Divine*
*Shine forth upon our clouded hills?*
*And was Jerusalem builded here,*
*Among these dark Satanic mills?*

**The Complete Illuminated Books of William Blake:-**
**Volume 1 Jerusalem**
Tate Gallery pbk £20.00
1854372602

**Volume 2 Songs of Innocence and Experience**
pbk £15.00 1854372610

**Volume 3 The Early Illuminated Books**
pbk £20.00 1854372629

**Volume 4 The Continental Prophecies**
pbk £20.00 1854372637

**Volume 5 Milton: A Poem**
pbk £18.00 1854372645

**Volume 6 The Urizen Book**
pbk £18.00 1854372653

**The Complete Poems of William Blake**
Penguin pbk £14.00
0140422153

**The Complete Writings (ed. Geoffrey Keynes)**
OUP pbk £13.99 0192810502

*Peter Ackroyd*
**Blake**
Minerva pbk £7.99 0749391766

*Kathleen Raine*
**William Blake**
Thames & Hudson pbk £6.95
0500201072

## JAMES BOSWELL (1740–1795)

For a century and a half after his death Boswell seemed fated to live
in the shadow of his greatest achievement. By creating so memorable
a portrait of Dr. Johnson he condemned himself to the position of
literary stooge, forever in attendance to note down the great man's
sayings but also forever in the background. *The Life of Samuel Johnson*
was published in 1791 and has since been elevated to the status of
the greatest biography in the language. Boswell had been collecting
material for the biography from the time of his first meeting with
Johnson at Davies's bookshop in Russell Street, Covent Garden in
1763 and the book owes much of its power to the immediacy and
vividness of the anecdotes and aphorisms that Boswell recorded.
The picture we have of London literary life in the eighteenth century
is indelibly marked by Boswell's portrait of Johnson, holding court at
the Turk's Head in Soho or the Mitre Tavern in Mitre Court off Fleet
Street, famously maintaining that when a man is tired of London he
is tired of life.

Yet, in this century, Boswell has been rediscovered as the recorder
of his own experiences in London, particularly during his visit in
1762–3, as a young Scot, eager for the diversions the capital could
offer. Many of Boswell's private papers and journals were found to
have survived in the possession of the family and the descendants of
one of his literary executors. Scholarly publication of these papers
began and Boswell's *London Journal* appeared in 1950. The Journal,
much of it written when he was in lodgings in Downing Street, is an
extraordinary record of high and low life in eighteenth century
London and a self-portrait just as remarkable as Boswell's portrait
of Johnson. Boswell lives London life to the full – drinking, whoring,
sightseeing, playgoing and drinking some more. As one critic
remarked, 'Boswell waked with a headache more often than any
human being on record.' Each dissipation is followed by resolutions
to be more sober and serious a character. Each resolution is,
inevitably, followed by the record of further excess.

Yet, amidst all this, Boswell is a wonderfully acute witness to
the drama and excitement and variety of the city. He records his

adventures with prostitutes ('At the bottom of Haymarket I picked up a strong jolly young damsel, and taking her under the arm I conducted her to Westminster Bridge... The whim of doing it there with the Thames rolling below us amused me much.') but he also records climbing the 311 stairs of the Monument:

> *It was horrid to find myself so monstrous a way up in the air, so far above London and all its spires. I durst not look around me. There is no real danger, as there is a strong rail both on the stair and balcony. But I shuddered, and as every heavy wagon passed down Gracechurch Street, dreaded that the shaking of the earth would make the tremendous pile tumble to the foundation.*

He visits Newgate to see the condemned Paul Lewis, 'a genteel, spirited young fellow' and then goes to Tyburn the following day to see him hanged and is 'thrown into a very deep melancholy.' He goes to the waxworks of Mrs Salmon, the eighteenth century equivalent of Madame Tussaud. He delights in Child's Coffee House near St.Paul's and records the conversation around him. He is moved to tears by Garrick's performance in Henry IV Part 2 and is appalled but fascinated by the cockfighting at the Royal Cockpit in St. James's Park. He travels to Greenwich with Johnson and to Ranelagh Pleasure Gardens with Lord Eglinton. He is interested in all the city offers. In the biography of Johnson, Boswell records himself as saying, 'I own, Sir, the spirits I have in London make me do everything with more readiness and vigour.' The proof of this is in the pages of the *London Journal*.

**Boswell's Life of Johnson**
OUP pbk £10.99 0192815377

**Boswell's London Journal**
Edinburgh UP pbk £12.95
0748602623

**The Journals of James Boswell**
Mandarin pbk £7.99
0749312556

**The Life of Johnson**
Penguin pbk £7.99 0140431160

## TOM BROWN (1663–1704)

Born in Shropshire and educated at Oxford, Brown then came to London and earned a precarious living as a writer of satirical verse and translator of works by Petronius and Lucian. He was a writer for whom the terms Grub Street and hack might have been invented. As the *Dictionary of National Biography* sniffily points out, 'his life was as licentious as his writings.' He was also a keen observer of urban life and his work in prose, *Amusements Serious and Comical, Calculated for the Meridian of London* (1700), is as vigorous and lively a depiction of the urban spectacle of the early eighteenth century as the better-known writings of John Gay and Ned Ward.

"Stand up there, you blind dog," says a carman, "will you have the cart squeeze your guts out?" One tinker knocks, another bawls. "Have you brass-pot, iron-pot, kettle, skillet or a frying-pan to mend?" Another son of a whore yelps louder than Homer's stentor, "Two a groat, and four for sixpence, mackerel." One draws his mouth up to his ears and bawls out, "Buy my flounders," and is followed by an old burly drab that screams out the sale of her "maids" and her "soul" at the same instant.
Tom Brown – Amusements Serious and Comical

### JOHN CLELAND (1709–1789)

Probably few readers have been drawn to Cleland's *Memoirs of a Woman of Pleasure*, better known as *Fanny Hill*, primarily for its lively passages about street life and low life in eighteenth century London. Cleland's fascination with sexual behaviour in its many forms ensured that the book was a bestseller in its own time and that attempts to publish it in the nineteen sixties met with prosecution for obscenity and resulted in a case that rivalled that of *Lady Chatterley's Lover*. Anyone today demanding sexual stimulation from their fiction would almost certainly not be satisfied by Cleland's narrative but the book remains interesting as a vigorous example of a genre of fictionalised memoirs about the dangers and delights of urban lives that dates back at least as far as Defoe.

**Fanny Hill, or Memoirs of a Woman of Pleasure**
Penguin pbk £2.99 0140432493
**Memoirs of a Woman of Pleasure**
OUP pbk £2.99 0192816349

## Restoration Comedy

Few genres of English literature are more urban than Restoration comedy. Nearly all the most notable examples are set in London. Even when the action takes place elsewhere London seems to lurk beneath the ostensible setting. Dryden's *Marriage a la Mode* is set in Sicily but, as one critic has pointed out, the characters are 'about as Sicilian as Hyde Park.' The themes which the comedies rehearse are urban themes. Metropolitan wit versus the innocence and foolishness of the country. The sexual and financial intrigue of a sophisticated and verbally adept elite. The Court versus the commercial classes of the city. Masks and deceit are central to the comedies – disguises adopted for purposes of intrigue, the facade of wit and manners beneath which characters manipulate others – and the complex hypocrisies of the city, contrasted with the simplicity of the country, have provided an important motif in London writing both before and since the Restoration.

Charles II's return to England in 1660 heralded a return of theatrical life which had been more or less dormant during the Commonwealth. By the late sixteen sixties the two patent theatres were presenting a succession of new dramas by new playwrights to audiences that, although not as socially varied as the Jacobean audience, came from a wider range of backgrounds than just the court and the aristocracy. Two writers who benefited from this were George Etherege and William Wycherley. Etherege (1636–1692) came from a solidly Royalist family but little is known of his early life before his first play, *The Comical Revenge*, was produced in 1664. His second comedy, *She Would If She Could* (1668), has some claim to being the first true Restoration comedy. All the elements are there. The contrast between the two country knights, Sir Oliver Cockwood and Sir Jolly Joslin (the names in these plays are not usually noted for the subtlety of their allusions) and the two men about town who idly pursue their womenfolk. The banter and repartee between the courting couples. The reflection of urban manners in the endless conversations about love, sex and marriage. The play is also seen to be taking place in specific London settings. The two rakes, Courtall and Freeman, take Lady Cockwood and her young kinswomen to a dance at the Bear, a tavern in Drury Lane where much of the comic action takes place. The play was a great success and earned Etherege preferment at court. He spent much of the rest of his career, when not involved in such courtly activities as brawling and duelling, as a diplomat abroad. *The Man of Mode* (1676), his last comedy, is notable for its portrayal of the hedonistic Dorimant, widely assumed to be based on the archetypal Restoration libertine-about-town, the Earl of Rochester.

William Wycherley (1641–1715) emerged, like Etherege, from a rather obscure background. Born in Shropshire he had been briefly at Oxford and had probably served as a soldier in Ireland and elsewhere before turning his talents to the stage. His first play, *Love in a Wood* (1671), is a comedy of intrigue in which a selection of

Restoration stock characters (an amorous widow, a gentleman wit, a city merchant) stumble into misunderstandings and deceits in St.James's Park. Wycherley became one of the members of the informal circle of wits, drinkers and womanizers which included Rochester, Etherege and others and he knew well the world of sexual and financial rapacity portrayed unflinchingly in his two best-known plays, *The Country Wife* (1675) and *The Plain Dealer* (1676). Both were condemned, even at the time, for their alleged obscenity and Garrick, when reviving *The Country Wife* in the mid-eighteenth century, felt obliged to bowdlerise it. The plot of *The Country Wife* is another variant on provincial innocence bamboozled by urban sophistication. The young Margery Pinchwife is brought to London by her husband and is immediately overwhelmed by the city and pursued by the witty Horner (another alleged portrait of Rochester) who pretends to impotence in order to present himself as a suitable chaperon. (It has to be admitted that the artlessness of the innocents in Restoration comedy sometimes stretches credulity.) After *The Plain Dealer* Wycherley wrote no more for the stage although he was to become a surprisingly close friend of Pope who was not even born when Wycherley's plays were first performed.

Much of what is usually described as Restoration comedy actually dates to later reigns than that of Charles II. The work of Vanbrugh, Congreve and Farquhar appeared in the decades from 1690–1710. Vanbrugh (1664–1726) was a man of many talents and is known as much for his work as an architect (Castle Howard, Blenheim Palace) as for his plays. His first, *The Relapse* (1696), is a witty variant of the city versus country theme. Loveless is a reformed libertine, living happily with his wife in the country, who is tempted back into his old ways when obliged to make a visit to town. In a second plot a London beau, Lord Foppington, travels from town to country to meet his future wife for the first time, only to find he has been pre-empted by his impoverished younger brother who has turned up, claiming to be Foppington. *The Provok'd Wife* (1697) puts on stage yet more sexual shenanigans and intrigues, some taking place in Spring Gardens, one of the many pleasure gardens in the city.

Restoration comedy reached its apogee in the work of William Congreve (1670–1729). Born in Yorkshire but brought up and educated in Ireland, Congreve came to England after the Glorious Revolution and gained acclaim for his first play *The Old Bachelor*, first performed in 1693. He was involved in the theatre for the next seven years, writing several plays and involving himself in the management of the Lincoln's Inn Fields Theatre. A combination of reasons – inheritance of money, comparative failure of *The Way of the World*, attacks on the immorality of the stage which singled him out for criticism – led to his retirement from the stage-world in 1700 but he remained a well-known literary figure, a friend of Pope, Swift and Steele. Congreve's masterpiece is *The Way of the World* which, in many ways, epitomises the attacks Restoration dramatists had made on 'the town' and its values, and does so with great wit and pragmatic intelligence. In a byzantinely complex plot, the basic premise is nonetheless clear. The lovers Mirabell and Millamant plan to marry and need the £6,000 pounds legacy that Millamant will receive only if she marries with the consent of her aunt Lady Wishfort. What stands in their path is the way of the world, the love of money that is the root of all evil. Mrs Marwood, spurned by Mirabell, conspires with Fainall, Lady Wishfort's son-in-law and Mirabell's supposed friend to thwart the lovers and divert the money in their direction. Mirabell and Millamant eventually triumph (of course) but only through a realistic assessment of the prospective success of their own relationship in a society so driven by money and status.

*The Way of the World* represents both the pinnacle of Restoration comedy and the moment when it began to mutate into something else. In the work of George Farquhar (1677–1707) we can see the last flashes of the cynicism and realism which had characterised it. His early plays are set in London (much of the action in **The Constant Couple** is set in St.James's Park) but his two best-known works, **The Recruiting Officer** and **The Beaux's Stratagem**, move out of town and into the provinces. Both are filled with the epigrammatic wit of earlier comedy but Farquhar is more genial than the earlier dramatists, more prepared to underwrite the values of romantic love. His plays look forward to the eighteenth century as well as back to Etherege, Wycherley and Congreve. His settings are significant. Perhaps it was only in the hothouse of the city, with its brittle sophistication and mad pursuit of worldly success, that the true spirit of Restoration comedy could thrive.

**Five Restoration Comedies**
A & C Black pbk £6.95 0713626100
**Three Restoration Comedies**
Penguin pbk £6.99 014043027X

## DANIEL DEFOE (1660–1731)

Born into the nonconformist, mercantile class of late seventeenth century London, Daniel Defoe enjoyed an extraordinarily chequered career as journalist, entrepreneur, bankrupt and spy. At various times in his life he was a hosiery merchant, fought in the Monmouth Rebellion, ran a business for the breeding of civet cats, was fined, imprisoned and pilloried for publication of an inflammatory pamphlet on religious dissent and acted as a clandestine agent for the Tory government of the day. He was in his late fifties and early sixties when he wrote the novels, including *Robinson Crusoe*, for which he is now best remembered. These include *Moll Flanders* and *Roxana*, both of which include scenes of London lowlife vividly realised in Defoe's plain and direct prose. Defoe eschewed the classical forms and allusions used by his Augustan contemporaries and, in much of his fiction, catered to the tastes of the burgeoning bourgeoisie with tales of calamitous ruin and debauchery, most usually ending in repentance and spiritual redemption.

*A Journal of the Plague Year*, first published in 1722, has been described as 'the best piece of work on the most terrible year London ever had.' Defoe was five years old when the Great Plague struck in 1665. It is estimated that 100,000 Londoners lost their lives, a figure equivalent to the entire populations of the next five largest towns in England. The Journal is presented as the memoir of a saddler living in Aldgate who conveys, with great compassion, the terrible suffering and anguish around him. Defoe was able to draw on several medical and historical accounts of the plague but the compelling style and the almost exclusive focus on the plight of the poor are uniquely his. So too is the extraordinary immediacy of the Journal. Incidents and anecdotes are located precisely within the city with a colloquial familiarity. 'Blowbladder Street', we are told, 'had its name from the butchers who used to kill and dress their sheep there (and who, it seems, had a custom to blow up their meats with pipes to make it look thicker and fatter than it was.)'

In other works Defoe could also deploy this precise topography of London to moral effect. In *Roxana* his eponymous heroine first lives as a society courtesan in an apartment in Pall Mall, her sinful lifestyle associated with the western side of London and the extravagances of the King's court. Later, renouncing her earlier life, she moves to the City where she is surrounded by the respectable merchants and tradesmen of Defoe's ilk. Among these same people Moll Flanders pursues her career of theft and, by her capture there, is eventually redeemed. Both Defoe's journalistic eye for the detail of city life and his ability to use those particular details to moral effect can be seen throughout his best London works.

*Andy Walker* Waterstone's, *Charing Cross Road*

**A Journal of the Plague Year**
Penguin pbk £4.99 0140430156

**A Journal of the Plague Year**
Oxford UP pbk £4.99
0192826824

**Moll Flanders**
Penguin pbk £2.50 0140433139

**Moll Flanders**
Oxford UP pbk £2.99
0192834037

**Roxana**
Penguin pbk £5.99 0140431497

**Roxana**
Oxford UP pbk £4.99
0192824597

**Passing through Token House Yard in Lothbury, of a sudden a casement violently opened just over my head, and a woman gave three frightful screeches, and then cried, 'Oh Death, Death, Death!' in a most inimitable tone, and which struck me with horror and a chillness in my blood. There was nobody to be seen in the whole street, neither did any other window open; for people had no curiosity now in any case; nor could any help one another; so I went on to pass into Bell Alley.**
Defoe – Journal of the Plague Year

## THOMAS DE QUINCEY (1785–1859)

Homelessness in London is not a new phenomenon. In 1802, at the age of seventeen, Thomas De Quincey arrived in Soho, fleeing the constraints of his family and of Manchester Grammar School. He spent two months on the streets, sleeping in shop doorways, before finding unpalatial accommodation in Greek Street. During this time he befriended Anne, a prostitute even younger than he was. Anne must have been the archetypal tart with the heart of gold since, as De Quincey later told it, her kindness and care for him saved his life when he collapsed, faint with hunger, on the steps of a house in Soho Square. Some weeks after this De Quincey departed London for Windsor and arranged to meet Anne three nights later at the corner of Titchfield Street. She didn't turn up on the appointed night or on any of the succeeding nights on which De Quincey waited at the meeting place. He never saw her again. De Quincey's dramatic tale of his life on the streets of the capital and the story of the young prostitute appear in the pages of his best-known book, *Confessions of an English Opium Eater*, which also recounts his enthrallment to opium. This addiction began at Oxford to which De Quincey went after reconciliation with his family. De Quincey also wrote, in later life, an account of his friendships with Wordsworth and Coleridge and was a prolific journalist. Much of this later life he spent in Edinburgh, contributing to the Edinburgh-based *Blackwood's Magazine*. Although his story of Anne and of life on the streets is highly stylised and intended to take its place in the self-consciously wrought form of the *Confessions*, it remains worth reading as some kind of record of a life which many lived but few committed to paper.

**Confessions of an English Opium-Eater**
Penguin pbk £4.99 014043061X

# PIERCE EGAN
## (1772–1849)

Tom and Jerry are today known as cat and mouse participants in cartoon mayhem. The original Tom and Jerry were regency rake Corinthian Tom, man about London, and his country cousin, Jerry Hawthorn, who were the central characters in Pierce Egan's *Life in London, or, The Day and Night Scenes of Jerry Hawthorn, Esq. and his elegant friend Corinthian Tom, Accompanied by Bob Logic, the Oxonian, in Their Rambles and Sprees through the Metropolis.* Egan, who is otherwise known as an early sporting journalist and writer on boxing, published the book in 1821 and its boisterous, good-humoured comedy proved immediately popular. It remains of interest because of the light it throws on the habits and language of a particular class of Regency Londoner and because its illustrations were done by Robert and George Cruikshank. There is, however, no edition currently in print. Examples of the illustrations can be seen in:

**The Graphic Work of George Cruikshank**
Dover £12.99 048623438X

# JOHN EVELYN (1620–1706)

The son of a Surrey gentleman, Evelyn was a Royalist during the Civil War, an early member of the Royal Society after the Restoration and a friend of the other great seventeenth century diarist, Pepys. His interests were many and varied and he was able to pursue them with the enthusiasm of the intelligent amateur throughout his long life. He wrote works on the art of engraving and the practice of arboriculture and was an enthusiastic proponent of various schemes for the improvement of the capital. *Fumifugium or The Inconvenience of the Air and Smoke of London dissipated* was published in 1661 and was an early attempt to suggest a solution for the perennial problem of London pollution. In the aftermath of the Great Fire Evelyn came up with a large and ambitious plan to transform and rationalise the city during its reconstruction. It was seriously considered by the King and his ministers but it was adjudged to involve too many complicated issues and disputes over property and ownership to be a practical proposition. *Evelyn's Diary* was first published in 1818 and the definitive edition, edited in six volumes by E. S. De Beer, appeared in 1955. Evelyn emerges much less strongly as a personality from the pages of his journals than the irrepressible Pepys does from his but he offers gripping accounts of the Fire and of events like the great Frost Fair of 1683–84, when the Thames froze over. His diary was also kept over a considerably longer period than that of Pepys and is a mine of information about public life and public figures in the late seventeenth century.

> *... the stones of Paul's flew like grenadoes, the lead melting down the streets in a stream, and the very pavements of them glowing with fiery redness, so as nor horse nor man was able to tread on them, and the demolitions had stopped all the passages, so as no help could be applied...*

Evelyn on the Great Fire

**The Diary of John Evelyn (3 Vols)**
Routledge hbk £175.00 0415149541

**The Diary of John Evelyn**
Boydell pbk £16.95 0851156398

# Eighteenth Century London: the Poets' View

*Poet and critic Peter Scupham looks at the city as it is mirrored in eighteenth century verse.*

*Houses, churches, mixed together,*
*Streets unpleasant in all weather;*
*Prisons, palaces contiguous,*
*Gates, a bridge, the Thames irriguous.*

*Gaudy things enough to tempt ye,*
*Showy outsides, insides empty;*
*Bubbles, trades, mechanic arts,*
*Coaches, wheelbarrows and carts.*

John Bancks's opening stanzas to his *A Description of London* (1738), with their easy jogtrot of particulars and sense of conversational intimacy are part of a mass of verse which has recently been brought back into circulation, particularly by Roger Lonsdale in his *New Oxford Book of Eighteenth Century Verse* and *Eighteenth Century Women Poets*. This new social, familiar poetry, its couplets so well adapted to the commercial society of equals which was taking the place of the tightly enclosed Court and Courtier world of the Stuarts, has given us a vivid panorama of early to mid-eighteenth century London – and if its practitioners had little to say about the kingdoms of the spirit, they had plenty to say about the kingdom of Anne and the Georges. For women, expected to write as amateurs and debarred from easy access to the classical education thought necessary for the 'higher'-and often more forgettable- poetry of the period, verse letters and epistles from town to country, country to town, were an attractive form, as in Anne Finch, the Countess of Winchelsea's 'Ballad to Mrs Catherine Fleming in London from Malshanger farm in Hampshire', published in 1729:

*From me, who whilom sung the town,*
*    This second ballad comes*
*To let you know we are got down*
*    From hurry, smoke, and drums,*
*And every visitor that rolls*
*In restless coach from Mall to Paul's,*
*    With a fa-la-la-la-la-la.*

It is often the minor writers of a period, themselves caught up in the hurly-burly, whose verses most effectively correct our inveterate tendency to fix periods as if they were tapestries, motionless landscapes of the imagination, and remind us of the bewildering dynamism of the past. As James Bramston, a country vicar, wrote in *The Art of Politicks*, published in 1729:

> *What's not destroyed by Time's devouring hand?*
> *Where's Troy, and where's the maypole in the Strand?*
> *Peas, cabbages and turnips once grew where*
> *Now stands New Bond Street and a newer square;*
> *Such piles of buildings now rise up and down,*
> *London itself seems going out of town.*

Heritage and television may slow down and simplify eighteenth century social life to a peep-show of balanced, sunlit houses, plump portraits and formal manner-codes, tempered by bluff squires, mollocking milkmaids and Tyburn Tree, but the view from the sash window had no such orderly security. The sense of eternal change, endless metamorphosis, was then, as now, the staple of London life.

This magnetic London, as the eighteenth century swung into view, was not only the largest city in England, but the largest in Europe with some 600,000 inhabitants – the second city, Norwich, had some 30,000 – and its triple nature grew more clearly defined as the century progressed. Ton, fashion, the carriage and flunkey world Fielding described as 'People of Fascination' moved west into the great squares whose names – Cavendish, Grosvenor, Berkeley – record the Tory land-owning magnates. The City was still the gated city: mercantile, Whig, talkative and thrusting, the centre of the trading universe. The shops of London were renowned for their eye-catching displays, and Mary Jones, in her *Soliloquy on an Empty Purse* (1750), recognises their blandishments entertainingly:

> *Safe shall I walk with thee along,*
> *Amidst temptations thick and strong;*
> *Catched by the eye, no more shall stop*
> *At Wildey's toys, or Pinchbeck's shop;*
> *Nor cheapening Payne's ungodly books,*
> *Be drawn aside by pastry-cooks:*
> *But fearless now we both may go*
> *Where Ludgate's mercers bow so low;*

*Beholding all with equal eye,*
*Nor moved at – "Madam, what d'ye buy?"*

Out to the east and north east grew the sprawling tribal communities of the labouring and depressed poor. Add to this picture, endless movement, filth, the din of metal rimmed wheels on cobbles, a hugely crowded Thames and the respectable or raffish glamour of tea-gardens and pleasure gardens – Ranelagh and Vauxhall for fashion, tea-houses such as White Conduit House in Islington for a general Sunday excursion like that celebrated here by William Woty in a contribution to *The Gentleman's Magazine* in 1760:

*Human beings here*
*In couples multitudinous assemble,*
*Forming the drollest group that ever trod*
*Fair Islingtonian plains: male after male,*
*Dog after dog succeeding, husbands, wives,*
*Fathers and mothers, brothers, sisters, friends*
*And pretty little boys and girls. Around,*
*Across, along the garden's shrubby maze,*
*They walk, they sit, they stand.*

Then, for the intellectual life of the town, sprinkle the whole with coffee-houses and taverns – particularly coffee-houses where coteries of wits, poets, actors, politicians (what trade or profession you will) talked their own shop from morning till night and kept the world of ideas in circular or forward motion. But though these worlds co-existed, they rubbed off and against each other to make up that creature London, felt on the poets' pulses as a physical entity, an organism with its own vital life. When Swift wrote his *A Description of a City Shower* (1710), we not only have the fashionable man imprisoned in his sedan-chair:

*Boxed in a chair the beau impatient sits,*
*While spouts run clatt'ring o'er the roof by fits;*
*And ever and anon with frightful din*
*The leather sounds, he trembles from within,*

but Swift, with his mordant sense that the powdered graces of life are merely a veneer on excrement, tells us in a triple-rhymed climax to his gallivanting couplets how:

*Sweepings from butchers' stalls, dung, guts and blood,*
*Drowned puppies, stinking sprats, all drenched in mud,*
*Dead cats and turnip-tops come tumbling down the flood.*

Swift, for the greater part of his life, was an unwilling exile in Ireland. John Gay, Swift's friend, Pope's friend, one of that argumentative, satirical band of Tory poets and pamphleteers which flourished in Queen Anne's London, has left two works whose vivacity keeps his London alive – ***The Beggar's Opera***, which he called his Newgate Pastoral and ***Trivia; Or the Art of Walking the Streets of London.*** First published in 1716, *Trivia* is a substantial poem of some 1300 lines which recreates the pullulating life of the streets by day and by night, with the mock-heroic figure of the walker-spectator threading that alarming maze. Road-rage is ever present:

*Now oaths grow loud, with coaches coaches jar,*
*And the smart blow provokes the sturdy war;*
*From the high box they whirl the thong around,*
*And with the twining lash their shins resound:*
*Their rage ferments, more dangerous wounds they try,*
*And the blood gushes down their painfull eye.*

The strength of the poem, as with so much verse of the period, as with the paintings of Hogarth, lies in the vitality and physicality of those commonplace details which have acquired a fascination by being so clearly there, so dead and gone yet so endlessly renewed: the bully, with his 'broad hat, edg'd round with tarnish'd lace', the housewife under her 'umbrella's oily shed', the 'swinging signs', so much an overhead part of early eighteenth century London, or 'the surly butcher's greasy tray.' In an essentially unpoliced city, danger was never very far away – particularly at night when the raffish street gangs, the Mohocks, Scourers and Hawkubites, were out for blood and chaos. Of course, the gentleman rakehell often created the danger, as Elizabeth Thomas describes in her ***Epistle to Clemena***, published in 1722. Aminta, unwisely married to the fortune-hunting Nefario, finds herself neglected while her husband, tavern-bound, sneaks off:

*To famed Pontack's or noted Monsieur Locket's,*
*Where Mrs Jilt as fairly picks his pockets.*
*Thus bubbled, in revenge he walks his round,*
*From loft three stories high to cellar underground;*
*Scours all the streets, some brother rake doth fight,*

*And with a broken pate conclude the night.*
*Or in some tavern with the gaming crew,*
*He drinks, and swears, and plays, till day doth night pursue.*

One of the most compelling nightpieces of Augustan London is the picture of young Samuel Johnson walking the streets from dusk to dawn in the 1730s with fellow-poet Richard Savage, both of them only too well acquainted with grinding poverty and those accompanying disappointments which fuelled both their resentments and their ambitions. As for danger, Johnson, who always carried a cudgel in his insomniac prowlings, once claimed to have beaten off four attackers till the watch came to the rescue. His rhetorical **London: A Poem, In Imitation of the Third Satire of Juvenal** (1738) is full of a sonorous disgust at the sad state of 'thoughtless ease and empty show' London exemplifies, but he knew the truth underlying the drama of his lines:

*Prepare for death, if here at night you roam,*
*And sign your will before you sup from home.*
*Some fiery fop, with new commission vain,*
*Who sleeps on brambles till he kills his man;*
*Some frolic drunkard, reeling from a feast,*
*Provokes a brawl, and stabs you for a jest.*

The unwary or incautious were lucky if they found a watchman to help, as Charles Woodward, drunk and tripping over a prostitute on his own front door, claims he did in **The Midnight Ramble**, published in 1731:

*"I'll light you home, sir, if you'll give me leave."*
*"Home, friend!" quoth I, "I live at this same house:*
*This is my trap, I am a city mouse;*
*But some damned, venomous cat, I fear, doth lie*
*To snap me up as I am passing by."*

This London of unsoftened vitality and corruption, so consciously seen by Johnson and other poets as akin to Juvenal's Rome, has closer links with the nineteenth century London of Dickens and Doré than with T. S. Eliot's Unreal City of isolation and withdrawal, where:

*Sighs, short and infrequent, were exhaled*
*And each man fixed his eyes before his feet*

'The fields lie sleeping underneath.' That slogan scrawled on 1960s London concrete finds its echo in an anonymous poem, *The Comparison*, published in 1729, though the author is exercising his ingenuity and fancy rather than rejecting some cancerous dystopia. (The 'kennel' is the gutter or centre-of-the-street drain):

> *Where busy crowds pressed on and thronged the way,*
> *Let groves and forests rise as thick as they;*
> *Let cascades play and streams come murm'ring down,*
> *Where noisy coaches rattled o'er the town;*
> *Let stinking kennels be transformed to brooks,*
> *Coxcombs (an easy change) to jays and rooks;*
> *Prating coquets be turned to cackling geese,*
> *And mobs huzzaing into buzzing bees;*
> *Let birds in concert serenade each street,*
> *Cows low at the Exchange and sheep at Guildhall bleat.*

The historian Dorothy George long ago pointed out that Tottenham Court Road, in Dr. Johnson's time, still 'ran chiefly through fields and was bordered with cow-houses and farms.' So, in 1754, the anonymous author of *A Description of the Spring in London* can tell us that, despite the ferment of expansion taking London's boundaries ever further into the fields:

> *The truant schoolboy now at eve we meet,*
> *Fatigued and sweating through the crowded street,*
> *His shoes embrowned at once with dust and clay,*
> *With whitethorn loaded, which he takes for May:*
> *Round his flapped hat in rings the cowslips twine,*
> *Or in cleft osiers form a golden line.*

England, as ever in transition, has not yet born the full brunt of that transformation the Industrial Revolution is preparing for her. There is still a sense of containment to London, despite the growth of that no-man's land of refuse, night-soil heaps, brick-making and scrubby market-gardening which separated city from country-mice. So, as a typical Londoner of his period, let us return to John Bancks (1709–1751), the weaver's apprentice from Reading who set up a bookstall in Spitalfields, worked as a journeyman bookbinder, turned author and ended his days in Islington, that genteel home of cow-keeping and tea-gardens. He invited us into his city; let him give us, in the closing stanzas of his *Description*, a valediction:

*Women black, red, fair and grey,*
*Prudes and such as never pray,*
*Handsome, ugly, noisy, still,*
*Some that will not, some that will.*

*Many a beau without a shilling,*
*Many a widow not unwilling,*
*Many a bargain, if you strike it:*
*This is London! How d'ye like it?*

**Eighteenth Century Women Poets (ed. Roger Lonsdale)**
Oxford UP pbk £9.99 0192827758

**New Oxford Book of Eighteenth Century Verse (ed. Roger Lonsdale)**
Oxford UP pbk £11.99 0192820540

**Johnson's Juvenal: London and The Vanity of Human Wishes (ed. Niall Rudd)**
Duckworth pbk £6.95 0906515645

## HENRY FIELDING (1707–1754)

Fielding was born in Somerset but made his way to London in the late seventeen twenties and for a number of years pursued a career as dramatist and satirist, lampooning the corruption and hypocrisies of Walpole's government. So successful was he in this, that the government introduced the Licensing Act of 1737 which effectively banned his plays from the stage and brought his career as a dramatist to an end. He turned instead to the novel and, in 1748 when he was made justice of the peace for Westminster, to the law. His court and his house were in Bow Street. Fielding was famously incorruptible in a time of great corruption and, together with his half-brother, the blind Sir John Fielding who succeeded him as magistrate when he died, Fielding struggled to impose some kind of honest dealing onto the chaotic world of eighteenth century law enforcement. He formed the group of thief-takers which later became known as the Bow Street Runners.

Fielding's experiences as a magistrate were put to effective use in *Jonathan Wild* (1743), a fictionalisation of the true story of the thief and betrayer of fellow thieves who was hanged in 1725. Wild's career through Newgate and the criminal underworld is traced up to his defiant death on the gallows and Fielding hints at parallels between Wild's criminality and the actions of the great men of town, implicitly condemning both for hypocrisy. *Joseph Andrews* (1742) has scenes of the iniquities and the glamour of London life and in *Tom Jones* (1749) all the characters end in London where Tom is involved with the ageing Lady Bellaston and the villainous Lord Fellamar attempts to force Sophia Western, the heroine of the novel, to submit to him. Not everybody was impressed by *Tom Jones*, which is now accepted as Fielding's greatest work and one of the finest novels in the language. 'I am shocked to hear you quote from so vicious a novel,' Dr. Johnson said to a friend and there were some who attributed the two earthquake shocks which hit London in 1749 to the malign influence of Fielding's book. In truth, although Fielding does show the reader the low life of Georgian London, he is not so 'realistic' in his depiction of it as, say, Hogarth or fellow novelist Smollett and his intention in the book seems impeccably moral. Fielding's London is primarily a London of deceit and masquerade, a London where nothing is quite as it appears and the country virtues of honesty and openness are open to abuse and exploitation by the vicious and the sinful. As such *Tom Jones*, as well as providing a panorama of urban life at the time, sits at the heart of a tradition of contrasting the provincial and the metropolitan which has continued to the present day.

**Amelia**
Penguin pbk £6.99 0140432299

**The History of Tom Jones**
Penguin pbk £3.99 0140430091

**Jonathan Wild**
Penguin pbk £5.99 0140431519

**Joseph Andrews**
Penguin pbk £4.99 0140431144

**Joseph Andrews & Shamela**
Oxford UP pbk £4.99 0192815504

**Tom Jones**
Oxford UP pbk £3.99 0192834975

**Where Lincoln's Inn, wide space, is rail'd around,
Cross not with venturous step; there oft is found
The lurking thief, who, while the daylight shone,
Made the walls echo with his begging tone,
That crutch, which late compassion moved, shall wound
Thy bleeding head, and fell thee to the ground...**
John Gay – Trivia

## JOHN GAY (1685–1732)

Born in Barnstaple, Gay moved to the capital as a young man
when he was apprenticed to a silk merchant in the Strand. From
publication of his first major work, **Wine**, in 1708, he moved in
literary circles and was a friend of Pope, Swift and other Augustan
luminaries. **Trivia**, a poem subtitled *The Art of Walking the Streets of
London* was published in 1716. The narrator conducts the reader
through the pleasures and (more frequently) the hazards
of the early eighteenth century townscape, advising on the way to
avoid the filth of the streets, to recognise the street cries, to steer
clear of the crime and violence and so on. Gay's best known work
is, of course, **The Beggar's Opera**. This skillfully combines realism
with romance in its depiction of the Newgate underworld in which
the stylish highwayman Macheath operates. Peachum, the receiver
of stolen goods and betrayer of Macheath, is clearly based on the
notorious real-life Jonathan Wild, about whom Fielding also wrote.
The affairs between Macheath and both Polly Peachum and Lucy
Lockit, together with the improbably happy ending to the piece,
belong firmly in the realm of fiction. *The Beggar's Opera* was, by
eighteenth century standards, a prodigiously successful work. It ran
for sixty two nights at the Lincoln's Inn Fields Theatre at a time
when most plays were lucky to last more than a few performances.
Gay attempted to repeat the success with a sequel, **Polly**, but was
thwarted by the authorities which banned it, detecting unforgivable
satire of Walpole's government.

**The Beggar's Opera**
Penguin pbk £5.99 0140432205

## OLIVER GOLDSMITH (1730–1774)

Dramatist, novelist, poet, hack journalist, Goldsmith was a man whose hopeless improvidence meant he was always on the brink of financial ruin and he was frequently obliged to write his way out of financial disaster. His best-known works are the novel *The Vicar of Wakefield*, the poem *The Deserted Village* and the play *She Stoops to Conquer*, but he also wrote *The Citizen of the World* (1762), a collection of letters which pretends to be the correspondence of a Chinese visitor to London. These provide a satirical, mock-naive view of the contemporary city and the customs of its inhabitants.

**The Citizen of the World** is not currently available.

> *The streets of Nankin are sometimes strewed with gold leaf; very different are those of London: in the midst of their pavements a great lazy puddle moves muddily along; heavy laden machines with wheels of unwieldy thickness crowd up every passage, so that a stranger instead of finding time for observation, is happy if he has time to escape from being crushed to pieces. The house borrow very few ornaments from architecture; their chief decoration seems to be a paltry piece of painting, hung out at their doors or windows, at once a proof of their indigence and vanity.*

Oliver Goldsmith – The Citizen of the World

# My Judgment of Solomon is rolled up in a ware-house in the Borough! My Entry into Jerusalem... is doubled up in a back room in Holborn! My Lazarus is in an upholsterer's shop in Mount Street! and my Crucifixion is in an hay-loft in Lisson Grove.

## Benjamin Haydon – Diary

## BENJAMIN HAYDON (1786–1846)

Haydon was a flamboyant painter driven to produce huge canvasses on biblical and historical subjects which, he was firmly convinced, would revolutionise what he saw as the effete British art of his day. Initially his epic paintings had some success but his increasingly florid and paranoid personality eventually alienated patrons and friends alike. Professional and financial problems mounted and, in 1846, he killed himself. Ironically he is now best remembered not as a painter but as a writer. His diary, first published posthumously, is filled with anecdote and observation and provides a vivid portrait of London literary life, particularly in the teens and twenties of the new century when Haydon was a friend of Wordsworth and Keats, Hazlitt and Leigh Hunt.

**Haydon's Diary** is currently out of print.

# WILLIAM HICKEY (c. 1749–1830)

For insight into the low-life of eighteenth century Covent Garden and its environs and for entertaining descriptions of what happened when the younger members of the upper classes entered them in search of fun, William Hickey's memoirs can not be beaten. First published nearly a century after his death, they tell of an adventurous life of travel and drama. They also tell, with appealing frankness and vividly remembered detail, Hickey's own thrills and spills, as a young man in search of wine, women and more wine. Many passages in the memoirs are also a useful antidote to nostalgia and a reminder of just how dangerous and violent the streets of London could be at the time.

**The Memoirs of William Hickey** are not currently in print.

*intoxicated as I was... (I) endeavoured to walk home. Unfortunately for me they were then paving anew the lower parts of Westminster, and I in consequence encountered various holes, and various heaps of stones and rubbish, into and over which I tumbled and scrambled. God only knows how, or how I contrived to get so far on my way as Parliament Street; but a little after seven in the morning, a party who had supped, and afterwards played whist all night... were just sallying forth to get into a hackney coach. Mr. Smith, one of the company... stepping to the rear of the coach to make water, descried a human figure lying in the kennel, whereupon he called to his companions, who, upon examination, found it was poor pilgarlic in woeful plight.*

89

## SAMUEL JOHNSON (1709–1784)

Dr. Johnson famously remarked that when a man is tired of London he is tired of life and, thanks largely to Boswell's biography of him, he is seen as the quintessential literary figure in the eighteenth century city. He also wrote a bitter satire, *London*, first published anonymously in 1738, in which he unfolds a bleak vision of urban decay and corruption, of a city in which 'all crimes are safe, but hated poverty'. The paradox is not as great as it might seem. Eighteenth century writers may have proclaimed the belief that the city was the seat of the polite virtues and that literature and the fine arts could only flourish in an urban setting. They also portrayed the city as diseased and insanitary, a place of madness and moral decrepitude, in sharp contrast to the pastoral simplicities, the honest, unassuming virtues of the countryside. As the century went on and London grew as a trading and mercantile city, it took on the role, earlier occupied by the Court, both of epitome of civilisation and moral cesspit. Johnson's poem, as well as being an exercise in imitation of a classical model, reflected one of the roles London played in the eighteenth century imagination.

Johnson himself was not born a Londoner. Like so many of the city's most eminent citizens over the centuries, he became one. He arrived in London, accompanied by David Garrick, in 1737, in flight from failure as a schoolmaster and in pursuit of literary glory. He was slow to find it and he knew only too well the perils of Grub Street hack-writing, lampooned by Pope in *The Dunciad* and evoked by Johnson himself in works such as his *Life of Mr Richard Savage*. For many years he wrote reams of poems, essays, reports of parliamentary debates, all for very little money and most of them for *The Gentleman's Magazine*, a miscellany edited by Edward Cave from offices and works in St. John's Gate, Clerkenwell. St. John's Gate is still in existence today.

Also still there to be visited is the house in Gough Square, off Fleet Street, where Johnson and a number of assistants worked for nearly a decade on the *Dictionary of the English Language*, finally published in 1755. Johnson's *Dictionary* was not the first such work in

English but it was the first to cite examples of the language in use and was not wholly superseded until the publication of the *Oxford English Dictionary*. The *Dictionary* established Johnson's reputation but he was not finally freed of money worries until he was awarded a crown pension of £300 a year in 1762. The following year he met Boswell in a bookshop in Russell Street, Covent Garden and the process by which Johnson was transformed into the legendary figure of the biography was begun. The period in which Boswell knew Johnson was the period in which Johnson emerged from the years of hack-writing to become what Smollett called 'the Great Cham of Literature'. The Johnson of the biography is eccentric, overbearing, opinionated, often lacking the most basic social graces. He is also a brilliant conversationalist, a large, generous and unforgettable character. Boswell's *Life of Johnson* is, amongst other things, a vivid evocation of a certain kind of London literary life in the period, a life lived in the streets and taverns of Fleet Street and Covent Garden, one conducted in the public spaces of London rather than behind the closed doors of the salon. Even if we had no writing by Johnson himself on urban life he would still deserve a place in any guide to London writing because of the portrait of him in Boswell's biography.

**Selected Poetry and Prose**
U. of California P. pbk £14.95 0520035526

> ## One thing extraordinary was this day, a man, a Quaker, came naked through the Hall, only very civilly tied about the loins to avoid scandal, and with a chafing dish of fire and brimstone burning upon his head, did pass through the Hall, crying, "Repent! Repent!"
> **Samuel Pepys**

## CHARLES LAMB (1775–1834)

The bust of Charles Lamb at the back of St. Sepulchre's church in Giltspur Street has an inscription in which he is described as 'perhaps the most loved name in English literature.' The truth is that, today, Lamb is little known and little read. Yet he is in many ways an archetypal London writer. Few writers have loved the city as Lamb did. He was born in Crown Office Row in the Temple and lived most of his life in London, only moving out to Enfield and to Edmonton in the last few years of his life. His *Essays of Elia*, originally published in the *London Magazine* between 1820 and 1823 and printed in book form in the latter year, are filled with observations, anecdotes and memories of the city. Lamb's style, mannered and deliberately embellished with archaisms and convoluted phraseology, can be difficult for a modern reader but essays like 'Christ's Hospital' (Lamb was at school there and met Coleridge, a lifelong friend, there), 'Some of the Old Benchers of the Inner Temple' and 'The South Sea House' remain worth reading for their idiosyncratic portraits of a long-gone London.

**Charles Lamb and Elia**
Fyfield Books pbk £9.95 1857540034

## GEORGE LILLO
## (1693–1739)

Lillo is remembered today solely for his play *The London Merchant, or the History of George Barnwell*, first produced in 1731. At about the same time that Gay was turning the exploits of Newgate highwaymen into ballad opera, Lillo, of whom little is certainly known, was writing the first drama in English in which the everyday life of the commercial classes of the city is the subject of tragedy. A London apprentice called George Barnwell is induced by a Shoreditch whore, Sarah Millwood, to steal his master's money and to murder his uncle. After squandering the money both are brought to justice and hanged. The play is unambiguously moralistic but precise in its London details and was a popular success for at least a century after its first staging. It has been recently revived.

**The London Merchant**
U. of Nebraska P. pbk £6.50
0803253656

# Went to hear Mrs. Turner's daughter... play on the harpsichon; but, Lord! it was enough to make any man sick to hear her; yet I was forced to commend her highly.

Samuel Pepys

## SAMUEL PEPYS (1633–1703)

Pepys was born in 1633 in a house in Salisbury Court, off Fleet Street, the son of a London tailor, and was educated at school near St. Paul's Cathedral and at Magdalene College, Cambridge. When his famous diary was begun, on the 1st January 1660, he was married and working in London as a lowly and poorly paid civil servant. The years in which he kept his diary were also the years in which his professional life flourished as he became a more and more significant and prosperous figure as a naval administrator. He ceased to keep his diary in May 1669, largely because he believed, wrongly, that he was going blind. After the period covered by the diary Pepys, despite one or two setbacks, continued to lead a successful career in public life before retiring, at the time of the Glorious Revolution, to a substantial property at Clapham. His *Diary*, in shorthand, was kept with his other papers at Magdalene College and a selection was deciphered and published in 1825. A ten volume edition was produced in the eighteen nineties but the standard edition now is the monumental, and unbowdlerised, eleven volumes transcribed and edited by Latham and Matthews between 1970 and 1983.

Few works give so vivid a portrait of a past London as Pepys's *Diary*. Partly this is a result of the range of people he meets and describes. Through his work for the Navy Board he came into contact with the leading figures of the day and there are revealing glimpses of the King and his court dotted through the pages of the diary. Through his active social life and his personal interests he introduces the reader to the more anonymous characters of Restoration London from his parish priest, Dr.John Mills, to Mary Mercer, his wife's maid. Partly the vividness is a result of the unguardedness of the diary. Written in shorthand, the diary was not intended to be published and it is a work of frankness and immediacy. Mostly the diary's charm and its liveliness of detail are the consequences of Pepys's personality. He can sometimes appear miserly and money-obsessed. He can sometimes appear to be slightly humourless. However his distinguishing quality would seem to have been an enormous zest and relish for life which are obvious throughout the diary, whether in descriptions of his playgoing and music-making or excursions with friends along the Thames, in accounts of Parliamentary debates or tales of his own sexual adventures. Pepys was interested in everything London offered him. He is an invaluable source for information about the great national disasters of the Fire and the Plague. He can also tell us about the food that people ate at the time and the clothes they wore. He notes down details of court ceremonies and of domestic pleasures with the same enthusiasm. And, because of the unselfconscious freshness of his prose, he is endlessly and delightfully quotable.

*I went out to Charing Cross, to see Major-General Harrison hanged, drawn and quartered; which was done there, he looking as cheerful as any man could do in that condition.*

**Diary Volume 1 (1660)**
Addison Wesley Longman
pbk £8.99 0004990218

**Diary Volume 2 (1661)**
Addison Wesley Longman
pbk £9.95 0004990226

**Diary Volume 3 (1662)**
Addison Wesley Longman
pbk £9.95 0004990234

**Diary Volume 4 (1663)**
Addison Wesley Longman
pbk £9.95 0004990242

**Diary Volume 5 (1664)**
Addison Wesley Longman
pbk £9.95 0004990250

**Diary Volume 6 (1665)**
Addison Wesley Longman
pbk £9.95 0004990269

**Diary Volume 7 (1666)**
Addison Wesley Longman
pbk £9.95 0004990277

**Diary Volume 8 (1667)**
Addison Wesley Longman
pbk £9.95 0004990285

**Diary Volume 9 (1668/9)**
Addison Wesley Longman
pbk £9.95 0004990293

**Diary Volume 10 (Companion)**
Addison Wesley Longman
pbk £9.95 0004990307

**Diary Volume 11 (Index)**
Addison Wesley Longman
pbk £9.95 0004990315

**The Shorter Pepys**
Penguin pbk £14.00 0140433767

# TOBIAS SMOLLETT (1721–1771)

Smollett was born near Dumbarton and, after brief attendance at Glasgow University and a spell in the navy, settled in London to earn his living as a surgeon and as a writer. After publishing two satirical poems on London life, Smollett wrote the first of his novels, *The Adventures of Roderick Random*, which appeared in 1748. He went on to publish several more novels, to translate Cervantes and to make his forceful presence felt in both journalism and the theatre. His health was poor and in the seventeen sixties he travelled much in Europe in the hopes of finding a climate in which it would improve. He was a notably ill-tempered traveller, hugely unimpressed by nearly all things foreign, and *Travels Through France and Italy* is entertaining in the way it mingles virulent prejudice with sharp observation. Smollett died in Italy in 1771.

One of Smollett's strengths as a novelist was the vitality with which he portrayed, in several books, the street life of eighteenth century London. Smollett's own experience of the city was varied. At different times he practiced as a surgeon in Downing Street, kept open house in Chelsea and spent three months in the King's Bench prison for libelling an admiral. His characters are similarly rooted in the specific realities of the city. Roderick Random undertakes a lengthy pub crawl through the taverns and alehouses of Covent Garden ending up at Moll King's by St. Paul's Portico, a notorious nightspot often mentioned in writings and portrayed in prints of the period. In *The Expedition of Humphrey Clinker*, an epistolary novel first published in the year of Smollett's death, characters visit Sadler's Wells to see the rope-dancers and tightrope artistes and admire the splendours of both Ranelagh and Vauxhall Gardens. Both Roderick Random and Humphrey Clinker spend time (unjustly) in London prisons and the horrors of eighteenth century incarceration are well drawn. Smollett's picaresque fiction is in the same tradition as Fielding's and his depiction of pullulating London life is just as vivid and often more brutally direct. His novels were enormously influential on the greatest of all London novelists, Charles Dickens.

**The Adventures of Roderick Random**
Oxford UP pbk £5.99
0192812610

**The Adventures of Roderick Random**
Penguin pbk £5.99 0140433325

**The Expedition of Humphry Clinker**
Penguin pbk £5.99 0140430210

**The Expedition of Humphry Clinker**
Oxford UP pbk £5.99
0192816640

## JOHN STRYPE
## (1643–1737)

In his long life Strype, who was rector of Leyton for nearly seventy years, wrote widely on church history, collected a huge array of historical documents and manuscripts and published biographies of major ecclesiastics including Cranmer. He also undertook new editions of Stow's *Survey of London*. He greatly enlarged and expanded Stow's original work from the late sixteenth century, indeed rewrote much of it, and his edition, published in 1720, contains much valuable material on the city in the seventeenth and early eighteenth century.

## HORACE WALPOLE
## (1717–1797)

What Pepys and Evelyn were to the seventeenth century, Horace Walpole was to the eighteenth century. Born into privilege (his father was the first Prime Minister Sir Robert Walpole), Horace Walpole was never inconvenienced by the need to work and could spend his time as a man about London, an insider in the social and political worlds, and in the gradual transformation of a small property at Twickenham into the elaborately 'gothic' castle known as Strawberry Hill. His letters, of which some four thousand survive and have been edited in a massive work of scholarship by Yale University Press, provide an extraordinarily lively portrait of the eighteenth century city. Many of the scenes of London life from the fiction of Fielding and Smollett can be matched by scenes from Walpole's Letters and Walpole, as observer and writer, loses little in the comparison.

**The Letters of Horace Walpole**
Everyman's Library hbk £10.99
1857152328

The complete correspondence in 48 volumes is available from Yale UP, each volume costing £75.

## NED WARD (1667–1731)

Ned Ward ran a tavern near Gray's Inn for thirty years in the first half of the eighteenth century and was a prolific writer of scurrilous, Grub Street verse. He is now remembered chiefly for *The London Spy*, a prose collection of vigorous, journalistic pieces about city life. In these vivid sketches a wide-eyed country bumpkin is introduced to a metropolis teeming with life and vitality. Ward offers an entertaining panorama of eighteenth century London life from the wits in the coffeehouses to the fishwives at Billingsgate, from the inhabitants of Bedlam to the courtiers of St. James. Thanks to the enterprise of an American publisher, Colleagues Press, *The London Spy* is currently available.

**The London Spy**
Colleagues Press pbk £14.95
0937191507

# Victorian and Edwardian City

The images in this
chapter are from
*London: A Pilgrimage*
by Gustave Doré and
Blanchard Jerrold

# HARRISON AINSWORTH
## (1805–1882)

Ainsworth was an enormously popular writer in his day, and for a generation or two after his death, but is now almost unread. To read him today is, by and large, to understand why he is neglected. His style of unsophisticated historical melodrama is difficult to take seriously. Yet, in books like *The Tower of London, Old St. Paul's* and *Jack Sheppard*, he did take well-known episodes of London history and attempt to do for them what Sir Walter Scott had done for the great stories of Scottish history. Scott was, far and away, the greater artist but Ainsworth should not be entirely dismissed and he did much to draw the attention of the Victorian, novel-reading classes to the history of the city.

The novels of Harrison Ainsworth are currently out of print.

# SIR WALTER BESANT (1836–1901)

Besant was one of those indefatigable Victorians whose prodigious energies were directed into a wide array of activities. He was an authority on French literature. He was one of the founders of the Society of Authors, an organisation which has, for more than a hundred years, worked to protect legal rights and copyrights for writers. He worked on a variety of philanthropic projects including the creation of the 'People's Palace' in the Mile End Road, which was designed to provide education and amusement to the poor of the East End. He wrote very extensively on the history and topography of London and began a process which resulted, in the years after his death, in the publication of a multi-volume survey of the city. As a novelist he worked initially in collaboration with James Rice and produced a number of books, well enough known in their day but now almost completely forgotten, even the memorably titled *Ready Money Mortiboy*. After Rice's death in 1882, Besant wrote many more novels of which, perhaps, only two, *All Sorts and Conditions of Men* and *Children of Gibeon*, retain more than an exclusively historical interest. Both books portray convincingly the poverty and deprivation of the eighteen eighties East End but do so within interesting stories of individual transformation and the ambivalent consequences of crossing class-boundaries.

**All Sorts and Conditions of Men**
Oxford UP pbk £6.99 0192832581
**Children of Gibeon** is currently out of print.

## CHARLES BOOTH
### (1840–1916)

Booth was a wealthy shipowner, born in Liverpool, who became interested in the condition of the poorer classes of Victorian London when he moved to the capital to open a branch of his business. *Labour and Life of the People* was published in 1889 and the entire, monumental work appeared in seventeen volumes between 1891 and 1902 as *Life and Labour of the People of London*. Booth worked in the same broad area as Mayhew but his approach to his material was more statistically based. Where Mayhew listened and recorded, Booth was keen to measure and quantify. The result is that Mayhew was the more entertaining, but Booth probably the more reliable, social investigator.

## G. K. CHESTERTON (1874–1936)

If twentieth century Fleet Street has seen any equivalent to Dr. Johnson it is probably G.K. Chesterton. Where Johnson dealt in robust common sense, Chesterton turned his uncommon powers of wit and paradox on all the major issues of the day – political, social, religious, literary – in what was a prodigious output of essentially ephemeral journalism. The figure of Chesterton and his eccentricities – his vast bulk, his piping falsetto voice, his legendary absent-mindedness (allegedly, while he was on a lecture tour, he once telegraphed his wife, 'Am in Market Harborough. Where ought I to be?') – feature largely in any romanticised account of the departed glories of Fleet Street in the early decades of the century. Yet, amidst the demands of journalistic deadlines, Chesterton found time to write more substantial work. He published poetry, literary criticism, religious polemic and, most famously, the Father Brown stories, in which an unassuming Roman Catholic priest solves apparently insoluble mysteries by using his logic and his knowledge of the human heart. (Chesterton became a Catholic himself in 1922.) He also published several novels which, in varying degrees, exhibit his love of fantasy and romancing. The first of his novels, *The Napoleon of Notting Hill* (1904), represents Chesterton's most interesting take on the London which he loved. The book is set in the future (1984 – a date which seems to have been peculiarly attractive to crystal-gazing novelists) and yet it seems curiously redolent of the past. Chesterton believed that the future would (or should) more resemble the past (or his own version of it) than the present. In his London of 1984 the King is selected on a rota basis. When Auberon Quin becomes king he establishes the London boroughs as independent states. Conflict follows particularly when Adam Wayne, the leader in Notting Hill, takes the idea of independence to its logical conclusion. The book is a diverting and fascinating expression of Chesterton's complicated, often contradictory, political and social views, his love of an imagined 'Merry England' and of the anarchic and individual, his hatred of bureaucracy, big business and the deadening hand of the modern state. It remains enormously enjoyable as an elaborate fable worked out in the streets of a real London.

**The Napoleon of Notting Hill**
Oxford UP pbk £4.99 0192831453

# JOSEPH CONRAD (1857–1924)

Born in the Ukraine to Polish parents, Joseph Conrad, christened Jósef Korzeniowski, may seem an unlikely author for one of the most compelling portrayals of London in English literature. Having gone to sea at the age of sixteen, he joined the English Merchant Marine in 1878 with, by his own account, barely six words of English at his command. 'Polish Joe', as he was known to his crew-mates, became a British subject in 1886. His maritime career dogged by ill health, he settled in England in 1895 and embarked on the literary career that was to produce *Lord Jim* and *The Nigger of the Narcissus*, the masterly *Nostromo*, set in Latin America, and *Under Western Eyes*, a novel about revolutionary intrigue in Russia and Geneva. Widespread critical acclaim came to Conrad late in life but he was an established figure in literary circles which included Ford Madox Ford, Arnold Bennett, John Galsworthy and H.G. Wells. It is to the latter that *The Secret Agent* (1907) is dedicated.

The kernel of fact at the heart of *The Secret Agent* is an explosion at the foot of the Royal Observatory in Greenwich Park in February 1894. The apparent instigator of the explosion and its only casualty was a man found kneeling on the ground with one hand blown off and appalling wounds to his stomach. Later identified as one Martial Bourdin, he was dead within the hour. Conrad was living in Pimlico at the time and, as well as reading speculations in the newspapers, he seems likely to have seen a pamphlet published several years later in which it was claimed that Bourdin was duped into carrying the explosive by his brother-in-law H.B. Samuels, a police informant posing as an anarchist.

In *The Secret Agent* the central character, Verloc, is an *agent provocateur* in the pay of the Russian embassy who is compelled to manufacture an outrage which will discredit the anarchist community in London. The aim is to turn public opinion against the government's tolerant stance towards refugees and dissidents from other countries. Verloc's seedy shop in Soho is the meeting place for a group of anarchists but they are too feeble or superannuated to serve his purpose. Instead Verloc dupes his simple-minded brother-in-law Stevie into carrying the explosive in an attempt to blow up the Royal Observatory at Greenwich. The bomb explodes prematurely and Stevie is killed. When Verloc's wife, Winnie, learns of her brother's death she murders Verloc. She plans to leave the country with Ossipon, one of the other Soho anarchists, but Ossipon steals her money and abandons her. Winnie, left alone, commits suicide by jumping off the cross-Channel ferry.

Almost overwhelming the action, however, is the vast and malign presence of London, described in the Author's note as 'a cruel devourer of the world's light.' When the sun does shine it appears bloodshot and its rays are rusty. After dark the city is 'an immensity of greasy slime and damp plaster interspersed with lamps and enveloped, oppressed, penetrated, choked and suffocated by the blackness of a wet London night.' Cloaked in an urban miasma Dickens would have recognised, Conrad's novel also prefigures the thrillers of Graham Greene. With its themes of betrayal, political intrigue and terrorism, *The Secret Agent* reminds us that there is nothing new under the bloodshot sun.

*Andy Walker* Waterstone's, *Charing Cross Road*

**The Secret Agent**
Penguin pbk £3.99 0140180966
**The Secret Agent**
Oxford UP pbk £4.99
0192816276

He went through Islington, strode up the hill at Highgate on which stands the stone in honour of Whittington; turned down to Highgate Hill unsteady of purpose, and uncertain where to go; struck off to the right again, almost as soon as he began to descend it; and taking the footpath across the fields, skirted Caen Wood, and so came out on Hampstead Heath. Traversing the hollow by the Vale of Health, he mounted the opposite bank, and crossing the road which joins the villages of Hampstead and Highgate, made along the remaining portion of the Heath to the fields at North End, in one of which he laid himself down and slept.

Bill Sikes' journey after the murder of Nancy in Oliver Twist

## CHARLES DICKENS (1812–1870)

Dickens is the greatest of London novelists. No other novelist has made the city so much his own. He may set parts of his novels outside the metropolis – Yarmouth and Canterbury in *David Copperfield*, a cathedral city not unlike Rochester in *Great Expectations* – but his fictions, with the solitary exception of *Hard Times*, are, in Peter Ackroyd's phrase, 'deeply invaded by the city.' It is as hard to imagine Dickens the novelist without London as it is for us to imagine the nineteenth century city without Dickens's novels. For Dickens, who was a prodigious walker of the city streets, London was a landscape in which he was never a stranger and he is always precise and detailed in the urban geography of his fiction. Almost any landmark of central London in the middle decades of the century makes its appearances in Dickens's books. Take Blackfriars Bridge, for instance, the first version of which Dickens would have crossed every day as a child on his melancholy way from the infamous blacking factory in which he worked to the Marshalsea prison in which his father was incarcerated for debt. It is above Blackfriars Bridge that Pip rows when in training for the rescue of Magwitch in *Great Expectations*. Clennam and Plornish drive over the bridge in *Little Dorrit*, on their way to see the Dorrits who, like Dickens's father, are in the Marshalsea. In *Bleak House* Jo the crossing sweeper, chivvied by the hypocrite Chadband, seeks refuge in a 'baking stony corner' of the bridge. 'And there he sits munching, and gnawing, and looking up at the great Cross on the summit of St. Paul's Cathedral, glittering above a red and violet-tinted cloud of smoke.'

Almost any street in central London carries its echoes of Dickens's fiction. Golden Square, for example, is where Ralph Nickleby lives – 'It is one of the squares that have been; a quarter of the town that has gone down in the world, and taken to letting lodgings.' In the same novel, *Nicholas Nickleby*, the Kenwigs live in one of the surrounding streets, probably Carnaby Street. It is in the vicinity of Golden Square that Peggotty, in *David Copperfield*, finally tracks down his errant niece, Little Em'ly. Essex Street, going down from the Strand, is where Pip in *Great Expectations* finds lodgings for Magwitch when the convict reappears in his life. Fountain Court in the Temple is the scene of the courtship of John Westlock and Ruth Pinch in *Martin Chuzzlewit*. In Oliver Twist, Mr Brownlow is standing at a bookstall near Clerkenwell Green when his pocket is picked by the Artful Dodger. Examples like these, picked almost at random, can be multiplied a thousandfold. No street in the town was without its significance to Dickens and, despite the vast changes to London in the years since his death, there is no street that does not carry some resonance for the attentive reader of his fiction.

Yet Dickens is also acutely aware of the power the city carries as metaphor for the restrictions, constraint and injustices of his society. Perhaps the most memorable and extended example of his use of the city as metaphor is the extraordinary opening to *Bleak House.*

> *London. Michaelmas term lately over, and the Lord Chancellor sitting in Lincoln's Inn Hall. Implacable November weather. As much mud in the streets, as if the waters had but newly retired from the face of the earth, and it would not be wonderful to meet a Megalosaurus, forty feet long or so, waddling like an elephantine lizard up Holborn Hill.*

The fog-enshrouded city is captured by Dickens brilliantly in this opening – 'Fog everywhere. Fog up the river, where it flows among green aits and meadows; fog down the river, where it rolls defiled among the tiers of shipping, and the waterside pollutions of a great (and dirty) city... Chance people on the bridges peeping over the parapets into a nether sky of fog, with fog all round them, as if they were up in a balloon, and hanging in the misty clouds.' He leads the reader from the literal description of the London fog to the fog that lies at the heart of the Chancery legal system and the heart of the case of Jarndyce v. Jarndyce in which so many of the characters are enmeshed:

> *The raw afternoon is rawest, and the dense fog is densest, and the muddy streets are muddiest, near that leaden-headed old obstruction, appropriate ornament for the threshold of a leaden-headed old corporation: Temple Bar. And hard by Temple Bar, in Lincoln's Inn Hall, at the very heart of the fog, sits the Lord High Chancellor in his High Court of Chancery.'*

Not only the city itself but also, often, its individual institutions carry this metaphoric force. In **Little Dorrit** the Marshalsea (where Dickens's own improvident father had been imprisoned) is very much a real place carefully realised. 'It was an oblong pile of barrack building, partitioned into squalid houses standing back to back, so that there were no back rooms; environed by a narrow paved yard, hemmed in by high walls duly spiked at top.' Yet it also reflects Dickens's sense of Victorian society confining and limiting the individual, of London itself as a place of imprisonment. As so many commentators have suggested, this sense of the darkness and oppressiveness of the city probably has its origins in his time in the blacking factory near Hungerford Stairs. When an adult Dickens could not bring himself to confide these experiences to anyone but his close friend and future biographer John Forster but he wrote pointedly of the desolation and helplessness he must have felt in his childhood. 'I often forget in my dreams that I have a dear wife and children; even that I am a man; and wander desolately back to that time of my life.'

Of course the city Dickens recreated in his books was not just a place of darkness and oppression, an early version of James Thomson's late Victorian *City of Dreadful Night*. It was also the stage on which the life and drama of the age was played out. Dickens was famously fascinated by the theatre. Throughout his life he attended theatrical productions of all kinds. He organised theatrical performances by family and friends that, because of his fame, were played before paying audiences. As a young writer one of the first jobs he undertook was the editing of the Memoirs of the legendary pantomime clown, Joseph Grimaldi. In later life the public readings Dickens gave were renowned for the theatrical power of his delivery. In his fiction London becomes a huge theatrical backdrop against which his characters play out the destinies he assigns them. One of the most frequent criticisms levelled against Dickens as a novelist is that his characters are not 'rounded' characters but 'flat' caricatures, silhouettes or puppets brought to life only through verbal or physical eccentricities. Compared with, say, Henry James, Dickens, it is true, seems uninterested in the inner lives of his characters and yet, to criticise him for this is to miss much of his greatness as a chronicler of urban life. Dickens sensed a profound truth about the city – that it can be best depicted in fiction as a huge theatrical space in which character and individuality can best be displayed as theatrical performance.

The London of Dickens is both a city of the imagination and a reflection of the realities of the early Victorian city. (Or, perhaps, the Regency city since, as Peter Ackroyd has pointed out, 'the London of his novels always remains the London of his youth.') It is his unmatched capacity to combine the realities of a city with the myths and metaphors it can embody, a historical city with a city of the imagination, that continues to make Dickens the London novelist against which all other writers on the city have to be measured.

**Barnaby Rudge**
Penguin pbk £4.99 0140430903

**Bleak House**
Penguin pbk £4.99 0140434968

**David Copperfield**
Penguin £3.99 0140434941

**Dombey and Son**
Penguin pbk £5.99 0140430482

**Great Expectations**
Penguin pbk £5.99 0140434895

**Little Dorrit**
Penguin pbk £3.99 0140434925

**Martin Chuzzlewit**
Penguin pbk £4.99 0140430318

**Nicholas Nickleby**
Penguin pbk £4.99 0140431136

**The Old Curiosity Shop**
Penguin pbk £3.99 014043075X

**Oliver Twist**
Penguin pbk £2.99 0140430172

**Our Mutual Friend**
Penguin pbk £5.99 0140434976

**Pickwick Papers**
Penguin pbk £4.99 0140430784

**Selected Journalism 1850–1870**
Penguin pbk £9.99 0140435808

**Sketches by Boz**
Penguin pbk £7.99 0140433457

**A Tale of Two Cities**
Penguin pbk £3.99 0140430547

PETER ACKROYD
# Dickens
Mandarin pbk £12.50 0749306475

***Nick Creagh-Osborne** of Waterstone's at Harrods looks at a biography of London's greatest novelist, written by a contemporary novelist who has charted the interactions of London past and present.*

Peter Ackroyd's magisterial biography of Charles Dickens is a lucid and penetrating psychological and factual study of its subject. Dickens and the era to which his name is often applied are presented and analysed like the London of Ackroyd's own novels. The Dickens of reality and the constellation of his fictional characters walk with the reader through a London which is a kaleidoscopic vision of both historical fact and contemporary experience.

Dickens arrived in London at the age of ten in 1822. Ackroyd describes the boy as 'entering his kingdom': a moment of great consequence after which neither Dickens nor London would be the same again. Dickens spent the greater part of the rest of his life in London. The city became his home, his stage, his muse, a quarry from which he mined his myriad characters, mimicking their gestures in the mirror and rehearsing their speech inflexions aloud before committing them to paper. Ackroyd shows clearly how London became for Dickens both a living reality and an imaginary world to which he could escape to indulge his fantasy and his invention. The two worlds became inextricably linked over the years as Dickens increasingly sought fictions in the everyday fabric of London life and escaped from childhood trauma into a make-believe world of love and security.

Dickens never recovered from two experiences of horror in his youth: an encounter with filth, poverty and abandonment in a blacking factory at Charing Cross and his father's incarceration in the debtors' prison at the Marshalsea in Borough High Street. Nevertheless, as Ackroyd shows the reader Dickens maturing from parliamentary reporter into sketch writer into, very rapidly, world-famous novelist, the impression is of a man of unbounded energy, a joyful man of expansive gestures and ringing tones with a penchant for

Gustave Doré's illustration of the Lascar's Room in *Edwin Drood*

brightly coloured waistcoats and an insatiable curiosity for all that surrounded him. The childhood scars remained, however, and in Dickens's middle years, the impression is of a man who became less and less able to hide their effects. The frightened child peers out and shows himself in the craving for mother figures, the restlessness, the endless walks and abrupt departures and in the consuming loneliness. Finally Ackroyd presents the searing picture of Dickens, in tears on his deathbed.

In many ways Dickens in life was a tormented, driven and miserable man but his novels live on. Our view of the city which he once made his kingdom is still shaped by his imagination and Ackroyd's biography is, arguably, the finest yet of the man behind that imagination.

## GUSTAVE DORÉ (1832–1883) and
## BLANCHARD JERROLD (1826–1884)

Doré was the foremost French illustrator of the nineteenth century, famed for his interpretations of Rabelais and Balzac, of Dante and Cervantes. Blanchard Jerrold, son of the dramatist and journalist Douglas Jerrold, was himself a journalist on the Daily News, the newspaper founded by Dickens, and, as that paper's Paris correspondent, came to know many figures in French cultural life, including Doré. When Doré visited England it was Jerrold who showed him around the capital and the ultimate outcome was *London: A Pilgrimage*, which was published in 1872. Doré's extraordinary images and Jerrold's prose combine to produce one of the most distinctive views of the Victorian city. It was the huge contrasts of nineteenth century London which excited the imagination of Doré in particular. There is no middle ground in Doré's vision. The privileged lead lives of paradisal leisure. The poor are trapped in scenes of hellish labour and deprivation. One of the greatest works by one of the greatest of all black-and-white illustrators, and a valuable insight into Victorian London, Doré and Jerrold's book deserves to be better known.

**London: A Pilgrimage**
Dover pbk £14.95 048622306X

> **Look out of this window, Watson. See how the figures loom up, are dimly seen, and then blend once more into the cloud-bank. The thief or the murderer could roam London on such a day as the tiger does the jungle, unseen until he pounces, and then evident only to his victim.**
>
> Conan Doyle – The Bruce Partington Plans

## SIR ARTHUR CONAN DOYLE (1859–1930)

Doyle came from a family of artists and illustrators – his uncle worked for *Punch* from the time of its first publication and his grandfather was a celebrated political caricaturist in the era of of Rowlandson and Cruikshank – but he trained originally as a doctor. He began writing in the eighteen eighties and Sherlock Holmes made his first appearance in *A Study in Scarlet* (1887). The character's huge popularity developed as short stories, later collected as *The Adventures of Sherlock Holmes* (1892) and *The Memoirs of Sherlock Holmes* (1894), appeared in the *Strand Magazine*. So great did Holmes's fame grow that Doyle, who was a prolific writer in many other fields, became resentful that he was identified solely as the creator of the saturnine detective. He attempted to kill him off by sending him over the Reichenbach Falls in the clutches of the criminal mastermind Professor Moriarty, but the public demanded his return and Doyle was obliged reluctantly to comply. Several further novels and collections of short stories appeared, including perhaps the most famous Holmes story, *The Hound of the Baskervilles* (1902).

The London Doyle creates for Holmes and Watson is twofold. Although cases do take them out to the Home Counties and beyond, they are indelibly associated with London and with a London that is, effectively the capital of the world, the centre of the British Empire at the height of its power. Doyle is careful to place his characters in the real London of the late nineteenth century. We are told that when, in July 1877 or 1878, Holmes came down from Oxford he took rooms in the capital and we are told precisely where – 'in Montague Street, just around the corner from the British Museum.' The site of the first meeting between Holmes and Watson, at Bart's Hospital, is so carefully described that later admirers of the stories have been able to mark the spot with a plaque. When Holmes goes to a concert it is specifically stated that it is to St. James's Hall, once in Picadilly, When he and Watson set out by rail to investigate the mystery at Baskerville Hall, it is specifically Paddington from which they depart. Much use is made of the Thames, most memorably in the river chase of Jonathan Small and his fiendish companion in *The Sign of Four*. Even their famous set of rooms at 221B Baker Street, although it has never existed, is very specifically located.

Yet the London of Holmes and Watson is also a mythological one. Just as the characters have escaped the boundaries of the fiction in a way that few characters, except some of Dickens's and some of Shakespeare's, have done, so Sherlock Holmes's London is greater than the sum of its individually realistic parts. The meditative calm of Baker Street, disturbed by the approaching footsteps of a new client. The breathless hansom-cab journeys through the fog-enshrouded streets towards some den of crime and infamy. The endless hustle and bustle of the streets and markets of the wealthiest city in the world. Doyle's feel for the atmosphere of late Victorian London is considerable but, in the same way that Holmes and Watson have become archetypal figures, the London they inhabit has become more real than the reality. The process has been helped by the proliferation of stage, film, radio and TV adaptations and by the wealth of Holmes-related material published since Doyle's death. It is probably not going too far to say that, for many first-time visitors to the city, their expectations of London have been determined as much by the mythical city created by Doyle and his adapters as by the real city of the present day.

**The Complete Sherlock Holmes**
Penguin pbk £10.99 0140056947

## FORD MADOX FORD (1873–1939)

Ford was born Ford Hermann Hueffer in London, son of The Times' music critic, Dr. Francis Hueffer (he later changed his name in the wake of anti-German feelings following the Great War), and grandson of the Pre-Raphaelite painter Ford Madox Brown. As a youth he was steeped in the aestheticism of his parents' circle, which included several Pre-Raphaelite writers and artists, including Dante Gabriel Rossetti (a relative on his mother's side), an influence he described as 'the hothouse atmosphere of Pre-Raphaelism, where I was being trained for a genius.' After writing several volumes of verse, fairy tales and biography, including his study of Rossetti, he met and collaborated with Joseph Conrad, whose impressionistic style was to be a great influence. After two novels written with Conrad, Ford produced *The Soul of London* (1905), a work that, unlike the realistic novels of his contemporaries, George Gissing and H. G. Wells, created 'a personal image of the place', with the city's myriad facets ('infinite miles of unmeaning streets, of horizons that are the blur of lamps in fogs... mists, great shadows, great clouds') filtered through the consciousness of an author who was 'passionately alive to all aspects of life.'

Ford's skill in combining travel-writing, history and personal impressions to produce a kind of proto-fiction (some sixty years before the New Journalism of Tom Wolfe and others) is so marked that at times we seem to be waiting for figures to grace the canvas, although we know that they won't actually appear. Despite editing the *English Review*, where he published work by the two spearheads of the emerging, London-based Vorticist movement, Ezra Pound and Wyndham Lewis, Ford never really wrote about the city of his birth again (although glimpses appear in the monumental *Parade's End*), preferring instead his adopted homes, France and latterly, America, but *The Soul of London* lives on, not just a paean to the ever-shifting metropolis but (perhaps more crucially) as a foretaste of the technique and style of his later novels.

**The Soul of London**
Dent pbk £5.99 046087621X

## GEORGE GISSING (1857–1903)

*Writer and critic Anthony Quinn looks at the vexed relationship between the author of New Grub Street and the city in which so many of his novels of the urban poor were set.*

On September 2nd 1893 George Gissing paid a visit to his former lodgings in Regent's Park. He recorded in his diary:

> *Morning looked in to see old Lane, the agent for Cornwall Mansions, and learnt from him that my successor in 7K committed suicide – not at home, but in the City. The atmosphere I left behind me, some would say, overcame the poor man.*

The plangent tone is characteristic. Gissing's relationship with London was, like so much else in his life, deeply vexed. When he returned from America as a twenty year old in 1877, London seemed to offer vistas of opportunity to this sensitive, bookish young man – here was the literary nerve-centre, a place of libraries and reading-rooms, of publishers, editors and aspirant novelists like himself. More importantly the city would provide him with the settings for his studies of the urban poor, which got underway with *Workers in the Dawn* in 1880. The true artist, Gissing later remarked in his 1887 novel *Thyrza*, 'will oftener find his inspiration in a London garret than amid the banality of the plutocrat's drawing-room.'

True enough, though to judge from the anguished pessimism which characterised Gissing's work throughout the 1880s, that inspiration came at a heavy price. The personal circumstances behind *The Nether World* (1889), his most accomplished novel of this period, are instructive. In March 1888 he was summoned to a boarding-house in Lucretia Street, Lambeth, where his estranged wife lay dead from a combination of alcoholism, syphilis and hunger. The sight of her pitiful corpse, surrounded by some pitiful tokens of her destitution, moved Gissing to write in his diary, 'Henceforth I never cease to bear testimony against the accursed social order that brings about things of this kind.' He made good the resolution in a novel that owed something to Dickens but whose setting, the slums of Clerkenwell, was drawn from his own bitter observation: 'The economy prevailing in today's architecture takes good care that no depressing circumstance shall be absent from the dwellings in which the poor find shelter. What terrible barracks, those Farringdon Road Buildings!... Pass by in the night, and strain imagination to picture the weltering mass of human weariness, of bestiality, of unmerited dolour, of hopeless hope, of crushed surrender, tumbled together within those forbidding walls.'

Gissing tends to be exact about place names in his novels, be it the Lambeth of *Thyrza* or the Camberwell of **In the Year of the Jubilee**. Perusal of a contemporary map will acquaint the reader with the topography of *The Nether World* – Tysoe Street, Shooter's Gardens, Wilmington Square, Myddleton Passage, Clerkenwell Green – some of which can still be located in a modern A-Z. From November 1879 to February 1881 Gissing himself lived at 5 Hanover Street, Islington, where the novel's misguided philanthropist Snowdon has lodgings. The street has since been renamed (and renumbered) 60 Noel Road, four doors along from where I write these words. Unlike Joe Orton's flat at number 25, no plaque commemorates the novelist's residence, a neglect that would doubtless afford his shade some grim amusement.

Of the emotional effects of poverty Gissing was painfully aware, yet in his late autobiographical novel **The Private Papers of Henry Ryecroft** he looks back on his penurious times in the capital with something close to affection. He fondly recalls one year from his 'garret-days' when he tutored a man for the London matriculation; each morning he would rise before dawn and make the hour's walk from his lodgings near Hampstead Road to be with his pupil in Knightsbridge at half-past-six. Once his day's coaching was done, he treated himself to a large breakfast, walked back home and worked 'as only few men worked in all London, with pleasure, zeal, hope...' In the same book he describes the joy of purchasing a first edition of Gibbon and carrying them, one volume at a time, from the bookseller's at the west end of the Euston Road all the way back to his rooms in Islington. He did not take public transport for the simple reason that he could not afford.to: 'In those days I hardly knew what it was to travel by omnibus. I have walked London streets for twelve and fifteen hours together without ever a thought of saving my legs, or my time.'

It is pertinent to note how much walking also figures in **New Grub Street** (1891), Gissing's great novel of literary London and one of the most heart-rending studies of marriage and money in the language. When his protagonist Reardon makes the six-mile walk from Islington – once again a geographical metonym for desperate straits – to the home of his estranged wife Amy in Westbourne Park, the prospect of a reconciliation all but disappears when she inwardly recoils at the shabbiness of his clothes and boots, muddied by his tramp along Euston Road. It is, arguably, the turning-point of the novel, and typical of the way in which London often seems to be conspiring in the misfortune of Gissing's characters. One thinks of Harold Biffen returning from a night walk to find his garret in Clipstone Street ablaze; of Marian Yule horror-struck amid the 'endless shelves' of the British Museum's Reading Room; of Alfred Yule's encounter with a destitute surgeon outside Camden Town station and the diagnosis of his oncoming blindness.

The East-West London divide in *New Grub Street* is indicative of a larger struggle between impecunious drudgery and respectability. At the beginning of the novel most of the central characters live around Regent's Park or Bloomsbury; later, however, they marry and move west towards Bayswater, Earl's Court and the Brompton Road. Even the heroic, penniless Biffen eventually strikes out westward at the end of the novel, walking – of course – through Kensington Gardens into Fulham and then across the Thames into Putney. Having taken one last look at the just-risen moon, he steals onto the heath, out of view, and kills himself. Thus the fate of the novel's most honourable, but least practical, character. The situation his creator forced on him, some would say, overcame the poor man.

**In the Year of Jubilee**
Everyman pbk £2.99 0460875337

**The Nether World**
Oxford UP pbk £6.99 0192817698

**New Grub Street**
Penguin pbk £6.99 0140430326

**New Grub Street**
Oxford UP pbk £5.99 0192829637

**The Private Papers of Henry Ryecroft**
Oxford UP pbk £4.99 0192517493

## GEORGE (1847–1912) and WEEDON (1854–1919) GROSSMITH

The two Grossmith brothers were known in their day for their work in the theatre – George took roles in some of the first productions of Gilbert & Sullivan's Savoy operas – but it is for their comic novel, *The Diary of a Nobody*, first published in 1892, that they continue to be remembered. The humour that emerges from their portrayal of the minor trials and tribulations of Charles Pooter, the accident-prone, lower middle-class resident of Brickfield Terrace, Holloway, is still effective. Unlike much Victorian humour the petty anxieties and humiliations, largely class-based, which afflict Pooter and his wife can still make a modern reader actually laugh. The precision of social observation, as demonstrated in the details of contemporary life recorded in Pooter's unself-conscious diary, is also fascinating. The illustrations, by Weedon, have their own charm and interest and are reproduced in most editions of the book.

**The Diary of a Nobody**
Penguin pbk £4.99 0140005102
**The Diary of a Nobody**
OUP pbk £4.99 019282404X

## W. W. JACOBS (1863–1943)

Something of the life of the late nineteenth century East End survives in the work of writers like Arthur Morrison, Israel Zangwill and W. Pett Ridge. Another writer who translated his own experiences of the docks and riverside life into the form of once-popular fiction was W.W. Jacobs. Jacobs was born in Wapping in 1863, the same year as Morrison, and his father worked on the docks and wharves there. Jacobs himself started his working life as a clerk in the Post Office. He began to publish short stories in the nineties and was soon successful enough to resign from the Post Office. He went on to publish a number of novels and many collections of short stories, including *Many Cargoes* (1896), *Light Freights* (1901), *The Lady of the Barge* (1902) and *Night Watches* (1914). Many of these often humorous stories were set in the world of the dockers and sailors of the East End. They appealed to a middle-class audience which enjoyed the frisson of reading about the less genteel areas of the city but did not want too pungent a dose of realism. Nonetheless Jacobs genuinely knew the world of which he wrote and this knowledge is apparent in the best of the stories. Jacobs was also a gifted writer of the macabre and at least one of his stories in this genre, *The Monkey's Paw*, continues to be well-known and regularly anthologised.

# HENRY JAMES (1843–1916)

Born in New York, Henry James studied briefly at Harvard Law
School and began to write essays and reviews when he was in his
early twenties. In 1869 he made his first return to the Europe that
he had visited as a boy with his family and, after spending some
time in Paris, he settled in London in 1876 (the year his first major
novel, **Roderick Hudson**, was published) and lived in the city for
the next twenty years. Even after moving to the town of Rye he
continued to spend long periods of time in London. After living
in England for much of his adult life he finally became a naturalised
British citizen in 1915 and died in the following year. James's great
subject as a novelist was the contrast between the old world and
the new and, more particularly, the interactions between the
inhabitants of the centuries-long civilisation of Europe and the
brasher, less sophisticated but more vital products of America.
Nearly all his greatest works (**Portrait of a Lady**, **The Wings of the Dove**,
**The Golden Bowl**) explore this subject with characteristic complexity
and subtlety.

His responses to the city in which he spent so much of his life
are similarly subtle. His first reactions to the place were not positive
– 'I may say that up to this time I have been crushed under a sense
of the mere magnitude of London, its inconceivable immensity,' he
wrote to his sister in 1869 – but he came to see the city as the one
indispensable home for a writer such as he. In his notebooks in 1881
he wrote:

> *It is difficult to speak adequately or justly of London. It is not a pleasant
> place; it is not agreeable, or cheerful, or easy, or exempt from reproach.
> It is only magnificent. You can draw up a tremendous list of reasons why
> it should be insupportable. The fogs, the smoke, the dirt, the darkness,
> the wet, the distances, the ugliness, the brutal size of the place, the horrible
> numerosity of society... For one who takes it as I take it, London is on
> the whole the most possible form of life. I take it as an artist and as a
> bachelor; as one who has the passion of observation and whose business is
> the study of human life. It is the biggest aggregation of human life – the
> most complete compendium of the world.*

Many of his novels contain scenes set in typically London
surroundings. In *The Wings of the Dove*, for example, the initial
meeting between Kate Croy and Morton Densher, who later plot to
manipulate an inheritance from a dying woman, takes place on a

minutely detailed Underground journey from Sloane Square through High Street Kensington and Notting Hill to Lancaster Gate. Yet the city is not wholly central to these novels and the demands of the plot transport the characters to other locales, often Venice and Florence and other less unregenerately modern cities. James's great London fiction is *The Princess Casamassima*, first published in 1886, which succeeds in encompassing a wide range of social classes (wider than James usually allows himself) and convincingly portrays a number of different London milieux. The central character is the orphan Hyacinth Robinson, brought up in drab lower class surrounds, who is drawn into a secret revolutionary movement where he shares his fervour for social upheaval (slightly improbably, it must be acknowledged) with the Italian princess of the title. Later in the novel Hyacinth, still sworn to the society but with changed beliefs, is thrown into a despairing dilemma by the revolutionaries' demands that he undertake an assassination. The novel, very unlike much of James's other fiction, brilliantly depicts its strange and shadowy city and is fascinating to read in conjunction with Conrad's very different take on the urban underworld of anarchy and revolution, *The Secret Agent*, published twenty years later.

**The Princess Casamassima**
Penguin pbk £8.99 014043254X

## RICHARD JEFFERIES (1848–1887)

Remembered as a naturalist (*Wild Life in a Southern County*), author of a children's classic (*Bevis: The Story of a Boy*) and autobiographer (*The Story of my Heart*), Jefferies deserves inclusion in this guide as the writer of a peculiar prophetic account of London's future. *After London* offers a vision animated by the same hatred of nineteenth century industrialism and urban squalor that stirred William Morris. However, where Morris, in *News from Nowhere*, envisaged a future London changed dramatically for the better by communist revolution, Jefferies foresees a bleaker destiny for the city. In *After London* the capital has become swampland and the central character traverses a landscape reverted to nature. Jefferies's pessimism and disbelief in the potential of the communities men and women create are made abundantly clear in what is a fascinating but bitter book.

**After London** is currently out of print.

## JEROME K. JEROME (1859–1927)

Born in the Midlands but brought up in east London, Jerome K. Jerome, on leaving school, joined the great army of the city's lowly paid clerks. Escaping to become an actor and journalist he made his name with the bestselling comic novel *Three Men in a Boat* (1889) which chronicled the minor misadventures of a middle-class trio and their dog, Montmorency on a boating expedition on the Thames. The book has retained its popularity throughout the century and more since first publication. Few London books, then or since, share its amiable light-heartedness, perhaps because the novel recounts the protagonists' escape, along the river, from the constraints of work and the city. As the narrator, George and Harris (to say nothing of the dog) meander along the Thames, so the narrative diverts into anecdote and tall story. The frustrations of trying to open a stubbornly resistant tin of food are counterpointed with tales of failure to unlock the secrets of Hampton Court maze. The enjoyment Jerome obviously takes in his story mirrors that of the reader. Many years on, what he wrote of his own pleasure in London at the time of writing the book is an antidote to the view, so often expressed in Victorian literature, of the capital as the 'City of Dreadful Night'. 'It was summer time, and London is so beautiful in summer. It lay beneath my window a fairy city veiled in golden mist, for I worked in a room high above the chimney-pots; and at night the lights shone far beneath me, so that I looked down as into an Aladdin's cave of jewels.' Jerome K. Jerome wrote much else, including a less successful follow-up to *Three Men in a Boat*, *Three Men on the Bummel* (1900) and a play, *The Passing of the Third Floor Back* (1907), in which a vaguely Christ-like figure passes away in a Bloomsbury boarding-house, but it is for his tale of a long-gone summer on the Thames that he is deservedly remembered.

**Three Men in a Boat**
Penguin pbk £3.99 0140012133

## JACK LONDON (1876–1916)

Jack London is, of course, best known as the author of boys' own adventures set in the frozen north, tales such as *The Call of the Wild* and *White Fang*. In his lifetime he was one of the most famous authors in the world and was a leading figure in the socialist movement, although his idiosyncratic brand of socialism owed as much to his garbled reading of Nietzsche as it did to his even more garbled reading of Marx. *The People of the Abyss* was the result of time spent by London in lodgings in Flower and Dean Street, Spitalfields and was published in 1903. London's impassioned indictment of the conditions he found in the capital's slums remains powerfully readable even if his documentary exactness can sometimes be doubted.

**The People of the Abyss**
Pluto Press £9.99 0745314155

## ARTHUR MACHEN (1863–1947)

London for Arthur Machen was both heaven and hell. A native of Gwent, he spent his early years among the hills of the Usk valley, arriving in London in 1881 at the age of eighteen. 'Country folk', he wrote later,'are in [one] respect like Londoners... it is only occasionally that either goes out determined to... stray for the very sake of straying.' At his first London address in Notting Hill, he often strayed 'for the very sake of straying' to alleviate his loneliness and boredom. His initial forays proved unfruitful: he speaks of getting 'terribly entangled with a canal which seemed to cross my path in a manner contrary to the laws of reason', and then, further afield, 'I came upon Kensal Green [cemetery] again and again; it was like the Malay, an enemy for months. I would break off by way of Portobello Road and entangle myself in Notting Hill, and presently I would come upon the goblin city: I might wander into the Harrow Road, but at last the ghost-stones would appal me. Maida Vale was treacherous, Paddington false.'

This 'goblin city', a shifting, menacing place whose threat is ever present yet undefined, features prominently in his work of the eighteen nineties: ***The Great God Pan*** (1894) and ***The Three Impostors*** (1895). In these novels, London is a demonic sprawl, where encounters in the street are never merely chance and its characters are prey to invisible forces which can effortlessly manipulate and kill. Yet as Machen himself notes in *The Great God Pan*, 'London has been called the city of encounters; it is more than that, it is the city of resurrections.' He began to see London in the same way that he saw the valleys of Gwent:

> *he was... aware of the enchantment that was transmuting all the world*
> *about him, informing his life with a strange significance and romance.*
> *London seemed a city of the Arabian nights, and its labyrinth of streets*
> *an enchanted maze; its long avenues of lighted lamps were as starry systems,*
> *and its immensity became for him an image of the endless universe.*

He would later call this the 'Ars Magna of London': an awareness of mystery and a sensitivity to its vastness and unknowability. In his subsequent works (and life), London became the means by which a person could come to find themselves, a mirror of sufficient complexity to reflect the darkest recesses of one's soul, 'a concrete image of the eternal things of space and time and thought.'

*He who cannot find wonder, mystery, awe, the sense of a new world and an*
*undiscovered realm in the places by the Gray's Inn Road will never find those secrets*
*elsewhere, not in the heart of Africa, not in the fabled hidden cities of Tibet.*
*"The matter of our work is everywhere present", wrote the old alchemists, and that is the truth.*
*All the wonders lie within a stone's throw of King's Cross Station.*

*Sean Martin*

**The Collected Arthur Machen**
Duckworth hbk £25.00 0715621203

**The Great God Pan**
Creation Press pbk £7.95 1871592119

**The Three Impostors**
Dent pbk £4.99 0460877186

## FREDERICK MARRYAT (1792–1848)

Marryat was a naval officer who used his own experiences in the war against Napoleon as the basis for a first novel in 1829. He went on to publish a number of sea and adventure stories in the next twenty years. Marryat remains in print, just, as a children's writer. *The Children of the New Forest,* his story set in the English Civil War, is a Puffin Classic. Virtually everything else by him is unavailable. One of the novels that most deserves a reprint is his 1834 story of life on the Thames, *Jacob Faithful.* Perhaps only Dickens, of Victorian novelists, has produced so lively and so evocative a picture of the Thames when it was a major thoroughfare of the city and provided thousands with their livelihood. Marryat also anticipates Dickens in his extraordinary description of the death by spontaneous combustion of Jacob Faithful's mother who goes up in flames on her husband's Thames lighter. Before this fiery death (and that of his father who leaps from his boat and drowns at the sight of his wife's engulfment) Jacob Faithful has spent his first ten years on the river and never stepped ashore. The rest of the book is a picaresque account of river life in which Faithful is apprenticed to a bargeman, to a wherryman and eventually pressed into the Navy.

**Jacob Faithful** is currently out of print.

## YOSHIO MARKINO
### (1874–?)

One of the most idiosyncratic and charming memoirs of Edwardian London is Markino's *A Japanese Artist in London* (1910). Markino had arrived in London in 1897, after a period in the USA, and existed for some years in genteel poverty before his atmospheric watercolours of urban life, published in a number of books, began to gain attention. From the commentaries attached to his paintings, written in his own particular form of English, Markino moved on to longer excursions into prose. *A Japanese Artist in London*, which an enterprising publisher has recently reprinted, gives us a portrait of the city created by an Anglophile from a radically different culture, a portrait written in a prose that is simultaneously naive and rather knowing.

**A Japanese Artist in London**
in Print Publishing hbk £14.95
1873047002

## RICHARD MARSH

Published in the same year as *Dracula*, *The Beetle* was for many years as popular a tale of Gothic horror as Stoker's novel. The book opens with a down-at-heel, unemployed clerk, turned away from a Hammersmith dosshouse, venturing into an apparently deserted house and stumbling across a vile hermaphroditic creature capable of transforming itself from man/woman to gigantic beetle. It ends with a frenzied chase across London, from the dives of Limehouse to St. Pancras station, as the heroes attempt to save the heroine from white slavery and unspeakable degradation at the hands of followers of the ancient cult of Isis. The novel's prose is purple, to say the least, but, like many works of late Victorian popular fiction, the book is interesting in its unconscious revelation of *fin-de-siècle* anxieties about sexuality and race. It is also grippingly told and is often surprisingly sophisticated in its use of different narrative voices. Marsh uses his London settings to great effect and the atmosphere he creates, stripped of its supernaturalism, is often reminiscent, particularly in the Limehouse chapters, of the fog-bound London of Sherlock Holmes.

**The Beetle**
Sutton pbk £5.99 075090688X

> ## Then about the life of London, I have found out it is larger than any other town. London is on the extremely larger scale altogether. She is just like a vast ocean where sardines as well as whales are living together.
> **Yoshio Markino**

## SOMERSET MAUGHAM (1874–1965)

The prevailing image today of Somerset Maugham is that of the worldweary traveller sipping Singapore Slings at Raffles hotel and turning his observations into a succession of well-made short stories. Or perhaps it is that of the grand old man of letters living out his twilight years on the Riviera. Yet it was the experience of his training at St Thomas's Hospital in the 1890s, and, in particular, obstetrics (where, to qualify, he had to attend at least twenty confinements in the slums around the hospital) that led directly to the writing of *Liza of Lambeth* (1897), the novel which launched his literary career.

As Maugham said in a preface to a later edition, 'This was the material I used in *Liza of Lambeth*. I exercised little invention. I put down what I had seen and heard as plainly as I could'. Set in Vere St, a long straight road of plain houses, each one containing several families, the story centres on the doomed love affair between the generous-hearted Liza and her new, married, neighbour Jim Blakeston. The plot is slight and shows the influence of the French Realists such as Guy de Maupassant, an influence which recurs through much of Maugham's later work, in particular the short stories. However, in the details of the time and the squalid environment, the gas-lit public houses, melodramatic theatres, an itinerant organ grinder, the bank holiday outing to Chingford, and above all in the street life of gossiping women, babies crawling round their feet, children playing improvised cricket in the road, there is a picture of the people of Victorian London that is preserved more clearly than in any fading photograph.

London is partly the setting for other Maugham books such as *Theatre* and *Of Human Bondage*, the massive novel of 1915 which again drew on Maugham's medical experiences to tell a semi-autobiographical story. *Cakes and Ale* contains a number of woundingly vindictive portraits of London literary life and short stories such as *The Verger*, in which an illiterate man, barred from his job in a fashionable church, goes on to unexpected success in less snobbish surrounds, also use London backdrops. None of his works, however, draws so heavily as *Liza of Lambeth* on the sights, smells and sounds of the London of Maugham's early years, a London that would disappear forever within his lifetime.

**Liza of Lambeth**
Mandarin pbk £5.99 0749304286

**Of Human Bondage**
Mandarin pbk £8.99 0749303441

## HENRY MAYHEW
## (1812–1887)

Mayhew was renowned in his day as a dramatist, wit and humourist, author of plays and farces, and was co-founder of *Punch*. He was a philanthropist and writer of novels, travelogues, stories and treatises on science. Born one of seven brothers, he was the son of a London attorney. Educated at Westminster, he ran away to sea and was subsequently articled to his father's firm. In 1841 he quit the law and founded *Punch* where he worked as contributor and co-editor.

The first decade of Victoria's rule was an era of social ferment. In the previous generation the Congress of Vienna in 1815, which ratified the defeat of Napoleonic France, had restored the status quo of aristocratic rule but had paid no heed to the newly emerging nationalist and social demands for change. Popular discontent erupted all over Europe in 1848, the Year of Revolutions. In Britain there was no revolution but there was a widespread fear amongst the governing classes that the Masses would one day rise up and eradicate aristocratic culture and civilisation.

Partly this fear was based on ignorance of the ways in which those Masses lived. One of the first authors to depict the life of the London poor was Charles Dickens. Another was his friend Henry Mayhew.

Mayhew ventured far out into the fetid slums and gimcrack, tumbledown world of London's overcrowded, pestiferous and decaying shanty-towns. In lanes, streets, back alleys, pubs and markets, he researched, questioned, interviewed, noted and categorised. The four volumes of ***London Labour and the London Poor*** are a systematic examination of the metropolitan poor and the enormous variety of ways in which they strove to make a living. Mayhew met costermongers who spoke backwards and in rhyming slang. In Somers Town he came across 'a perfect nest of rat catchers' and in Battersea he interviewed Jack Black, 'rat and mole destroyer to Her Majesty.' Today many of the professions listed by Mayhew are likely to remind the reader of an oriental bazaar rather than the streets of London. He met water-carriers, nutmeg graters, a dog finder, sellers of birds' nests, bone grubbers, rag gatherers, street reciters, street musicians, a writer without hands, a doll's eye maker, dancing dogs, and a long-song seller. He came across street vendors of cat's meat, fly papers, beetle wafers, 'green stuff', and gold and silver fish. The level of detail in his enquiry is illustrated by his subdivisions of the one trade of crossing-sweeper – able-bodied male, able-bodied female, occasional, afflicted and juvenile.

*Nick Creagh-Osborne*
*Waterstone's at Harrods*

**London Labour and the London Poor**
Penguin pbk £9.99 0140432418

**London Labour and the London Poor Volume 1**
Dover pbk £9.95 0486219348

**London Labour and the London Poor Volume 2**
Dover pbk £9.95 0486219356

**London Labour and the London Poor Volume 3**
Dover pbk £9.95 0486219364

**London Labour and the London Poor Volume 4**
Dover pbk £9.95 0486219372

**The Morning Chronicle Survey of Labour and the Poor (6 volumes in paperback)**
Caliban Books £180.00
0904573826

# HERMAN MELVILLE (1819–1891)
## Israel Potter
Northwestern UP pbk £9.99 0810115913

*Moby Dick* was published in 1851. A few years later Melville produced a strange, and now little-read, novel which appeared in the pages of *Putnam's Monthly Magazine*. *Israel Potter* was based on an obscure pamphlet which was published in New York in the eighteen twenties and told the story of a soldier from the American War of Independence who had been obliged to suffer a long exile in London. Melville's Potter is a Yankee volunteer who fights at Bunker Hill, serves with John Paul Jones and finds himself, through misfortune, stranded in London for decades, unable to afford passage home. Melville did not know London well but the power of his dark imagination is such that he provides, in the later parts of the novel, an apocalyptic view of the city as prison and inferno. Here he describes a London Bridge that could be situated in one of Dante's circles of hell:-

*Hung in long, sepulchral arches of stone, the black, besmoked bridge seemed a huge scarf of crape, festooning the river across. Similar funereal festoons spanned it to the west, while eastward, towards the sea, tiers and tiers of jetty colliers lay moored, side by side, fleets of black swans... As ant-hills, the bridge arches crawled with processions of carts, coaches, drays, every sort of wheeled, rumbled thing, the noses of the horses behind touching the backs of the vehicles in advance, all bespattered with ebon mud, ebon mud that stuck like Jews' pitch.*

# WILLIAM MORRIS (1834–1896)

Throughout the Victorian period pride in, and celebration of, London as the heart of the empire and of a Britain transformed by the Industrial Revolution co-existed with horrified revulsion from the ugliness and squalor that industrialisation brought with it. Few writers were more driven by a hatred of industrial production and the alienation of the worker from his work than William Morris. *News From Nowhere* (first published in volume form in 1891) was his vision of a future London and a future England freed from the filth of its factories and slums. At the time he wrote the book Morris was the leading light in the Socialist League and it embodies his dream of what a truly socialist society might be. The narrator awakens in his Hammersmith house to find himself in a paradisal London of the early 21st century. Men and women live in freedom, work is pleasure and fulfilment rather than meaningless and degrading toil, central government has been abolished. The narrator travels through a dramatically changed city which Morris brings vividly to life. Famously the Houses of Parliament have been transformed into a dung market. In the second part of the book the narrator hears of the revolution that was required to bring about this utopia (it took place in 1952) and the work concludes with a journey up the Thames through a countryside returned to its pre-industrial beauty. Of all literary visions of a future London, Morris's is, perhaps, the most appealing and, sadly, the least likely to materialise.

**News from Nowhere**
Cambridge UP pbk £14.95
0521422337
**News from Nowhere**
Penguin pbk £7.99 0140433309

## ARTHUR MORRISON (1863–1945)

Arthur Morrison's work has often been classified (and therefore dismissed with the vagaries of fashion) as a product of the late Victorian school of Social Realism, the English heirs to Balzac and Zola. Born in Poplar in London's East End in 1863, Morrison gained notoriety with the publication of the story 'Lizerunt' in *Tales of Mean Streets* (1894) because of its description of the descent into street prostitution of a factory girl. In 1896 he was again the centre of controversy over the authenticity of his description of slum life in his finest novel, *A Child of the Jago*. He tells the moving and horrifying story of Dicky Perrott, an aspiring criminal who falls under the influence of a reforming priest, Father Sturt, only to be drawn back into the slum underworld. The real Sturt, Father Arthur Jay, the vicar of Holy Trinity, Shoreditch, came forward to support the accuracy of Morrison's account. In 1899 Morrison published *To London Town*, a more sentimental and less effective novel which he saw as the culmination of his London trilogy. Further London fiction appeared in 1902 with publication of *The Hole in the Wall* in which the seedy milieu of an East End pub is unsentimentally evoked.

Although Morrison continued to write, and his sub-Conan Doyle *Martin Hewitt* detective series was widely read, he gradually turned his energies to collecting and writing about Japanese art. Several critics have, in recent decades, attempted a re-evaluation of Morrison's work, most notably V. S. Pritchett. Pritchett's description of *The Hole in the Wall* as 'a minor masterpiece' may be over-generous but Morrison was undoubtedly a gifted and original writer and, were it a valuation of the much stronger novel *A Child of the Jago*, it would surely stand.

**A Child of the Jago**
Dent pbk £6.99 0460877720
**Tales of Mean Streets**
Acadamy, Chicago pbk £8.99 089733440X

*Paul Baggaley*

Hung in long, sepulchral arches of stone, the black, besmoked bridge seemed a huge scarf of crape, festooning the river across. Similar funereal festoons spanned it to the west, while eastward, towards the sea, tiers and tiers of jetty colliers lay moored, side by side, fleets of black swans... As ant-hills, the bridge arches crawled with processions of carts, coaches, drays, every sort of wheeled, rumbled thing, the noses of the horses behind touching the backs of the vehicles in advance, all bespattered with ebon mud, ebon mud that stuck like Jews' pitch.

Herman Melville

## G. W. M. REYNOLDS (1814–1879)

Who was the most popular novelist of the early part of Victoria's reign? Dickens would be the obvious guess but the awesomely prolific G. W. M. Reynolds had a larger readership, particularly among those classes to whom Dickens had little or no appeal. In his career as hack novelist, journalist and political activist on behalf of the Chartist movement, Reynolds churned out millions of words. His novels *The Mysteries of London* and *The Mysteries of the Courts of London* were published in weekly penny instalments, as well as in volume form, over a period of more than a decade, and sold tens of thousands each week. Inspired by Eugene Sue's stories of the Parisian underworld, *Les Mystères de Paris*, first published in 1842, Reynolds sent his hero Richard Markham into a London that was portrayed with a curious mixture of social realism and wild gothic melodrama.

> *It was now midnight, and the streets were nearly deserted. The lamps, few and far between, only made darkness visible instead of throwing a useful light upon the intricate maze of narrow thoroughfares... (Markham) soon perceived that he had mistaken his way, and at length found himself floundering about in a long, narrow street, unpaved, and here and there almost blocked up with heaps of putrescent filth. There was not a lamp in this perilous thoroughfare; no moon on high irradiated his path; black night enveloped everything above and below in total darkness.*

**The Mysteries of London**
Keele UP hbk £30.00 1853311111 (an abridged reprint)

# A Child of Her Times: W. Pett Ridge's Mord Em'ly.

*Michael Moorcock, author of the contemporary classic of London fiction, **Mother London**, writes about a forgotten Victorian classic.*

London S.E. Winter '98. Resisting all efforts to cheer it up, the New Kent Road grimly meets the Old. Warrens of dejected streets surround tenement rookeries where shifty crooks prey off the hooked, the fearful, the sick, the ruined and the unemployed. Young girls with babies are hopeless addicts, going for the easy money of casual prostitution. Truant youths savour the streets, on the lookout for unguarded vehicles, houses, shops, or vulnerable individuals. The police can't catch them. Most crime goes unreported. But ordinary people manage to survive and even improve their lives. The media urgently demand solutions to welfare dependency, health and education problems, teenage crime, child abuse and domestic violence. Can the public or the private sector provide the best cure? Meanwhile -

> *The members of the Gilliken Gang, who, in the slow, thick stream of traffic in Walworth Road, had been noticeable only for the peculiar whistle given when one happened to be out of sight of her colleagues, turned into Trafalgar Street. The leader, a round, white-faced young woman of fifteen, upset a sieve of Brussels sprouts from a stall with a calm, methodical air, as though performing a State duty. Some of her followers had less than her years; all wore black, braided jackets (pinned), maroon skirts, hats with plush decorations and smart boots. It was near to being a uniform.*
> *"Mord Em'ly! Seen anything of them Bermondsey bahnders?"*
> *"Not yet I ain't." Mord Em'ly was a short girl, with a green plush bird in her hat that nodded as she hurried up to the leader of the Gilliken Gang. She seemed pleased at being singled out...*

Things haven't changed much. The date, of course, is 1898. The novel is **Mord Em'ly**. Its author W. Pett Ridge was the most famous literary Londoner of his day. He walked everywhere. He knew the city from suburbs to centre. He knew everyone. An energetic social reformer, he was a good friend of H. G. Wells, J. M. Barrie, W. S. Gilbert, Jerome K. Jerome, E. Nesbit and many contributors to *The Pall Mall Gazette, The Idler, Westminster Gazette*, journals of what we'd call today the moderate left. All testified to his experience and talent. 'There is nobody else in London,' said J. M. Barrie, 'with his unique literary ear.'

*Mord Em'ly* was his best-loved book. Reprinted regularly, it became a major silent film and last appeared in paperback in 1992. Mord Em'ly herself is spirited, witty and pugnaciously charming. Living wretchedly with her drunken mother in Pandora Buildings, Walworth, she's caught stealing a meringue. The reform school's repressive methods fail to break her so she's put into service as a housemaid. She proudly resists. Returning to her old territory, she finds Gilliken in the Salvation Army. Other friends are now whores. She's not attracted to either prospect. Getting a job as a waitress, she's courted by a socialist soap-box orator and a wholesome young liberal-minded boxer. She begins a better life, determining her own destiny.

Born in Kent in 1860, 'Pett' wrote down, for fifty years, an unmatched record of lower-class London life. He heard the subtleties of Cockney and could repeat the conversations of charwomen, costers, vanmen, railwaymen, telephonists, shopgirls and petty crooks. His books, such as *Nearly Five Million* (1907), often combined fact and fiction. *A Storyteller, Forty Years in London* (1926) gives us a revealing picture of the rewards and frustrations of a still familiar London literary life. Train buffs seek out the work he based on his railway years – *Love at Paddington, Top Speed, London Only, Lost Property, The Bustling Years*. His stories of *Thomas 'Enry* (1910), from Kings Cross delivery boy to parcels clerk, are autobiographical.

Like so many of his contemporaries from poor backgrounds, he educated himself at the Birkbeck Institute's evening classes. With his clever sketches of London life, he soon gained a name. For all his huge literary output – much of which was never collected – he was actively involved in the life of the city, rigorously helping underprivileged Londoners help themselves. He married late, fathered a daughter and a son (whom I knew) and had a heart attack in September 1930, leaving his family all but penniless. Friends rallied round but failed to get his widow and school-age children a civil list pension.

In its warm obituary, *The Daily Telegraph* remarked on his philanthropic work, his brilliance as an after-dinner speaker, the lasting value of his novels which, 'besides being good reading in themselves, have the further value of being a record of the impressions of a man of humour, veracious, and entirely unsentimental, as to the conditions of life among the London poor.'

An exemplary Londoner, his public reputation soon faded. His kindly books live on.

# The French & London

*Phil Davies of Waterstone's, looks at eight very different French writers and their experiences of London.*

Between 1715 and 1920 a number of famous French writers lived in London. Voltaire and Rousseau, Stendhal, Mallarmé, Rimbaud and Verlaine, Alain-Fournier and Celine, all crossed the Channel to spend time in the city. Why did they come? Diverse sets of circumstances were reflected in diverse motives. Yet, paradoxically, what they all had in common is what they all lacked. None had a positive desire to come and explore the ways and places of a foreign capital. Of none of these writers was it true that a love of things English or a wish to know more of London provided the primary motives for their visits.

Voltaire, who, more than any of the others, took delight in what he found during his three-year stay, chose exile in London as an alternative to incarceration in the Bastille. Not, one would guess, a difficult choice. And, as soon as word reached him from the court of Louis XV that it was safe to do so, he took the first available packet for Calais. Rousseau, rendered an intellectual vagabond by his opposition to the *ancien régime*, made an attempt to settle in London. In spite of an establishment favourably disposed towards him and despite the friendly ministrations of the even-tempered David Hume, Rousseau hated his brief stay. His chief problem was that, in addition to the very real hostility he aroused in the conservative mind, he also had to deal with the threats and fears generated by his own personality, riven as it was by hysteria and paranoid delusion. Stendhal, undoubtedly appreciative of many aspects of English life before he came, first visited London when he was suffering from the disappointments of a failed love affair. For Rimbaud and Verlaine, London was a convenient bolt-hole from the petty demands of French bourgeois life, particularly those of Verlaine's doting but provincially minded wife. The capital was a mere backdrop for their joint exploration of a world of alcohol and sex, poetry and hashish. Mallarmé came to improve his English so that he could read Edgar Allan Poe in the original. Thus a French poet's visit to London was one of the reasons an American writer came to exercise such a powerful influence on the Symbolists of late nineteenth century Paris. Unfortunately, Mallarmé's fluency in English, acquired in London in the 1860s, imprisoned him in a career as a teacher in a *lycée*, a career which he found a greater and greater burden as the years passed. Alain-Fournier's family sent him to London to learn English in the hope of enlarging his job prospects. As for Celine, his trip to London began in October 1914 when a shell knocked him flat as he was relaying messages between the 125th and 66th infantry regiments. After months of painful recuperation he was given a desk job at the French consulate in Bedford Square.

For these French writers, then, London was a place of refuge or it was somewhere to hide and let mental or physical wounds heal, it was a means of circumventing the demands of respectability or it was just somewhere to learn English and lay the foundations of a career. For none of these very different writers was London a place one visited because one was attracted to the culture, to the place itself and to its people.

Yet, despite the unhappy occasion of his trip to London in 1726, Voltaire was delighted by what he found. The weather at Greenwich he compared favourably with balmy days in the South of France. The Thames, he thought, put all French rivers to shame. The tolerance and industry that he saw as characteristic of so much of English life he ascribed to the predominant influence of those of the middling sort and he trumpeted the virtues of the middle classes in a series of letters whose publication was famously compared to a bomb thrown at the European *ancien régime*. Voltaire was also impressed by the lack of snobbery among the English aristocracy and noted the contrast with France where relentless jostling for position at court and obsession with the minutiae of social gradation were all-pervasive. During his time in London he was an enthusiastic theatre-goer and was present at Drury Lane on the first night of Gay's *The Beggar's Opera*, one of the century's great theatrical successes. Voltaire made many friends in England, including Alexander Pope. Together with Pope's mother they made a cheerful, if slightly incongruous, trio for dinner in Pope's house at Twickenham. He also encountered Londoners' notorious antipathy to foreigners. Wandering around Fleet Street and the Inns of Court one day, he aroused the curiosity of some street traders. He was identified as a foreigner – and as a Frenchman, representative of the ancient enemy – and a hostile crowd gathered. They chased him towards the Fleet. However Voltaire's eloquence and his sympathy for all things English saved his skin. He scrambled up a lamppost and addressed his pursuers. 'Good Englishmen,' he began, 'Am I not already unfortunate enough not to have been born among you?' By the end of his speech his would-be attackers were applauding him.

Rousseau's visit to London was shorter and altogether less successful. George III and Queen Charlotte were eager to meet him but he had to be almost dragged to court by his friend Hume. During his stay in London Rousseau appeared to be most concerned about the well-being of his dog Sultan. He was convinced that Sultan would run off and get lost. While the two of them were staying with a grocer named Pulleyn, in Chiswick, this is exactly what happened. Rousseau was distraught. Hume placed an advertisement in the newspapers and, happily, dog and philosopher were soon reunited. Rousseau's problems were exacerbated by his limited grasp of English. David Garrick was honoured by the philosopher's appearance at one of his performances and threw a party for him, after the play, at the Adelphi, off the Strand. The great actor was taken aback when he realised the extent of his guest's incomprehension of the play he had just attended and was baffled by constant, anxious references to an otherwise unidentified Sultan.

By contrast, Stendhal had a much better understanding of the English and their language. For many years he contributed articles on music and painting to periodicals on both sides of the Channel. London, in 1817, when he first visited, was a very different city from the one seen by Rousseau and Sultan in the 1760s. Stendhal saw little evidence of the social mobility and openness admired by Voltaire ninety years before. He deplored the rigidity of the English class system and its nurturing of a spirit of narrow-minded snobbery. The English, he thought, cared neither for the suffering of their own lower classes nor for the promotion of aesthetic and spiritual values. For Stendhal this was summed up by their indifference to the plight of that epitome of human greatness then languishing on St. Helena – Napoleon. Yet he seems to have been impressed by what he saw of the ordinary people. He delighted in the ordinary Londoner's disdain for militarism. The authorities might choose to name a bridge Waterloo but, to the rest of London, it was still the Strand Bridge. And he ate with relish the steak-and-kidney pie he bought for 3s 6d in Whitechapel. Stendhal had come to London in the aftermath of a failed love affair and it was here, beyond the pale of respectable society, that he found some solace. Expecting to find distraction at a house of doubtful reputation in Westminster Street (then a muddy lane lined with hedge-row and hawthorns), he discovered a haven of domestic order and comfort in the house of the Appleby sisters. He grew intimate with one sister in particular who was insistent that he should take her back to Paris. She was prepared, she said, to subsist, if necessary, on a diet of apples to avoid becoming a burden on his meagre finances. Stendhal was tempted but did not take her up on her offer. On subsequent trips to London in the 1820s he did not re-visit the Misses Appleby. History does not record what became of them.

Unlike Voltaire and Rousseau, Stendhal paid no visits to court. And no celebrities were knocking at his door, eager to make his acquaintance. Mallarmé cut even less of a figure in London society. He moved to the city in the winter of 1862. London had grown enormously in the course of the nineteenth century. The estates of Kensington and Chelsea had long been laid out and one-time villages like Camden and Kentish Town had now been embraced by the sooty arms of road and railway. The major railway termini had begun to make their mark, leaving great gashes across the face of old London. The Holborn Viaduct was being built and the Thames was about to be constrained by the Victoria Embankment. Mallarmé took a flat on the second floor of 9 Panton Square, between Leicester Square and Piccadilly Circus. His flat-mate, Marie Gerhard, and he lived together in a dry-run for their marriage which was solemnised the following year at Kensington, now Brompton, Oratory. During their brief stay the couple kept largely to themselves. Yet, of all the writers described in this article, Mallarmé was the one who found London most congenial to his aesthetic needs. 'I love this perpetually grey sky.' he wrote. 'You don't need to think. The bright blue sky and the stars are really frightening things. You can feel at home here, and God cannot see you. His spy, the sun, does not care to come out of his shadows.' He and Marie spent many happy evenings and daylight hours, curtains drawn, toasting muffins by the fire and quietly contemplating the London fog seeping under the window sill and gathering on the drapes, the tables and the comfy chairs.

In 1871, some years after Mallarmé's return to France, two more poets crossed the Channel and arrived in London. One was in his late teens, the other was a married man in his thirties. Rimbaud and Verlaine lived in Camden Town. Despite a meagre understanding of English, they attempted to supplement their, or rather, Verlaine's miserable means – Rimbaud exulted in the possession of nothing and sponged enthusiastically off his friend – by advertising themselves as teachers of French. It is not known if anyone applied for lessons. If anyone did, he probably regretted it. Verlaine was drunk most of the time and the two developed a passion for the pubs and illicit drinking dens of Soho. A favourite dive was situated at the Charing Cross Road end of Old Compton Street. There they drank pernod and recited their poems to one another. Despite their liquid intake, their stay was a productive one poetically. It was in London that Rimbaud wrote *Les Illuminations* and he completed *Une Saison en Enfer* soon after his return to Paris. The beginning of the end of the affair between the two poets came with an argument over a piece of fish. Verlaine, drunk and obstreperous, so enraged Rimbaud with complaints about the stink of the fish a local stall-holder had persuaded him into buying for supper, that the younger man headed straight back to France. Later the two met in a hotel room in Brussels. In the presence of his long-suffering mother, Verlaine fired three shots at his estranged lover, hitting him only once, in the wrist. Rimbaud left once more for France. Verlaine was taken to a Belgian prison.

In the summer of 1905 Alain-Fournier started work in Turnham Green at Sanderson's, the wallpaper manufacturer and retailer. He lodged with a senior colleague in the firm, a Mr. Nightingale, at 5 Burlington Road, Chiswick. At first he was charmed by the leafy suburb and the placid, domestic routines of his middle class hosts but these soon began to pall. He missed people in France, one person in particular. The food in England was tasty enough but there was never enough of it. He thought English girls too free and easy in their manners, their dress sense too boyish and severe. He liked more reserve and otherworldliness in women, a suggestion of a fragile and inaccessible beauty. The one thing he liked unreservedly was tea. A year after his return to France he still craved a good, strong cup of English tea.

Ten years after Alain-Fournier's departure Celine arrived. An early casualty of the war, he left the army three-quarters disabled. Throughout the rest of his life he was to be plagued by chronic and acute headaches, insomnia and a buzzing in his ears that were the results of head injuries inflicted by an exploding shell. The French government found him a job in Bedford Square at the consulate, checking and ratifying passport applications. This was in May 1915. Celine lived at 71 Gower Street, sharing rooms with a friend whom he regaled with hour-long recitations from the works of Hegel, Fichte and Nietzsche. However the areas that attracted Celine most were the Docks, Commercial Road and Whitechapel. In short he was drawn to the places he could mix with pimps and prostitutes, longshoremen and market porters, street traders, petty crooks and beggars. He also found a substantial expatriate community, men supporting themselves largely by the sexual efforts of their women. These characters, their lives and their stories, were re-shaped years later by Celine's buzzing, aching brain into *Guignol's Band* and *London Bridge*. In later life Celine encouraged rumours about his time in London. Whether it is true that he and his flatmate went to bed with Mata Hari in return for assistance with a passport application is impossible to tell. Certainly he was not averse to using his position at the consulate to gain sexual favours. In January 1916 he married Suzanne Nebout to enable her and her sister to stay in London. In all likelihood he was going to bed with them both. Later the same year Celine returned to Paris, leaving his bride behind. The marriage was, in time, conveniently forgotten.

## CLARENCE ROOK
### (1862–1915)

In the last decades of the nineteenth century the comfortable middle classes of the Victorian city became increasingly concerned about the problems posed by outcast London, the barbarians at the gate, whose swelling numbers seemed to threaten law and order. Any number of novels, newspaper articles and tracts examined, with varying degrees of hysteria, the perceived dangers of the criminal classes. Clarence Rook's *The Hooligan Nights* (1899) is remarkable both because it claims to tell the story of a Lambeth hoodlum largely in his own words and because it is mostly free of the moralising judgements usual in such literature. How far the book, with its stories of petty criminality and gang-fighting, is a social document and how far it is a work of fiction is a matter of debate but what is not debatable is the vigour and liveliness of its prose. Little is known about Rook other than that he was a journalist of wide experience. His book was reprinted in the eighties by Oxford University Press but is currently out of print.

## GEORGE AUGUSTUS SALA (1828–1896)

Sala's early career was as a scene painter and book illustrator but he soon showed the talent and facility as a journalist which enabled him to pump out millions of words for the newspapers and magazines of Victorian England. A protégé of Dickens on *Household Words* in the early eighteen fifties, he graduated in 1857 to *The Daily Telegraph* for which he was a correspondent in the American Civil War and the Franco-Prussian War. He wrote for and edited numerous other periodicals, produced several travel books and an autobiography, unimaginatively but inarguably called *Things I Have Seen and People I Have Known*. His most successful book is *Twice Round the Clock* (1859), a series of sketches subtitled *The Hours of the Day and Night in London*. In this book Sala was working in a tradition of amiable observation of high and low metropolitan life that travelled back through Pierce Egan to Grub Street writers like Ned Ward and Tom Brown. Unlike those writers he had to work for a Victorian audience which didn't like its low life to appear too low. Despite the self-imposed constraints on realistic reporting this involved, Sala's book remains a sequence of readable and graphic snapshots of the nineteenth century city.

# WILLIAM MAKEPEACE THACKERAY (1811–1863)

Thackeray was born of Anglo-Indian parents in Calcutta and sent to London to Charterhouse School, then in its original buildings in the centre of the city. This was not a happy experience for Thackeray and the school appears, thinly disguised, in his fiction under the names of Grey Friars and, revealingly, Slaughterhouse. After time at Cambridge (he left without a degree) and as an art student in London and Paris, Thackeray began to have some success as a journalist and to publish collections of satirical sketches and parodies such as **The Yellowplush Papers** (observations of a footman on the lives of his social superiors) and **The Fitzboodle Papers**, supposedly narrated by a bachelor clubman. Longer fiction began with **Catherine**, his own variant on the genre of 'Newgate' fiction (stories often taken from real-life criminal cases) and culminated in the achievement of **Vanity Fair**, published in 1847-8. His other major novels include a historical novel, **The History of Henry Esmond**, set in the early eighteenth century, and **The Newcomes** which describes the varying fortunes of the descendants of a self-made man, Thomas Newcome. From the publication of *Vanity Fair* onwards Thackeray was seen as Dickens's only rival as a major novelist but he published less as the 1850s went on and he died suddenly in 1863, aged only 52.

Thackeray's London is much less distinctive than the imaginative realm created by his great rival. Whereas Dickens's city often appears to be the only space his imagination could comfortably inhabit (and therein lies the peculiar power and intensity of his vision), Thackeray's novels deal with, in some senses, a wider world. Dickens's London is a world to itself. Thackeray's London is placed in a larger context.

> *When the eagles of Napoleon Bonaparte, the Corsican upstart, were flying from Provence, where they perched after a brief sojourn in Elba, and from steeple to steeple until they reached the towers of Notre Dame, I wonder whether the Imperial birds had any eye for a little corner of the parish of Bloomsbury, London, which you might have thought so quiet that even the whirring and flapping of those mighty wings would pass unobserved there?... Yes; Napoleon is flinging his last stake, and poor little Emmy Sedley's happiness forms, somehow, part of it.'*

(Vanity Fair)

The result is that the city, in its particulars, is presented less vividly to the reader. Yet Thackeray knew some aspects of the city – its upper and upper middle-class worlds, its gentlemen's clubs – better than Dickens and these appear convincingly in *Vanity Fair*. And the city itself provides Thackeray with the ideal image of Vanity Fair itself, the world of surface and deceit in which morality and honesty take second place to greed and hypocrisy.

**Vanity Fair**
Penguin pbk £2.99 0140430350
**Vanity Fair**
Oxford UP pbk £2.50 019281642X

## ANTHONY TROLLOPE (1815–1882)

Trollope is most often imagined as the novelist of the country and the small cathedral city, of mildly erring clergymen and hen-pecked bishops going about their business in the rural setting of Barsetshire. Certainly the Barsetshire novels remain amongst Trollope's best and most admired fiction. It's also true that the only one of Trollope's forty seven novels set entirely in the capital is the obscure and largely unfunny comic novel *The Struggles of Brown, Jones and Robinson*. However Trollope was himself a Londoner who lived much of his life in the capital (apart from his time in Ireland) and he knew the city intimately. At least one of his contemporaries, the critic R. H. Hutton, recognised the importance of London to the novelist. 'In Miss Austen's world, how little you see of London... In Mr. Trollope's novels... nothing can be done without London.' This is most true of the Palliser novels which describe a world centred on the city. The novels in the series (*Can You Forgive Her?*, *Phineas Finn*, *Phineas Redux*, *The Eustace Diamonds*, *The Prime Minister* and *The Duke's Children*) look at the London where the political and social élites mix and mingle, in which the hereditary aristocracy in the shape of Plantaganet and Glencora Palliser meets and does business with coming men like the handsome and charming Irish MP, Phineas Finn. Trollope may not have moved in the most elevated social circles himself but the world of gentlemen's clubs, the world in which the affairs of empire were discussed over brandy and a good cigar was one with which he was familiar and he put the material he gathered in such clubs as the Cosmopolitan to good use in the *Palliser* series which, Disraeli's novels not excepted, represent the best fictional recreation of nine-teenth century political London.

**Can You Forgive Her?**
Oxford UP pbk £3.99
0192815857

**Phineas Finn**
Oxford UP pbk £3.99
0192815873

**Phineas Redux**
Oxford UP pbk £3.99
019281589X

**The Eustace Diamonds**
Oxford UP pbk £3.99
0192815881

**The Prime Minister**
Oxford UP pbk £3.99
0192815903

**The Duke's Children**
Oxford UP pbk £3.99
0192815865

London is the most interesting, beautiful and wonderful city in the world to me, delicate in her incidental and multitudinous littleness, and stupendous in her pregnant totality

H. G. Wells – The New Machiavelli

## H. G. WELLS (1866–1946)

Wells was born in Bromley, the son of a cricketer turned unsuccessful tradesman, and had to work hard to fulfil his talent. After an unhappy period apprenticed to a draper and as a student teacher at a grammar school, he won a scholarship to the Normal School of Science in Kensington (now Imperial College) to study zoology. Amongst his teachers was 'Darwin's Bulldog', T.H. Huxley, who made a deep impression. After graduating Wells continued to teach but also embarked on a journalistic and literary career. His early successes were all in the field of scientific romance (*The Time Machine*, *The War of the Worlds*) but he later displayed equal talent for novels, like *Kipps* and *The History of Mr Polly*, which drew on his knowledge of the lives and dreams of the lower middle classes. Wells was a lifelong socialist (although an idiosyncratic, Wellsian one) and became, for much of the first half of the century, an example, like Shaw, of the writer as public figure.

Much of Wells's output can be seen as a response to questions of what Britain was and what Britain should become and hence, since London was the heart of the nation and the empire, what the capital was and should become. Even a book like *The Time Machine*, set far in the future, could be interpreted as a dark reflection of the city, with the effete Eloi, the pampered upper classes, threatened by the Morlocks, representing the dark, undifferentiated urban masses huddled in their ghettos. And, although it is not a 'London' novel in any sense, *The History of Mr Polly* presents a dream of rural England (the Potwell Inn to which Alfred Polly retires) which stands, implicitly, opposed to the relentless growth of the city. *Ann Veronica* (1909) has much of its action set in a convincingly realised London and presents a variant on a well-worn fictional theme. The young central character leaves suburbia for the city, for the demands of independence and the search for love, sex and marriage. Wells's twist is that the character is a woman.

The novel which Wells himself described in later life as 'perhaps my most ambitious novel', *Tono-Bungay* (also published in 1909), is also the novel in which he tackles most directly the problems of England the nation and London the city. The book is narrated by Wells's alter ego, George Ponderevo, who shares many biographical details with his creator. He is brought up in a country house where his mother is a housekeeper and is apprenticed to a tradesman. He escapes by attaching himself to his uncle, Edward Ponderevo, whose success with a quack medicine (*Tono-Bungay*) propels him upwards in society. Wells uses this story (and its later ramifications) as a parable with which to examine broader social and political issues. What strikes George Ponderevo (and Wells) about London is that it is simultaneously a city in which change is effortlessly assimilated by older structures and a city threatened by its own 'tumorous growth-process.' London, particularly the West End, may remind George of the social certainties of Bladesover, the country house in which he grew up, but it is also a London which is 'something disproportionately large, something morbidly expanded, without plan or intention', a place of 'endless streets of undistinguished houses, undistinguished industries, shabby families, second-rate shops, inexplicable people.' Few novels better embody Edwardian anxieties about the city than *Tono-Bungay* which deserves to be a much better-known example of Wells's fiction than it is.

**Tono-Bungay**
Dent pbk £5.99 0460872591

## RICHARD WHITEING

A number of middle class writers this century, most notably Orwell, have 'gone native' in an attempt to chronicle the lives of the poor and the dispossessed. Many novelists in the first half of the century, such as Patrick Hamilton, have used the London boarding house as a setting to tell the stories of its transient and multifarious inhabitants. Richard Whiteing, in *No. 5 John Street*, first published in 1899, had already combined the two approaches in an attempt to show the life of the Victorian poor. His narrator is a journalist who is asked to prepare a report on everyday life for a visiting foreign ambassador. He dons another identity to go and live among the struggling but resilient residents of *No. 5 John Street*. The novel is filled with characters saved from caricature by Whiteing's obvious fondness for them and was very popular in the decades immediately following its publication. It is now largely forgotten and is currently out of print but deserves rediscovery.

## ISRAEL ZANGWILL (1864–1926)

Born in the East End to immigrant parents, Zangwill grew up to be a well-known playwright and novelist and a leading spokesman for Jewish and Zionist causes. Many of his books contain vignettes of Jewish life in the Victorian and Edwardian city but he is best remembered for his 1892 novel *Children of the Ghetto* in which he drew on his own childhood memories to produce a vivid portrait of the immigrant Jews of Whitechapel and their daily struggles. Zangwill's book had a particular impact on first publication because of the novelty of its subject matter and it remains readable today, largely because of his vigorous use of language and his skill in creating believable characters.

**Children of the Ghetto**
Wayne State UP pbk £22.50 0814325939

# London in War and Peace

The images in this chapter
are courtesy of the National
Museum of Photography,
Film and Television, Bradford
through the Science & Society
Picture Library, London

## MARGERY ALLINGHAM (1904–1966)

Of all the writers of the 'golden era' of detective fiction it is Margery Allingham who most effectively uses London, not only as a backdrop to the action but as an integral part of the plot, a force that shapes the lives and actions of her characters. In the same way that writers like Agatha Christie use a country house or a village as an enclosed environment in which the characters play out the drama, so Allingham takes a London street or square and places the action of her whodunit within it. These streets and squares are as fictional as her characters but they are so convincingly realised that the reader feels he ought to recognise them if only he knew London a bit better. Many of the books featuring her urbane and civilised detective Albert Campion, books like *The China Governess* and *More Work for the Undertaker*, have these London settings. However there is little doubt that Allingham's best fiction, and her best London fiction, is *The Tiger in the Smoke*. This is not a conventional whodunit, although it abounds in mysteries to be solved. Albert Campion, Inspector Luke and other characters familiar from other novels appear in the book and the action takes place over three days in the early fifties. The tiger of the title is the escaped convict Jack Havoc and the smoke is both London and also the smog that is enveloping the city. The book is a brilliant evocation of period and atmosphere and the action moves swiftly from the markets and the squalor of the East End to the apparent refuge of the secluded St.Petersgate Square in the west. Allingham shows an eye for the telling detail and an ability to convey a deep sense of urban unease. The book is ample confirmation that Campion is the best London detective since Sherlock Holmes.

**The Tiger in the Smoke**
Penguin pbk £5.99 0140166173

## SAMUEL BECKETT (1906–1989)

Sense of place is not something readily associated with Beckett's writings. Nor are the places he explores those of the exterior world but the less easily describable landscapes of solipsistic consciousness and the outer reaches of thought and language. Yet his first novel, *Murphy* (1938), is set in a recognisable city and that city is not Dublin or Paris but London. Before finally settling in France, Beckett had spent the early thirties eking out a precarious living as a reviewer and translator in Germany, France, Ireland and London and his period in London is reflected, with characteristic Beckettian black humour and pessimism, in *Murphy*. The central character is forced from his savagely restricted life in a 'medium-sized cage of north-western aspect' in the west of London, a life which he endures with a kind of nihilistic relish, into the world of work, at a mental hospital, and a room with Celia, the woman who loves him, off the Caledonian Road. None of this is to Murphy's liking. No novel has presented so unflinchingly, and with such paradoxically rich comedy and word play, a character for whom the possibilities of city life mean nothing.

**Murphy**
Calder pbk £6.99 0714500429

# ARNOLD BENNETT (1867–1931)

Most of Bennett's best known work is set in the Potteries, the five towns in which he grew up and which he recreated in novels like *The Old Wives' Tales* and the *Clayhanger* sequence. Thus it is easy to forget how metropolitan a man Bennett became and that one of his finest novels is set firmly in the heart of the city. Bennett moved to London in the late eighteen eighties and, apart from a lengthy residence in Paris in the first decade of the century, he lived in the city to the end of his life. His journals, first published immediately after his death, describe a professional life of disciplined literary work and a social life spent amidst the great and good of literary and artistic London. They also include a number of striking descriptive passages in which Bennett, rather in the manner of a nineteenth century explorer encountering remote tribesmen, relates his visits to Limehouse, the East End and other parts of the city outside his usual habitat.

Some of Bennett's lesser novels have London settings (*Imperial Palace* takes place in a hotel markedly like the Savoy) but the one book which ensures his inclusion in any survey of London literature is *Riceyman Steps*, first published in 1923. The novel centres on the miserly Henry Earlforward who inherits a secondhand bookshop in Clerkenwell and enters, in middle age, upon the courtship of a widow who has moved into a nearby shop. Henry's emotional desiccation and his obsession with money and possessions mean that the marriage which ensues is doomed from the outset.

**Riceyman Steps**
Penguin pbk £6.99 0140182594

## ELIZABETH BOWEN (1899–1973)

One of the particular strengths of the Anglo-Irish novelist and short-story writer Elizabeth Bowen was her skill at evoking place and landscape, both the Ireland in which she grew up and the London in which she lived for many years. Her two most famous novels are *The Death of the Heart* (1938) and *The Heat of the Day* (1945). The former is a story of innocence let loose amidst upper-middle class London sophistication. The second, set in the same milieu but one dislocated and deracinated by the war, is one of the most effective and evocative novels of the city in the Blitz. The love affair of Stella Rodney and Robert Kelway is doomed both by the large-scale upheaval in which it is conducted and by the sinister machinations of Stella's other suitor who reveals that Kelway is a spy. Themes of love and betrayal play themselves out against the backdrop of a city in which everyone seems to have lost their bearings. Many of Elizabeth Bowen's best short stories, such as 'Mysterious Kor', first published in Penguin New Writing in 1944, are set in the war. Although her social range is limited – she rarely moves outside the upper middle-class into which she was born – she is one of those writers who has most effectively memorialised the London of the Blitz.

**The Death of the Heart**
Vintage pbk £6.99 0099276453
**The Heat of the Day**
Penguin pbk £6.99 0099276461

## NORMAN COLLINS

Of all the novels that Collins wrote, and he was a prolific novelist, it is *London Belongs To Me* (1945) that is most deserving of inclusion in a guide to London writing. Other novels (*Bond Street Story* of 1965, for example) use London settings very effectively to tell London stories. However Collins begins *London Belongs to Me* by using Dunbar's famous line, 'London thou art the flower of cities all', as an epigraph and he states explicitly in his preface that he wants the novel to be about 'real Londoners.' 'Real Londoners', he writes, 'who sleep the night in London as well as work the day there. Real Londoners – some in love, some in debt, some committing murders, some adultery, some trying to get on in the world, some looking forward to a pension, some getting drunk, some losing their jobs, some dying, and some holding up the new baby.' The setting for the book is a terraced house in Kennington, No. 10 Dulcimer Street, and the novel tells of the unheroic, ordinary lives of those who live there, from landlady Mrs Vizzard to retired City clerk Mr Josser, on the eve of the Second World War. The chief drama, beyond the impending war, is the haphazard tragedy that befalls young, semi-delinquent Percy Boon. Read today, *London Belongs to Me* seems largely a period piece and the tradition in which Collins was working, ultimately derived from Dickens via H.G. Wells, was past its sell-by-date even at the time he was writing. However Collins was a vigorous writer and his characters do have a life and energy that are engaging. As a middlebrow saga of London life at a particular moment of history, *London Belongs to Me* is still worth reading.

The work of Norman Collins, including **London Belongs to Me**, is currently out of print.


## JAMES CURTIS

Large areas of London life never made it into pre-War fiction, were never validated or made more real by memorialisation on the printed page. Middle class and upper-middle class life were relentlessly scrutinised but inhabitants of less genteel milieu tended to be overlooked. In novels like *The Gilt Kid*, *You're in the Racket, Too* and *There Ain't No Justice* James Curtis examined the worlds of unsuccessful criminals dreaming of the big heist, of drinkers in low-life pubs, of drifters caught in the shady world of small-time boxing. Curtis's slightly self-conscious use of slang ('Blimey, if all the bogeys was like that, you'd never have to do no time at all.') can grate and the political message in his novels sometimes seems forced but his novels are strong on sense of place (*There Ain't No Justice* shows its readers round the less salubrious parts of Shepherd's Bush) and remain lively reading.

The novels of James Curtis are not currently available.

# From Gaslight to Neon: A brief look at London Crime Fiction

*by Richard Shephard of Waterstone's, Hampstead*

Other gaslight detective fiction, such as Fergus Hume's ***The Mystery of the Hansom Cab***, was published around the same time but Conan Doyle's ***A Study in Scarlet*** (1887) remains the best known of early crime fiction and introduced his immortal creation Sherlock Holmes, indisputably London's most celebrated detective. It was Holmes's untimely (and brief) 'death' at the Reichenbach Falls in ***The Final Problem*** (coupled with the handsome fees paid by *The Strand Magazine*) that spurred on other writers to create similar detectives. Arthur Morrison, author of such realist London novels as ***A Child of the Jago*** (1896) and ***The Hole in the Wall*** (1902), produced Martin Hewitt, who appeared in four books, a plump, genial sleuth who was the opposite to the gaunt, aquiline Holmes. Morrison's collection ***Tales of Mean Streets*** (the title pre-empted Raymond Chandler's famous phrase by more than fifty years) concerned itself with the London poor but was just as atmospheric as the Hewitt yarns.

Like Morrison, George R. Sims (1847–1922) wrote novels detailing the miseries of metropolitan poverty, most notably ***The Devil in London*** (1908) in which Satan arrives in the capital and comments wryly on the social conditions he sees (perhaps Mikhail Bulgakov saw a copy of this?) but also produced a series of stories featuring Dorcas Dene, an ex-actress turned detective. One of the few female sleuths (as well as one of the worst named), Dene was a memorable character, but her 1897 adventure ***The Haverstock Hill Murder***, although not lacking in local colour, in its obsessive topography reads as if it were narrated by a cab driver.

In the early part of the century there were scores of authors who based their detective fiction in London, including A. E. W. Mason, Marie Belloc Lowndes (sister of Hilaire Belloc and author of ***The Lodger***, the classic fictionalisation of Jack the Ripper), the hugely prolific Edgar Wallace, Sax Rohmer whose ***Fu Manchu*** stories often have East London's Chinatown as a setting, and the popular E. W. Hornung, who ignored the advice of his brother-in-law Arthur Conan Doyle ('You must not make a criminal a hero'), and created A. J. Raffles, cricketer, jewel thief, resident of The Albany, Piccadilly, a Robin Hood character whose chief vice is boredom.

Two writers who produced seminal works of London crime fiction in the thirties were Gerald Kersh, whose 1938 novel ***Night and the City***, twice adapted for the screen, became a cult classic, rivalling the best American thrillers in its urban noir setting, and the mysterious Cameron McCabe, 'author' and anti-hero of the astonishing ***The Face on the Cutting Room Floor*** (1937). Described by critic and author Julian Symons as a 'dazzling, unrepeatable box of tricks… the detective story to end all detective stories', and by poet and critic Herbert Read as 'Hegelian', McCabe's tale was discovered, in the mid-seventies, to have been written by one Ernst Bornemann, a German author, film-maker and jazz musician. Starting in a King's Cross film studio, the plot zigzags feverishly, zooming through the city like badly spliced celluloid before suddenly disappearing from the screen, the empty reel still spinning, leaving the reader full of images and questions. Though out of print for years, it remains a uniquely surreal piece of London fiction.

Since the war crime writers of very different styles have produced novels set in London. John Creasey, under his own name or one of many pseudonyms, produced a staggering 560 novels, including those written as J. J. Marric, featuring Commander George Gideon of Scotland Yard. Robin Cook ushered in the sixties with a number of lowlife thrillers before changing his name to Derek Raymond and producing the *Factory* novels, tough police novels set amidst a very realistic and violent London underworld. Raymond has proved to be a lasting influence, paving the way for Julian Barnes to don his mac and produce, as Dan Kavanagh, the *Duffy* novels, all showcasing a likeable and bisexual private eye, and for Mark Timlin whose South London books featuring investigator Nick Sharman form an agreeably slapdash series. Also possibly influenced by Raymond, but equally his own man, is John Milne, author of several novels set in London. These include the 1983 novel *London Fields* (a title later purloined by Martin Amis) and the excellent *Dead Birds* and *Shadow Play*, both starring Jimmy Jenner, a seedy, one-legged private eye. Paul Charles and Lauren Henderson have written entertaining mysteries and both Mike Phillips and Victor Headley have produced novels written from a black Londoner's perspective. Phillips's books detail journalist Sam Dean's adventures while Headley's *Yardie* books are compelling stories of drug dealing and gang warfare.

Finally many American crime writers have given us their own versions of London. The most successful are Elizabeth George and Martha Grimes, although, topographically, their books sometimes require a suspension of disbelief and any reader obsessive enough to follow in the footsteps of their characters may find himself not with his feet nestling under a table at the Savoy but soaking in the mudbanks of the Thames. Possibly the most entertaining American chronicler of a crime-ridden London returns us, by a roundabout route, to Sherlock Holmes. Horror author and H. P. Lovecraft acolyte August Derleth wrote stories of *Solar Pons* (try saying it quickly) which present virtually an alternative universe to that inhabited by Conan Doyle's sleuth. Continued after Derleth's death by the aptly-named Basil Copper, the Pons adventures are narrated by one Lyndon Parker M. D. and usually start in the rooms he shares with Pons at 7B Praed Street. A spiritualist in later life, Conan Doyle may still be turning in his grave.

*Paul Charles*
**I Love the Sound of Breaking Glass**
Do-Not Press pbk £7.00 1899344160

*Paul Charles*
**Last Boat to Camden Town**
Do-Not Press pbk £7.00 1899344306

*Basil Copper*
**The Dossier of Solar Pons**
Academy Chicago Publications Pbk £6.99
0897332520

*Victor Headley*
**Fetish**
The X Press pbk £5.99 1874509204

*Victor Headley*
**Here Comes the Bride**
The X Press pbk £5.99 1874509360

*Victor Headley*
**Yardie**
Pan pbk £5.99 033033042X

*Victor Headley*
**Yush!**
Pan pbk £5.99 0330337335

*Lauren Henderson*
**The Black Rubber Dress**
Arrow pbk £5.99 0099244322

*Lauren Henderson*
**Dead White Female**
NEL pbk £5.99 0340649151

*Lauren Henderson*
**Freeze My Margarita**
Hutchinson hbk £10.00 0091801893

*Lauren Henderson*
**Too Many Blondes**
Sceptre pbk £6.99 0340649178

*F.W. Hornung*
**The Collected Raffles Stories**
Oxford UP pbk £5.99 0192823248

*Fergus Hume*
**The Mystery of a Hansom Cab**
Breese Books pbk £6.95 0947533427

*Dan Kavanagh*
**The Duffy Omnibus**
Penguin pbk £9.99 0140158243

*Marie Belloc Lowndes*
**The Lodger**
Oxford UP pbk £5.95 019282371X

*John Milne*
**Alive and Kicking**
No Exit Press hbk £9.99 1874061882

*John Milne*
**Dead Birds**
No Exit Press pbk £6.99 1874061874

*Mike Phillips*
**An Image To Die For**
HarperCollins pbk £5.99 0006496717

*Sax Rohmer*
**The Fu Manchu Omnibus Volume 1**
Allison & Busby pbk £9.99 0749002719

*Sax Rohmer*
**The Fu Manchu Omnibus Volume 2**
Allison & Busby pbk £9.99 0749002220

*Sax Rohmer*
**The Fu Manchu Omnibus Volume 3**
Allison & Busby pbk £9.99 0749002271

*Mark Timlin*
**Ashes by Now**
Gollancz pbk £4.99 0575057831

*Mark Timlin*
**Dead Flowers**
Vista pbk £5.99 0575603232

*Mark Timlin*
**Find My Way Home**
Vista pbk £5.99 0575601760

*Mark Timlin*
**Paint It Black**
Vista pbk £5.99 0575600144

*Mark Timlin*
**Pretend We're Dead**
Gollancz pbk £4.99 0575058285

*Mark Timlin*
**Sharman and Other Filth**
Vista pbk £5.99 0575601019

*Mark Timlin*
**A Street That Rhymed at 3a.m.**
Vista pbk £5.99 0575601361

*Elizabeth George* is published by Bantam Press and Hodder & Stoughton. *Martha Grimes* is published by Headline. For book titles by **Conan Doyle**, **Arthur Morrison**, **Gerald Kersh** and **Derek Raymond**, see separate entries on these writers. Books by **George R.Sims**, **A.E.W. Mason**, **Cameron McCabe's** **The Face on the Cutting Room Floor**, titles by **John Creasey** and *August Derleth's* Solar Pons stories are unavailable.

## HENRY GREEN (1905–1973)

Born Henry Vincent Yorke in Tewkesbury, Gloucestershire, Green was educated at Eton and Oxford and his first novel *Blindness* was published in 1926, while he was struggling through his final undergraduate year. His ultimate failure to graduate combined with his early literary success to separate him from contemporaries such as future novelists Evelyn Waugh and Anthony Powell. His first London novel, *Party Going,* was published in 1938, although Green had been working on it since 1931. Possibly influenced by Joyce's *Ulysses,* the book's time-span was a mere four hours, all of them spent at a London station, where the party-goers are boarding a train. In 1929 Green had moved to London to work at the city offices of the family business and in 1938 he volunteered to join the Auxiliary Fire Service. This experience was recorded in his 1943 novel *Caught,* one of the most brilliant of all fictional accounts of the Blitz. In 1960 Green intended to write a non-fiction book entitled *London in Fire 1940–1945* but it never materialised. We are left instead with a fragment (ember, perhaps), published posthumously in the volume *Surviving.* Here, as in *Caught,* his portraits of the destruction wreaked by fire-bombs afford ample demonstration of his descriptive powers, not often encountered in his other, dialogue-led fiction and they give the city, with its violent spectrum of colours, its 'huge yellow cobra tongues of flame' and 'yard-high maple leaf of flame..veined in violet' an unearthly, surreal appearance. One bizarre incident is described by Green's son Sebastian: 'Henry once entered a burning house, axe in hand, to find a naked girl, oblivious to smoke and flames, making love to a Great Dane..' (Unsurprisingly this never appeared in any of Green's writings, published or unpublished.) Arguably London brought out the best in Green as a writer and it is entirely reasonable that this city of contrasts and oddities should so inspire an author who had once said that 'life is after all, one discrepancy after another.'

*Richard Shephard Waterstone's, Hampstead*

The London fiction of Henry Green is not currently available.

# GRAHAM GREENE (1904–1991)

*Simon Roberts of Waterstone's, Notting Hill Gate on two London novels by Graham Greene*

The short-story writer and habitué of Fitzrovia, Julian Maclaren-Ross, describes meeting Graham Greene at his Clapham residence in 1938. They walk across the Common to fetch jugs of beer from The Windmill, the pub which Greene was to use as the model for The Pontefract Arms in his 1951 novel, ***The End of the Affair***. During their post-lunch conversation Maclaren-Ross reports Greene as saying: 'I try to restrict myself to home ground if I can, English backgrounds, London whenever possible: I've always made that a rule... Oh, I know, I've broken the rule several times. But all the same I think an English novelist should write about England, don't you?' (*Memoirs of the Forties*). There is something both wholly English and yet, at the same time, other-worldly about the London of ***It's A Battlefield*** (1934), a novel in which the city is presented as a character with a more concrete sense of itself than any of the lonely, guilty lives that people it.

As the worlds of each of the main characters connect themselves around the battle to save Drover, a Communist bus-driver awaiting execution for the murder of a policeman, so London draws them together, flickering across their individual consciousnesses like a cinema film, wielding its power indiscriminately like a God. For the jaundiced Assistant Commissioner the city appears as a battlefield on which to defend poverty and brutality, only to be defeated by the realisation that 'the peace of Sunday in Pall Mall was like the peace which follows a massacre, a war of elimination; poverty here had been successfully contested, driven back on the one side towards Notting Hill, on the other towards Vauxhall'; for the emigré Jules, it is a place to experience a sense of belonging, however briefly: '...Jules could stand and laugh and gossip, feel himself for ten minutes part of the street, part of London, part of a country, not one abandoned by his mother's death to fight his way in a land which was his only by accident of birth'; and for the fantasist Conder, a shabby newspaper journalist, the London landscape is his only true reality: 'He clung to the drab street; a bus went by and in an upper window across the way a man was shaving. This was real, this he had to keep hold of.'

Greene's topography is exact, as witness the route the Assistant Commissioner takes as he realises he is being followed by Conrad, Drover's increasingly paranoid brother: 'He turned sharply up St. James's Street, walked rapidly towards the Circus, took the turning by Fortnum and Mason's and waited.' *It's a Battlefield*, as an evocation of thirties London is not merely a litany of familiar street-names and landmarks but manages to elevate the city's patchwork of districts onto a plane that is both believable and imaginary: '...as the car left the crowds and the tram-lines, he was saddened for a moment like a man leaving his home. Candahar Road, Khyber Terrace, Kabul Street, the Victorian villas wavered in the mist like a shaking of shakos in old imperial wars.' Nevertheless, as a depiction of a capital, this arguably experimental novel presents a vision of London in which solitary lives are fought out, not altogether successfully, and in which the Outer Circle Line runs through territory more normally associated with Dante:

> *"It would give me the creeps," Mrs Simpson said, "spending all the day with murderers and thieves. Why, I dream sometimes that you're bleeding on the doorstep."*
> *"Come, come, Mrs Simpson, this is London"*
> *"Them as knows what London is," Mrs Simpson said, "would not be surprised to find their nearest and dearest bleeding."*

The London of *The End of the Affair* plays a less pivotal role than in the earlier novel, having a more prosaic reality as a location which Greene uses as a backdrop to Maurice Bendrix's triangular relationship with Sarah and Henry, her dull civil servant husband. Unlike *It's A Battlefield*, *The End of the Affair* is not chiefly a work of the imagination but a thinly fictionalised account of Greene's own affair with Lady Catherine Walston, American wife of the British peer Harry Walston. The London scenery, although authentic, functions as a piece of territory, a region in which the course of an unhappy and bitter passion is charted by the isolated first-person narrator.

*The End of the Affair* alternates between London's seamier and more respectable locations – Vigo and Sackville Streets on the one hand (Savage's private detective agency, Bendrix's encounter with a Mayfair prostitute), Clapham's imposing North Side and Rules Restaurant in Maiden Lane (where, until recently, there used to exist the 'Greene' table) on the other. There is a particularity about each location that suggests Bendrix/Greene's obsessive desire to recall the specifics of the doomed affair. The narrator's memory of the lovers' hurried taxi ride to a hotel, having abandoned their lunch in Rules, is a case in point:

> *We caught a taxi by Charing Cross station and I told the driver to take us to Arbuckle Avenue – that was the name they had given amongst themselves to Eastbourne Terrace, the row of hotels that used to stand along the side of Paddington station... The doors of these hotels were always open and you could get a room at any time of day for an hour or two. A week ago I revisited the terrace. Half of it was gone – the half where the hotels used to stand had been blasted to bits, and the place where we made love that night was a patch of air.*

'A patch of air' is a good description of Clapham Common itself. It divides the Miles residence on the fashionable North Side from Bendrix's bed-sit at the 'wrong', south side and is traversed, often in rain, by the three main characters as if crossing a no-man's land between belief in God (Sarah's Catholicism) and atheism (Bendrix's hostility to Sarah's conversion). On the Common itself, amid the political and religious speakers, is the rationalist Smythe who, as Bendrix cynically points out, essentially preaches 'nothing', only to abandon his creed when he believes his facial disfigurement has been 'cured' by a lock of Sarah's hair, stolen from her after her death. London, or at any rate the acreage of Clapham Common, is still a battlefield but the war being waged has become an overtly religious one.

*The End of the Affair* 'fails to take a straight course' and so we see London pre-war, post-war and during the Blitzkrieg (prominent in Greene's 1943 novel, *The Ministry of Fear*). In one of the novel's most striking passages it is, in effect, London under the Blitz that precipitates the end of the affair. It is June 1944 and the city is under threat from the V1 pilot-less planes:

> *I never heard the explosion, and I woke after five seconds or five minutes in a changed world. I thought I was still on my feet and I was puzzled by the darkness: somebody seemed to be pressing a cold fist into my cheek and my mouth was salty with blood... I had no memory of Sarah and I was completely free from anxiety, jealousy, insecurity, hate: my mind was a blank sheet on which somebody had just been on the point of writing a message of happiness. I felt sure that when my memory came back, the writing would continue and that I should be happy. But when memory did return it was not in that way... I remembered Sarah and Henry and the dread of love ending.*

In the only, but significant, instance of London under siege having a direct influence on the novel's action (Sarah vows to believe in God and give up Bendrix if he survives the raid), Greene exposes the devastating effects of both mortal and spiritual love on human beings.

Greene's London of the thirties and forties is hardly the London we know in the nineties. Or is it? Towards the end of the novel Bendrix, in a short dream sequence, describes Oxford Street:

> *...all the shops were full of cheap jewellery, glittering under the concealed lighting. Now and then I saw something beautiful and I would approach the glass, but when I saw the jewel close it would be as factitious as all the others...*

Plus ça change.

**The End of the Affair**
Penguin pbk £6.99 0140184953
**It's a Battlefield**
Penguin pbk £6.99 0140185410

# WALTER GREENWOOD
**(1903–1974)**

Greenwood is best known for his 1933 novel *Love on the Dole* in which he drew on his own experiences in his home town of Salford to examine the effect of the Thirties depression on family life. The book was both a critical and commercial success and dramatisations, and eventually a film version, appeared. Greenwood was propelled into the limelight as an early exponent of kitchen sink realism, a precursor of the Northern writers of the late fifties. Although he published other fiction nothing was ever to have the impact of *Love on the Dole*. One of his later novels, of interest to the devotee of London fiction, is *Only Mugs Work*, a not entirely successful but intriguing attempt to widen the geographical scope of his writing, which is a self-proclaimed melodramatic tale of Soho low-life.

**Only Mugs Work** is currently out of print.

# PATRICK HAMILTON (1904–1962)

Hamilton was born in Sussex and educated at Westminster, a conspicuously middle class beginning for a writer who was once described by J.B. Priestley as 'above all the novelist of the homeless.' His first novel, *Craven House*, was published in 1926 and, with its shabby boarding house setting, immediately established his fascination with the seedier side of life and, particularly, urban life. This bore fruit in a trio of London novels: *The Midnight Bell* (1929), *The Siege of Pleasure* (1932) and *The Plains of Cement* (1934). Set mainly in a pub near Euston station, they were later published together as a trilogy under the title *Twenty Thousand Streets Under the Sky*. With these books, and his classic *Hangover Square*, published in 1941, Hamilton transformed the squalid streets and pubs of London into a stage on which his characters played out their compellingly miserable lives. Subtitled 'A Story of Darkest Earl's Court', *Hangover Square* is masterly in its evocation of shiftless lives lived between the pub and the solitude of dismal boarding houses. Its narrative of schizophrenia and sexual obsession, in which George Harvey Bone is driven to the brink of madness by drink and by his fixation on aspiring actress Netta Longdon, is superbly controlled by Hamilton.

Earlier, in 1937, Hamilton, at the peak of his commercial fame and with royalties pouring in from his play *Rope*, had been knocked down by a car in a street just off Earl's Court Road. Seriously injured, he never fully recovered from the accident and was, in later years, as Priestley noted, 'no longer a social drinker but an unhappy man who needs whisky as a car needs petrol.' He died in 1962 and, six years later, Doris Lessing praised his writing and its uniquely-handled subject matter, stating: 'He wrote more sense about England in the 1930s than anybody else I can think of, and his novels are true now. You can go into any pub and see it going on.' Thirty years after this judgement, Hamilton's relevance remains.

*Richard Shephard* Waterstone's, Hampstead

**Hangover Square**
Penguin pbk £7.99 0140183973
**Twenty Thousand Streets Under the Sky**
Vintage pbk £7.99 0099288656

The wheels and tracks clicked out the familiar and unmistakable rhythm – the sly, gentle, suggestive rhythm, unlike any of its others, of a train entering a major London terminus, and he was filled with unease and foreboding as he always was by this sound. Thought and warmth must give place to action in cold streets – reality, buses, tubes, booking-offices, life again, electric-lit London, endless terrors.

Patrick Hamilton – Hangover Square

## R. C. HUTCHINSON
### (1907–1975)

An ambitious novelist who strove to tell resonant stories of individuals caught up in broader historical movements (his best known book, *Testament*, is set in the Russian Revolution) Hutchinson has been unfairly neglected in recent years. *The Elephant and Castle*, long out of print, is an often powerful examination of the social and racial divisions of Thirties London. Through the relationship, and eventual marriage, of a West End girl and the son of Italian immigrants in Southwark, Hutchinson shows that the distances between West London and South London are geographically small but culturally huge. The narrative heads inexorably towards tragedy.

**The Elephant and Castle** is out of print.

## ALDOUS HUXLEY (1894–1963)

The majority of Aldous Huxley's early novels – *Crome Yellow*, *Antic Hay*, *Those Barren Leaves* and *Point Counter Point* – are either set in London or examine the life of the capital's literati at the time and the books often include thinly disguised portraits of contemporaries such as D.H. Lawrence, Katherine Mansfield and Bertrand Russell. Remarkably vicious satires for their period, the novels are still very caustic and funny today.

London in these novels stands for what Huxley, in *Those Barren Leaves*, terms 'the heart of reality.' Or it would be more accurate to say that their experience of London is what his characters often mistake for reality, seeing the endless carnival of parties and evening social functions, followed by dreary days in plush offices, as the great work of life.

In *Point Counter Point* a party is described as 'a jungle of innumerable trees and dangling creepers…a jungle of noise' where conversation is the chattering of parrots and monkeys. Later in the novel one of the characters, Spandrell, instead of going out, reads the Births, Deaths and Court announcements in The Times, despite the fact that 'his shelves were full of books, all the London library was at his disposal.' The life of the mind beckons but is overwhelmed by trivial news from the world of society. 'Pascal and Blake were within reach, on the book-shelf. But "Lady Augusta Crippen has left England on the Berengaria to visit the Governor-General of South Melanesia."'

In *Those Barren Leaves* the horror of the daily grind overwhelms Francis Chelifer as he sits at his desk in Gog's Court: 'Why am I doing this ? What is it all for? Did I come into the world, supplied with a soul which may very well be immortal, for the sole purpose of sitting at this desk?' He concludes that the sole perk of his job is that he may sometime be able to afford a weekend in Brighton.

The absurdity of this life drives the Huxley 'hero' to leave London, as indeed Huxley himself did in 1923. In *Those Barren Leaves,* before his retreat into the mountains, Calamy finds himself becoming aware of 'other things': 'They loomed up enormously behind the distracting bustle of life, silently on the further side of noise and chatter. But what were they?… Through the fluttering veil of movement it was impossible to do more than dimly guess; one might as well try to look at the stars through the London smoke. If one could stop the movement, or get away from it, then surely one would be able to see clearly the large and silent things beyond.'

It is this 'stopping the movement' which forms the climax of *Time Must Have a Stop* (1944). In one of Huxley's most poignant chapters, Sebastian is shown meditating during an air raid. Outside, 'the guns on Primrose Hill were banging away with a kind of frenzy', whilst, in his flat, Sebastian experiences 'an almost effortless achievement of silence' that takes him into 'the intensely active tranquillity of the living and eternal Silence.' Realising that he cannot adequately explain it, he hopes that through the act of writing about it, he will be able to remind himself what he 'once had intuitively understood and, in others, evoke the wish and create some of the conditions for a similar understanding.' In all the novels, which often portray very vividly and precisely the perils and pleasures of the city, this desire remains, that we should not become so enmeshed in the jungles of our own making that we can no longer see the stars above London.

*Sean Martin*

**Antic Hay**
Flamingo pbk £5.99
0006547427

**Eyeless in Gaza**
Flamingo pbk £7.99
0006547303

**Point Counter Point**
Flamingo pbk £8.99
0006547281

## GERALD KERSH (1911–1968)

Born in 1911 in Teddington, Middlesex, Kersh died in 1968 in New York State, a naturalised American, having moved there after the war. His life would make an interesting biography: when not passing his time as a nightclub bouncer, cook, wrestler, soldier, film scenarist and journalist (popular with Fleet Street editors, he could churn out copy on almost any subject), he wrote over twenty novels and scores of short stories, including *They Die With Their Boots Clean*, his painfully honest account of his war-time experiences. His younger brother Cyril Kersh was also a journalist and fictional chronicler of urban life. Several of Gerald Kersh's novels are London-based but two stand out. His masterly comic novel *Fowler's End* (1957), centred on a run-down cinema in north London, has been much admired by other novelists such as Michael Moorcock and was described by one critic as 'one of the outstanding novels of this century.' Kersh's reputation, however, was established by his 1938 classic *Night and the City*. Set on the fringes of the fight game in a seedy pre-war London steeped in grime and squalor, the novel is an entirely successful amalgam of ingredients: a tinge of Greene, a dash of Hammett and a lick of Dante. The city's infernal presence is described in harsh, surreal terms – 'Bursting like inexhaustible fireworks, the million coloured bulbs of the electric signs blazed in perpetual recurrence over the face of the West End.' Like American hard-boiled writer David Goodis, Kersh is a master of what critics have termed 'thing language', in which inanimate objects seemingly come to life ('Cinema vestibules became black with people... The darkness of the April night got thicker. It seeped down between the street lamps, poured into basements, and lay deep and stagnant under the porches and arches of the back streets...'), often posing a threat to the people around them who, through their own weakness or the caprices of fate, become victims ('Night closed down upon the city.') Although *Night and the City* has been filmed twice, as a passable film noir starring Richard Widmark in 1950 and as a lacklustre 1992 version featuring Robert De Niro and Jessica Lange, it has never achieved the success or exposure it deserves. Kersh's view of the city is uniquely his and his disturbing and original talent remains ripe for 'rediscovery.'

**Night and the City**
Brainiac Books pbk £5.99 187405701X

*Richard Shephard* Waterstone's, Hampstead

## WYNDHAM LEWIS (1882–1957)

Of mixed American/English parentage, Lewis was born on his father's yacht off the coast of Nova Scotia and lived in New England until 1888, when his parents moved to England. They separated when he was eleven and Lewis was educated at various schools, later studying at the Slade School of Art. While establishing himself as a promising Futurist painter (particularly in Europe), Lewis also wrote short stories, publishing them in *The English Review* (then edited by Ford Madox Hueffer) and later in a collection *The Wild Body* (1927). After infamously quarrelling with Futurist leader Marinetti, Lewis produced *Blast: The Review of the Great English Vortex*, a scathing critique of contemporary art and writing, which included contributions from his Vorticist ally, the poet Ezra Pound. In the 1920s Lewis was, as he put it, 'always underground...buried in the Reading room of the British Museum or out of sight in some secret workshop.' Among the diatribes he concocted during this period was a small magazine called *Enemy* which was to prove an accurate, if sadly prophetic, title. Lewis was never to be short of enemies in his career. His 1930 novel *The Apes of God*, with its satirical caricatures of literary figures, including T.S. Eliot and James Joyce, horrified the good burghers of Bloomsbury. The following year he published a book expressing his admiration for Hitler, cementing his estrangement from the Leftish literary establishment and later prompting W.H. Auden to describe him as 'that lonely old volcano of the Right.' His mordant political epic *Rotting Hill* was written after the Second World War when he was in Canada, driven into exile from Britain for his fascist sympathies. Aside from these books, Lewis's main contribution to London letters were snippets published in his 1937 memoir *Blasting and Bombardiering* (he had served as a gunner in World War I), including the brilliantly misanthropic account of 'The Crowd' and its reaction to the declaration of war:'The Crowd, that first mobilisation of a country, now is formed in London... Every night it serpentines in thick well-nourished coils, all over the city, in tropic degustation of news.'

**Rotting Hill**
Black Sparrow Press pbk £12.99 0876856466

# GEORGE ORWELL [ERIC BLAIR] (1903–1950)

Orwell's best-known works are, of course, the political fable *Animal Farm* and the vision of a totalitarian future, *1984*. He also wrote of his experiences in the Spanish Civil War (*Homage to Catalonia*) and the journey into another England that was *The Road to Wigan Pier*. However his life in London in the late twenties and early thirties, and the books which reflect that, can be seen as marking decisive stages in the ongoing transformation of Eton-educated Eric Blair into the democratic socialist George Orwell. Coming as they did after his hated service in the Imperial Police in Burma, his experiences of 'fairly severe poverty' in the capital deepened his dislike and moral disapproval of the imperial and capitalist Britain which had schooled him to join its ruling elite but which he increasingly rejected. Back from Burma, via Paris, Blair/Orwell took up residence just off the Portobello Road, from where, dressed in threadbare clothing, he would make regular forays into the streets and dosshouses of the East End. These excursions would later provide him with some of the material for his first book, *Down and Out in Paris and London* (1933). Even after this had been published Orwell found it difficult to make a living from writing and he took work as a tutor and as a part-time bookshop assistant at Booklovers' Corner in Hampstead. *Keep the Aspidistra Flying* (1936), the story of the literary dreams and harsh financial realities of Gordon Comstock, a bookshop assistant, offers clear parallels with Orwell's own life. And perhaps the character of the insurance clerk, George Bowling, in Orwell's last novel before the war, *Coming Up for Air* (1939), who sets off in search of his fantasy of an unspoiled rural England, reflects some of Orwell's own deeply ambivalent feelings about city life. After the war Orwell attained, briefly, the status of bestselling and acclaimed author and *Animal Farm* and *1984* will always be his most widely read works but those earlier books which reflect something of certain kinds of London life in the depressed Thirties remain worth reading.

**Down and Out in Paris and London**
Penguin pbk £6.99 0140182306

**Keep the Aspidistra Flying**
Penguin pbk £6.99 0140182330

## ANTHONY POWELL (b.1905)

It is often assumed that the London evoked in many of the volumes of Powell's massive *roman fleuve* **A Dance to the Music of Time** is a narrow world of upper class parties and debutantes' balls. Certainly the narrator Nicholas Jenkins, in the earlier volumes, is to be found in Belgrave Square more frequently than the average Londoner. However the books are not as limited in the social range they encompass as this might suggest. From the dingy respectability of the Bayswater hotel in which Jenkins's Uncle Giles stays in **The Acceptance World** to Soho establishments like Casanova's Chinese Restaurant in the novel of the same name, from the South Kensington salon of Lady Molly Jeavons in **At Lady Molly's** to Fitzrovian pubs haunted by the writer X. Trapnel (a character based on Julian Maclaren-Ross) in **Books Do Furnish a Room**, Powell takes the reader on a tour of the London where upper middle class society and bohemia collided in the decades before and after the Second World War. Just as, in one sense, the sequence can be read as an ironic and often very funny lament for the passing of time and the price that exacts from all its characters, London is seen as a place of change and decay in which events, particularly the war, alter and destroy the city which Jenkins first inhabits.

**Dance to the Music of Time Volume 1**
Mandarin pbk 074932399X

**Dance to the Music of Time Volume 2**
Mandarin pbk 074932404X

**Dance to the Music of Time Volume 3**
Mandarin pbk 0749324090

**Dance to the Music of Time Volume 4**
Mandarin pbk 0749321477

## J. B. PRIESTLEY (1894–1984)

Priestley presented the image of a bluff and blunt Northerner, a man unafraid of calling a spade a spade and one temperamentally at odds with the London literary establishment. In fact he moved to London in his twenties and established his reputation as a journalist and critic before the publication of *The Good Companions* in 1929, a picaresque tale of a concert party's travels round the country, made him a bestselling novelist. For the rest of his long career he may have been at odds with some versions of the literary establishment (Bloomsbury, modernism) but, as novelist, dramatist and social commentator, he was, in the mind of the public, the epitome of that dying breed, the Man of Letters. Priestley's London novel is *Angel Pavement*, which was published in the year after the great success of *The Good Companions*.

**Angel Pavement** is currently out of print.

**Mr Smeeth... continued to stare idly through the railings of Bunhill Fields, where the old nonconformists are buried in mouldering eighteenth century elegance, to which they had at least conformed in death, if not in life; and where, among the divines and elders, not only Defoe, but also Bunyan and Blake, the two God-haunted men, lie in the sooty earth, while their dreams and ecstasies still light the world.**

J. B. Priestley – Angel Pavement

# Unreal City: London in Twentieth Century Poetry

*Poet Christopher Reid looks at the ways twentieth century poets have grappled with the city as subject matter.*

Towards the end of the nineteenth century, it looked as if London might at last become a subject for serious poetry. Taking their lead from the French – both writers and painters, Impressionists and Symbolists – such young poets as were disposed to do so could now see an alternative to the fancy-dress medievalism of Tennyson and William Morris. Talents as diverse as those of Arthur Symons, John Davidson, W.E. Henley, Richard Le Gallienne, began to find beauty, or the potential for it, in the gaslight and grunge of the city that lay before their very eyes. After the long Victorian pageant, modernity had arrived.

But not for long. Instead, Georgianism happened. Either the Nineties poets died, or their gifts died on them. Whatever the cause, metropolitan moods and impressions gave way to the sanitised rusticity of the Georgians, as artificial as seventeenth-century pastoral. And then there was the Great War, fought in a very different setting from that which had produced **The Yellow Book** and producing in turn poetry of a very different order. London was now decidedly off the agenda.

It was not like that in the other arts. Elgar's indefatigably dashing overture *Cockayne* and the big, foggy, impressionist canvas of Vaughan Williams's 'London' symphony both embrace the city as an epic or heroic subject. The painters who associated themselves with Sickert, the Camden Town Group, remained true to their urban inspiration – and their successors are active today. But in poetry there has been no such inheritance. A remarkable fact about many of the finest twentieth-century British poets is how resolutely non-metropolitan they have been. Looking for London in their work is a matter of noting exceptions, though among those may be some glorious ones.

London is certainly a feature of the early work of the two great poets most indebted to the same French writers as had inspired the Nineties 'decadents': T. S. Eliot and Ezra Pound. *'The Shop Girl'* (**Lustra**, 1916) who evokes from Pound a favourable comparison with 'the harlots of Baudelaire' is characteristic, as are the 'weeping multitudes' Eliot describes (*'A Cooking Egg'*, **Poems**, 1920) who 'Droop in a hundred A.B.C.'s' (a chain of cheap eating places), their 'buttered scones and crumpets' rhyming disadvantageously with the 'eagles and trumpets' of a nobler vision. And, of course, there is **The Waste Land** (1922). But already qualifications need to be made, for although the crowd crossing London Bridge, the gossips in the pub, the idly 'throbbing' taxi that is likened to 'the human engine' and the drifting logs that are washed 'Down Greenwich Reach/Past the Isle of Dogs' are all obvious London properties, the force of the poem is to co-opt everything into a generalised denunciation of 'unreal' urban civilisation. It is an emblematic London we are shown, 'unreal' not just in the mystical sense.

If naturalism in poetry is what you are after, then the 1930s are where it is most likely to be found. A view of humanity as shaped and driven by social factors, and an insistence on the documentary or testimonial duty of the artist, were in the air. Out of that came the work of two sharply-contrasted poets, Louis MacNeice and John Betjeman. Neither, it hardly needs saying, limited himself to London topics, but Betjeman's knowing studies of the manners and style of the city and its suburbs and MacNeice's more politically astute observations are among the pieces of evidence that define the period for us. The sections of MacNeice's *Autumn Journal* (1938) that show us what the city both looked like and felt like – his noting of the trees being cut down on Primrose Hill, for instance, in readiness for an anti-aircraft gun-emplacement, tells us so much about the actual texture of pre-war anxiety – remain marvellously fresh. If London, for Macneice, was 'littered with remembered kisses', it is now strewn, for those who have read the poem, with snapshots of this kind and is a richer place because of them.

An appreciation of the historical layerings of London, its submerged but still traceable past, its ghosts and buried treasures, has informed the lyrics of numerous more recent poets. John Heath-Stubbs's *Lament for The Old Swan, Notting Hill Gate,* for example, celebrates the recent past (recent in 1950) in an elegy for a favourite Bohemian drinking-place, now demolished. U.A. Fanthorpe attunes herself to more ancient times when, in *Rising Damp* (1981), she names the underground rivers of London – 'Effra, Graveney, Falcon, Quaggy' etc. – and relates them to the rivers of Hades. The drive in both cases is the need to find private, sustaining significance in one's otherwise de-spiritualised surroundings. On a broader scale, Gavin Ewart's book *Londoners* (1964), a survey of his personal territory, from the West End as far south as Strawberry Hill, is ostensibly mere factual record, but from its data it conjures up something like an improvised tribal mythology. When, in *Regent's Park Terrace,* a poem from the late forties, Bernard Spencer allows the noises heard from his London flat – they include the 'stony hoofing' of dray horses, 'screaming' railway trains and the 'cavernous' roaring of lions from the nearby Zoo, as well as 'the little teeth/of a London silence' – to 'make the ear /their road', immediate domestic circumstances dissolve and a vividly particularised, primitive rapport with the city is achieved.

With all this yearning for transcendence evident, at least intermittently, on the lyric level, why hasn't the London of our century yet found its epic poet? Yes, there have been gestures in that direction. Ken Smith's forty-page-long *Fox Running* (1980) is a sort of quest-poem, possibly autobiographical in origin, which scurries, breathlessly unpunctuated, through the boroughs of (mainly) North London. In *Vale Royal* (1995) Aidan Andrew Dun adopts a more Blakean or cabbalistic approach, reading the area north of King's Cross for its ancient, hidden meanings. The attempt is ambitious, but London itself – the London we know now, with its grimy brick terraces and bullying road traffic – barely registers on the poet's sensory equipment, so alert is he to the intimations of some ulterior reality. And something similar could be said about Smith's method: while the plight of his hero, Fox, may be authentic and engaging, the London through which he moves has as much physical reality as the names in an A-Z street guide. We could be almost anywhere.

Perhaps the most deliberate attempt to create a coherent, inclusive vision from idiosyncratic London experience, and the one that comes closest to epic scale, is to be found in David Jones's second book *The Anathemata* (1952). This is a work of great complexity – and, at times, of great obscurity. Jones himself subtitled it 'fragments of an attempted writing'. Multilingual, imbued with memories of the London-Welsh poet's ancestral history and of London itself in the time of Roman occupation, Christian (Roman Catholic) in its sense of ritual, Modernist in its reliance on discontinuity as a structural principle and on pieced-together book-learning, it seems to receive voices – identifiably London-dockland voices – out of the air, blending them into a capacious spiritual cantata. Jones's city is as 'unreal' as that of Eliot, his publisher and encourager – or, indeed, that of Aidan Andrew Dun. Although Jones was a skillful and original painter and print-maker, the poem is singularly lacking in visual particularity; it's the voices, with their Cockney timbre and lilt, that lend it what substance it has. Yet even they, burdened as they are with Latin and Welsh words, with the jargon of old ship-building and seamanship, with mythological and archeological lore, tend to dissolve from the palpable present into an idealised state beyond time. Once again, London reality – it must be there, somewhere – proves as hard to grasp as the gorgeously-tinted fog from which the nineteenth-century Impressionists showed us it was constructed.

**Ezra Pound – Selected Poems**
Faber pbk £8.99 0571109071

**T. S. Eliot – Collected Poems**
Faber pbk £8.99 0571105483

**Louis MacNeice – Collected Poems**
Faber pbk £15.99 0571113532

**The Best of Betjeman**
Penguin pbk £7.99 0140183086

**U. A. Fanthorpe – Selected Poems**
Penguin pbk £6.99 0140586253

**David Jones – The Anathemata**
Faber pbk £9.99 0571101275

Unreal City,
Under the brown fog of a winter dawn,
A crowd flowed over London Bridge, so many,
I had not thought death had undone so many.
Sighs, short and infrequent, were exhaled,
And each man fixed his eyes before his feet.
Flowed up the hill and down King William Street,
To where St. Mary Woolnoth kept the hours
With a dead sound on the final stroke of nine.
T.S. Eliot – The Waste Land

## V. S. PRITCHETT

V. S. Pritchett was born in Ipswich but spent much of his childhood in various London suburban homes (the title of his volume of memoirs **The Cab at the Door** refers to the frequent upheavals as the household moved about town) and went to Dulwich College. Pritchett wrote biographies, travel books and novels but will be best remembered as one of the great short-story writers of the century. Many of his stories illuminate London lives with their acute and ironic observation of the eccentricities, the unexpressed emotions and the often hidden individualities of seemingly ordinary people. He also wrote **London Perceived** (1962) which one critic described, soon after publication, as 'the most perceptive and brilliant... general essay on London to appear since the war.' Pritchett's impressionistic and individual view of the city, reminiscent in form, if not style, of Ford Madox Ford's *The Soul of London*, is of particular interest because it was written when the capital was on the verge of the major re-development of the sixties and seventies. The book reminds the reader today of the London that has gone and of the London which resists the changes imposed upon it.

**The Cab at the Door / Midnight Oil**
Random Ho. hbk £13.95 0679601031
**The Pritchett Century: Selected Writings**
Chatto hbk £25.00 0701166363

## WILLIAM SANSOM (1912–1976)

In the forties and fifties Sansom was recognised as a fluent and gifted short-story writer. Now he is almost forgotten and his work is entirely out of print. Born in London he travelled widely and many of his short stories are set abroad but the best of them, and *The Body*, his novel of 1949, use the city as backdrop. Indeed his first collection of stories was based on his wartime experiences as a fire-fighter in the Blitz. Sansom's particular talent was for observation of the bizarre and eccentric amidst the apparently banal and commonplace and he also had a gift for mimicking the speech of ordinary Londoners which often threatened to stray into condescension but never quite did. He deserves re-assessment and a return to print.

### STEVIE SMITH (1902–1971)

The cultish poet/novelist Stevie Smith lived at 1 Avondale Road N13 in respectable, if unfashionable, Palmers Green with her 'Lion Aunt' Margaret for most of her life. Outwardly her life was as unremarkable as Larkin's, a poet with whom she shares 'the authority of sadness' (Larkin's own comment on Stevie's verse) to be found in, say, *Not Waving But Drowning*. And, like Larkin the poet-librarian, Stevie the poetess-secretary (she worked for the publishers Newnes) produced a distinctively English body of work.

Yet perhaps she is too idiosyncratic to be considered strictly as a 'London' writer. **Novel On Yellow Paper** (1936), like Woolf's *Mrs. Dalloway*, has a London setting but its depiction of a middle/upper middle class London social scene at a particular time (the thirties) is secondary to the stream-of-consciousness chatter of Pompey Casmilus, Stevie's alter ego, who flicks a gossipy tongue over life, love, sex, death, books, friends and acquaintances. Pompey/Stevie cannot easily be pinned down and nor can her London, a place both appealing and depressing. 'I get much more furious in London than I do in the country. Oh beastly London – and yet at times so fine. Oh how I wish I had some money, then I could buy a haystack and go to sleep on it.'

Stevie's London, in her novels but even more so in her poetry, encompasses the fashionable centre and the less modish suburbs. But whether visiting the National Gallery at lunchtime (*Deeply Morbid*) or strolling by Hanover Gate at dusk (*Yellow Paper*), whether walking through Edmonton cemetery or her local park, her tone is most frequently a mixture of comic innocence and self-conscious melancholy. In the character of the 'deeply morbid' secretary, Joan, Stevie caricatures herself as 'all alone all alone', drawn in by the Turners at the National to create a blissful escape from office routine and social whirl:

> *She stood up straight*
> *The sun fell down*
> *There was no more of London town*
> *She went upon the painted shore*
> *And there she walks for ever more*
> *Happy quite*
> *Beaming bright*
> *In a happy happy light*
> *All alone*

Stevie's work may seem quaint and dated now but the poetry, in particular, should continue to address and inspire any reader who has experienced the joy and weight of solitary existence – in Palmers Green or Parsons Green.

**Novel on Yellow Paper**
Virago pbk £5.99 0860681467
**Collected Poems**
Penguin pbk £12.99 0140183655

*Simon Roberts Waterstone's, Notting Hill Gate*

## H. M. TOMLINSON
### (1873–1958)

Like W.W. Jacobs and Arthur Morrison, Tomlinson was born in the East End in the latter part of the nineteenth century and became a vigorous and versatile writer of fiction and non-fiction whose work is now, largely and unjustly, forgotten. He wrote convincingly of ships and the sea, of the Thames and the London riverside and books of essays and reflections like *London River* (1921) and novels like *Gallions Reach* (1927) deserve reprinting as records of a way of life which has disappeared into history. As a journalist for many years Tomlinson was an eloquent teller of tales of a Fleet Street which has also now gone.

## JOHN SOMMERFIELD

The thirties were, pre-eminently, a political decade. Many writers of the time were overtly political and committed to the parties of the left. Many novelists of the time were influenced by the movies and used literary equivalents of cinematic techniques in their fiction. In *May Day* (1936) John Sommerfield produced what has been called the classic revolutionary novel of the decade and he does so in a novel which makes dramatic use of a narrative which, like a camera tracking, follows the characters across London from early morning to late at night. The energy and sense of the city as a scene of daily political struggle is consider-able and the book deserves to be much better known than it is. As the critic Ken Worpole has memorably written, *May Day* is 'as if *Mrs. Dalloway* had been written by a Communist Party bus driver.'

**May Day** is not currently available.

# EVELYN WAUGH (1903–1966)

*"Oh, Nina, what a lot of parties."*
*(...Masked parties, Savage parties, Victorian parties, Greek parties, Wild West parties,*
*Russian parties, Circus parties, parties where one had to dress as somebody else, almost*
*naked parties in St.John's Wood, parties in flats and studios and houses and ships and*
*hotels and night clubs, in windmills and swimming-baths... .dull dances in London*
*and comic dances in Scotland and disgusting dances in Paris – all that succession and*
*repetition of massed humanity... Those vile bodies... )*

Evelyn Waugh – Vile Bodies

Nobody has caught the febrile inconsequentiality of a certain kind of London night-life better than Evelyn Waugh in his satiric fantasies of Bright Young Things in twenties Mayfair. In **Decline and Fall** (1928) and **Vile Bodies** (1930) extravagantly named characters like Miles Malpractice and Margot Metroland, Agatha Runcible and Archie Schwert inhabit a hedonistic world of parties and nightclubs, isolated from any knowledge of London outside the social domain that lies between Park Lane and Bond Street. Waugh's picture of this world is exaggerated for comic effect yet curiously convincing just as his own attitude to it is at once fascination and disgust, an ambivalence displayed by all the great satirists. Look how terrible this is, he seems to say, look how empty and trivial these lives are. Yet there is also the voice of Waugh, the product of a Hampstead intellectual family (his father was a publisher), impressed by the capricious escapades of the upper classes, the voice of Waugh, the outsider, anxious to gain admission to the charmed circle. Of course the original reason for Waugh's success as a novelist and the reason his earlier books remain worth reading today is the same – they are very, very funny. The scenes in *Vile Bodies*, for example, set in Lottie Crump's hotel in Dover Street (Lottie Crump was based on Rosa Lewis, the famed proprietress of the Cavendish Hotel in Jermyn Street) remain much funnier than most of the comic fiction of today. In the late thirties Waugh married for the second time and moved to the West Country where he set about establishing himself as a kind of caricature country squire. Metropolitan decadence no longer held the fascination it had for the younger novelist, although one only has to read **Brideshead Revisited** to see that the obsession with aristocracy, particularly Catholic aristocracy, had grown stronger rather than faded by the forties. Other novels have London scenes (**Put Out More Flags** is particularly good on an official London in a state of ludicrous bureaucratic shambles during the 'phoney war') but it is in his first two novels that Waugh most successfully created a fictional city of his own.

**Decline and Fall**
Penguin pbk £6.99 014018242X
**Vile Bodies**
Penguin pbk £6.99 0140188606

# VIRGINIA WOOLF (1882–1941)

Virginia Woolf lived much of her life in London and her work often reflects the city and her responses to it. Her father was the eminent Victorian critic and scholar Sir Leslie Stephen and the family home was in Hyde Park Gate. On her father's death in 1904 Virginia, together with her sister Vanessa and her brothers Thoby and Adrian, moved to Gordon Square, Bloomsbury, then an unfashionable neighbourhood. The house became the London meeting-place of Thoby's Cambridge friends, men like Lytton Strachey, Leonard Woolf and Clive Bell, the nucleus of what came to be known as the Bloomsbury Group. After Thoby's sudden death in 1906 and Vanessa's marriage to Clive Bell, Virginia moved to Fitzroy Square and later, after marriage to Leonard Woolf and a serious mental breakdown, perhaps triggered by the strains involved in completing her first novel, to Hogarth House in Richmond. Here she and Leonard founded the Hogarth Press, which was to publish work by both the Woolfs and by a number of major writers, including Katherine Mansfield and T. S. Eliot. In 1924 another move took the Woolfs and the Press back to Bloomsbury. They had also acquired a country home near Lewes in Sussex and it was near here, in 1941, that Virginia Woolf, plagued again by the mental distress that had been a recurrent feature of her life, filled her pockets with stones and drowned herself in the River Ouse.

The city is a presence in much of her work. Her diaries and letters are filled not only with the gossip and detail of London literary life but with brief, impressionistic sketches of the city. *Night and Day*, a novel published in 1919, is an account of two friends, one the daughter of a famous literary family and the other involved in the suffragette movement, and their contrasting lives in London. *Jacob's Room* (1922), the first novel in which she moved towards the experimentation and stream of consciousness which characterises her best-known fiction, has a central figure based on her brother Thoby and shows the social milieu, in London, Cambridge and abroad, in which he is formed. *The Waves* (1931), perhaps her finest novel, has important sequences set in a French restaurant in town and at Hampton Court. A more conventional work, *The Years* (1937), tells the story of one family, the Pargiters, from the last decades of the nineteenth century to the nineteen thirties and includes descriptions of their London life.

However the novel in which the city permeates the text, and in which the rhythms of the day described are echoed by the sounding of Big Ben, is *Mrs Dalloway*, first published in 1925. The narrative, if not the way it is structured, is deceptively simple. Clarissa Dalloway, a society London hostess, is preparing for an evening party. Her suitor of thirty years previously, Peter Walsh, has returned from a long absence in India and awakened her memories of her adolescence and of the choices which have shaped her life. Clarissa's story is counterpointed by that of Septimus Smith, a severely disturbed veteran of the Great War, who wanders London, his distressed wife in tow, imagining messages aimed at himself in the ordinary events of a city day. An aeroplane sky-writing advertising slogans is bringing him news of great import, the birds in Regent's Park are speaking to him in Ancient Greek (Woolf herself suffered this delusion during one breakdown) and dogs in the Park metamorphose alarmingly into men. Clarissa and Septimus Smith never meet but at the party which concludes the book she hears casual mention of his suicide.

Yet the simplicity is deceptive. The novel's use of interior monologue and memory opens it out in time, from the single day in which Clarissa plans her party and Septimus Smith approaches his suicide to the longer perspectives of Mrs Dalloway's past and to Smith's catastrophic war experience. The sense of the city as huge and impersonal and yet a place in which the smallest events can create subtle networks between the people who inhabit it is beautifully achieved. The sight of the sky-writing plane can link, however briefly, an elderly woman feeding the squirrels in Regent's Park to a man attending his garden in Greenwich:

> *There's a fine young feller aboard of it, Mrs Dempster wagered, and away and away it went, fast and fading, away and away the aeroplane shot; soaring over Greenwich and all the masts; over the little island of grey churches, St. Paul's and the rest... Away and away the aeroplane shot, till it was nothing but a bright spark; an aspiration; a concentration; a symbol (so it seemed to Mr. Bentley, vigorously rolling his strip of turf at Greenwich) of man's soul; of his determination, thought Mr. Bentley, sweeping round the cedar tree, to get outside his body...*

In its economical evocation of individuals in the city and its use of sophisticated fictional techniques to link those individuals and make their inner lives real to the reader, *Mrs Dalloway* is one of the great London fictions of the century.

**The Diary of Virginia Woolf Volume 1**
Penguin pbk £9.99 0140052828

**The Diary of Virginia Woolf Volume 2**
Penguin pbk £9.99 0140052836

**The Diary of Virginia Woolf Volume 3**
Penguin pbk £9.99 0140052844

**The Diary of Virginia Woolf Volume 4**
Penguin pbk £9.99 0140052852

**The Diary of Virginia Woolf Volume 5**
Penguin pbk £9.99 0140052860

**Mrs Dalloway**
Penguin pbk £4.99 0140185690

**Night and Day**
Penguin pbk £5.99 0140185602

**The Waves**
Penguin pbk £3.99 0140185623

**The Years**
Penguin pbk £5.99 0140185615

# London's Historians

*Stephen Inwood, author of the recent **A History of London**, looks at the work of some of his predecessors.*

Although historians from Tacitus onwards described episodes in London's history it was not until 1598, exactly four hundred years ago, that the first real history of London was published. Its author, John Stow (1525–1605), was a City tailor and antiquary, who had lived through a period of rapid religious and social change. Stow's *Survey of London* rejected Geoffrey of Monmouth's fabulous account of London's pre-Roman origins, which earlier writers had accepted. Instead, he tried to extract from ancient and medieval manuscripts (especially William FitzStephen's description of London in the 1170s) a true account of London's Roman, Saxon and medieval history. The bulk of the *Survey* was a street-by-street tour of the City, in which medieval history was interwoven with contemporary descriptions and Stow's memories of the rustic and monastic London of his boyhood. Despite his unique contribution to the study of London, Stow lived and died in poverty, and (a familiar story) 'made no gains from his travails'. Although he writes with nostalgia for the London of his youth, Stow lives up to his claim 'that his only pains and care was to write truth', and deserves to be seen as one of the greatest of London's historians. By far the best modern edition of Stow's *Survey*, C. L. Kingsford's edition (1908, reprinted 1971), is out of print, but there has been an Everyman edition (Dent, 1956) and a recent (rather unsatisfactory) paperback (Sutton pbk £9.99 0750908270).

Stow's work provided the foundation for most historical writing about London for the next 150 years. New and expanded editions of the *Survey* appeared in 1618 and 1633, and both James Howell's *Londinopolis* (1657) and Thomas Delaune's *Angliae Metropolis* (1690) borrowed freely from it. An enlarged and revised edition of Stow was published in 1720 by John Strype, a clergyman and collector of old documents. This work was itself reissued, 'brought down to the present time by careful hands', in 1754. Londoners and their visitors were hungry for history, and the first continuous narrative of London's past, William Maitland's long and painstaking *History of London* (1739), went into several editions, and was reissued in a revised form under the authorship of John Entick in 1766. Other writers offered their own accounts of the growing metropolis: John Noorthouck, an indexer and proof-reader, in 1773, and Thomas Pennant, a naturalist, in 1790. A more original contribution came from Daniel Lysons, curate of Mortlake and

Putney, and chaplain to Horace Walpole. His *Environs of London* (1792–6) dealt with London's hinterland, and the towns and villages that would soon be engulfed in the spread of the great wen.

Most nineteenth-century historians followed Stow in choosing a place-by-place approach rather than a chronological one. James Malcolm's *Londinium Redivivum* (1803–7) tackled London alphabetically, and so did Peter Cunningham's useful *Handbook for London* (1849), which was revised and updated by Henry B.Wheatley in 1891 as *London, Past and Present*. Charles Knight's *London* (6 volumes, 1841–4) gathered together a large assortment of essays on London locations, customs and historical themes. Walter Thornbury and Edward Walford's six-volume *Old and New London*, which first appeared as a part-work between 1873 and 1878, used Stow's historical guide-book or walking tour approach. Walford, who wrote volumes 3–6, added two volumes on *Greater London* in 1883–4. The whole set was republished as *London Recollected* and *Village London* in 1985–7. John Timbs' successful *Curiosities of London* (1855, with a second and enlarged edition in 1885) and James Thorne's *Handbook to the Environs of London* (1876) used an alphabetical arrangement. Their twentieth-century successors are H. A. Harben's authoritative *Dictionary of London* (1918), William Kent's useful *Encyclopedia of London* (1937, 1951 and 1970), and Ben Weinreb and Christopher Hibbert's excellent *London Encyclopedia* (Macmillan pbk £25.00 0333576888) which presently holds the field among single-volume London reference books.

Until the mid-nineteenth century most of London's historical writing was produced by antiquarians, enthusiasts, opportunists or plagiarists. But in the nineteenth century English historical writing became more scholarly and methodical, and the opening of public archives made historical research less dependent on private collections of old documents. Scholars and archivists began to publish editions of the City's medieval records from which a new and more professional study of London's history could be created. Among these, H. T. Riley's *Memorials of London and London Life, 1276–1419* (1868), and R. R. Sharpe's edition of the City of London *Letter Books* (11 volumes, 1899–1912), were outstanding achievements. Sharpe's *London and the Kingdom* (3 volumes, 1894–5) is an account of the City's constitutional and political history based on these records. Towards the end of the century several scholarly societies began publishing series of works which would, over time, enormously enrich the study of London's past. The Survey of London started in 1894 as a private initiative before coming under the control successively of the London County Council, the GLC and eventually the Royal Commission for Historical Monuments. In its first hundred years it published forty four detailed architectural and topographical studies of individual London parishes. The London Topographical Society, founded in 1880, produces excellent reproductions of maps, drawings, and other visual materials, and publishes, in its five-yearly *London Topographical Record,* scholarly articles on the history and fabric of London. The *Victoria County History,* which was started in 1899, only produced one volume (in 1909) on the County of London, but its twenty large volumes on Middlesex, Kent, Surrey and Essex constitute, in effect, an enormously detailed economic, social and ecclesiastical study of the Greater London area.

In the twentieth century the professionalisation of historical study has combined with the growth in available source material and the rising interest in social, economic and cultural issues to produce a great increase in specialised studies of particular themes in London's history. Dorothy George's *London Life in the Eighteenth Century* (Penguin pbk £9.99 0140137319), originally published in 1925, was one of the first and most influential of these, and Norman Brett-James' *The Growth of Stuart London* (1935), T. F. Reddaway's well-timed *The Rebuilding of London After the Great Fire* (1940), John Summerson's masterly *Georgian London* (1945, and a good new edition in 1988), Sylvia Thrupp's *The Merchant Class of Medieval London,* published in 1948 (University of Michigan pbk £15.99 0472060724), Valerie Pearl's *London and the Outbreak of the Puritan Revolution* (1961), H. J. Dyos' *Victorian Suburb: a Study of the Growth of Camberwell* (1961) and Gwyn Williams' complicated *Medieval London: From Commune to Capital* (1963), were also important in creating a new scholarly approach to the history of London. In the later 1960s, two multi-volume histories were launched. Cassell's more popular series produced five books, covering *Roman London* (R. Merrifield, 1969), *Medieval London* (T.Baker, 1970), *Elizabethan London* (M. Holmes, 1969), *Regency London* (S. Margetson, 1971) and *Victorian London* (P. Metcalf, 1972). Secker and Warburg's more scholarly series has (so far) only yielded three of its projected eight volumes: Christopher Brooke's *London, 800–1216* (1975), George Rudé's *Hanoverian London, 1714–1807* (1971), and Francis Sheppard's *London, 1808–1870: The Infernal Wen* (1971).

Since the appearance of these still valuable studies, the history of London has moved rapidly on, embracing issues of class, work and gender which Maitland and Thornbury never dreamed of. In the last twenty five years the history of Roman and Saxon London has been revolutionised by archeological discoveries, and by the writings of Museum of London specialists like Peter Marsden, Gustav Milne,

Dominic Perring and Alan Vince. Our knowledge of medieval London has been enriched by John Schofield's *The Building of London from the Conquest to the Great Fire* (1984, 1993), Mary Lobel's atlas of *The City of London from Prehistoric Times to 1550* (1989), Gervase Rosser's *Medieval Westminster, 1200-1540* (1989 Oxford UP hbk £45.00 0198201567), Martha Carlin's *Medieval Southwark* (1996 Hambledon Press hbk £38.00 1852851163) and by the essays of Caroline Barron, Elizabeth Veale, Pamela Nightingale and Derek Keene. For Tudor and Stuart London, there has been interesting work on religion and culture, including Susan Brigden's excellent *London and the Reformation* (1989), A. Gurr's *Playgoing in Shakespeare's London* (1996 2nd Edn Cambridge UP pbk £16.99 0521574498) and D. L. Smith, R. Strier, D. Bevington (eds), *The Theatrical City: Culture, Theatre and Politics in London, 1576–1649* (1995 Cambridge UP hbk £40.00 0521441269). Some of the most important recent works on this period have focused on issues of stability and participation in an expanding city. Ian Archer's *The Pursuit of Stability* (1991), Steve Rappaport's *Worlds Within Worlds* (1989) and Jeremy Boulton's *Neighbourhood and Society* (1987) a study of Southwark, and articles by M. J. Power and Valerie Pearl examine the surprising equilibrium of late Tudor London at a time of rising prices and booming population. Eighteenth-century London was a little neglected until recent years, but two fascinating books by Peter Earle, *The Rise of the English Middle Class* (1989) and *A City Full of People* (1994), brought the period 1650–1750 back to life, and Leonard Schwarz's *London in the Age of Industrialisation: entrepreneurs, labour force and living standards, 1700–1850* (1992 Cambridge UP hbk £35.00 0521403650) at last offered an interpretation to stand alongside that of Dorothy George. Crime and punishment have attracted some of the best recent work on eighteenth century London, including J. M. Beattie's *Crime and the Courts in England, 1660–1800* (1986 Princeton UP pbk £21.95 0691101663) and Peter Linebaugh's fascinating and individual *The London Hanged* (1991 Penguin pbk £11.00 0140132627).

The wealth of recent writing on Victorian London defies brief summary, but some works have had a distinctive and prolonged impact on our view of the period. In the 1970s these included G. Stedman Jones' *Outcast London* (1971), H. Dyos and M. Wolff (eds), *The Victorian City* (1973) F. M. L. Thompson's *Hampstead: Building a Borough, 1650–1964* (1974), D. J. Olsen's *The Growth of Victorian London* (1976) and A. S. Wohl's *The Eternal Slum* (1977). The 1980s produced some important works on London government: K. Young and P. Garside's *Metropolitan London: Politics and Urban Change, 1837–1981* (1982), David Owen's *Government of Victorian London* (1982), and John Davis' *Reforming London: the London Government Problem, 1855–1900* (1988 Oxford UP hbk £40.00 0198229372).

In the 1990s Anne Hardy's *The Epidemic Streets* (1993 Oxford UP hbk £45.00 0198203772) clarified Victorian London's medical history, David Green's *From Artisans to Paupers:Economic Change and Poverty in London, 1790–1870* (1995 Scolar Press hbk £45.00 1859280331) analysed patterns of poverty from a geographer's perspective and David Kynaston's two unusual volumes on *The City of London* (1994 Volume 1 Pimlico pbk £15.00 0712662006 1995 Volume 2 Pimlico pbk £14.00 0712662715) brought the world of finance to life at last. Finally, the growth of oral history and history 'from below', much of it pioneered by History Workshop and by feminist historians, has opened up new perspectives on London's past, and given women, children and the poor a greater place in it. Jerry White's two admirable studies, *Rothschild Buildings* (1980) and *The Worst Street in North London* (1986 Routledge pbk £16.99 071020700X), should be mentioned, along with Raphael Samuel's *East End Underworld*, Judith Walkowitz's *City of Dreadful Delight: Narratives of Sexual Danger in Late Victorian London* (1992 Virago pbk £16.99 1853815179) and E. Ross's *Love and Toil: Motherhood in Outcast London, 1870–1918* (1993 Oxford UP pbk £16.99 0195083210). Four volumes by Steve Humphries, Gavin Weightman and others, *The Making of Modern London* (1983–6), covering the period 1815–1985, also used oral testimony to very good effect.

Much of the best and most pioneering writing on London's history appears in articles, either in scholarly journals (*The London Journal, Guildhall Studies, Urban History*), or in collections of essays dedicated to a particular scholar or centred on a specific theme. Of these, some of the most important of recent years are A. E. J. Hollaender and W. Kellaway, *Studies in London History* (1969), A. L. Beier and R. Finlay, *London, 1500–1700* (1986), F. J. Fisher, *London and the English Economy, 1500–1700* (1990 Hambledon Press hbk £32.00 185285023X), J. Stevenson, *London in the Age of Reform* (1977), D. Feldman and G. S. Jones, *Metropolis London* (1989), A. Saint, *Politics and the People of London* (1989 Hambledon Press hbk £37.50 1852850299) and Longmans' very useful volumes of reprinted essays in urban history: R. Holt and G. Rosser, *The English Medieval Town* (1990 Addison Wesley Longman pbk £16.99 0582051282), J. Barry, *The Tudor and Stuart Town* (1990 Addison Wesley Longman pbk £16.99 0582051304), P. Borsay, *The Eighteenth-Century Town* (1990 Addison Wesley Longman pbk £16.99 0582051347), R. J.Morris and R. Rodger, *The Victorian City* (1993 Addison Wesley Longman pbk £16.99 0582051320).

Plainly, the history of London is a much wider and more demanding subject in the 1990s than it was at the beginning of the century, when Sir Walter Besant published his massive *Survey of London* (10 volumes, 1902-12). Few would attempt such a task today. Yet worthwhile single-volume histories of London are still written, and it is surely important that historians should make specialist research and new perceptions of the past available to general readers in this way. Modern readers have several good accounts to choose from. Christopher Hibbert's well-illustrated but dated *London: The Biography of a City* (1969 Penguin pbk £15.00 014005247X) has been popular for almost thirty years, though Felix Barker and Peter Jackson's large and beautiful *London: 2,000 Years of a City and its People* (1974) beats it for text and pictures. *The Times London History Atlas* (ed. H. Clout, 1997 2nd Edn Times Books hbk £25.00 0723009058) gives a crisp and enjoyable illustrated account of London's history, and Roy Porter's passionate and very readable *London: A Social History* (1994 Penguin pbk £15.00 0140) brings the skills of a leading academic historian to the subject. It rather overshadowed J. Richardson's useful *London and its People* (1995). Finally, my own 1,000 page *A History of London* (Macmillan hbk £30.00 0333671538) brings to the subject, I hope, a fullness of discussion and detail which has been missing from general histories of London since the days of Sir Walter Besant.

Stephen Inwood is Principal Lecturer in History, Thames Valley University, London. His **A History of London** was published by Macmillan in 1998.

All titles currently in print have bibliographical details attached.

# Feeling Blitzed – Fitzrovia in the Forties

*by Simon Roberts, Waterstone's Notting Hill Gate*

> *Tambi said: "Now we will go to the Black Horse, the Burglar's Rest,*
> *the Marquess of Granby, the Wheatsheaf, then the Beer House... "*
> *"Where are all these pubs?" I asked him.*
> *"In Fitzrovia. The other side of Oxford Street."*

Julian Maclaren-Ross - Memoirs of the Forties

The writers and artists who haunted the pubs in and around Rathbone Place and Charlotte Street at the end of the thirties and during the war years may collectively, if misleadingly, be termed 'Fitzrovians'. Misleadingly because, unlike the Bloomsbury Group, they never shared a set of defining characteristics. Tempting as it is to imagine Dylan Thomas, Julian MacLaren-Ross, Tambimuttu, George Barker et al. gathered together under one roof discussing their art, this would impose a non-existent coherence onto a disparate and often desperate bunch. Dylan and co. were not on a par with, say, Wilde's aesthetes of the eighteen nineties who had an instantly recognisable dress code and set of artistic values to match. On the occasions when the writers, artists, editors, poets and their hangers-on did chance to congregate for a night in Fitzrovia, they collided with each other as individuals who were there for the gossip, the contacts and the beer.

The area itself, for all its fleetingness as a habitation (few 'Fitzrovians' were true locals) and romantic mythology as a place (Hugh David, in his definitive history of bohemian society in London, refers to it as a 'district of the mind') has distinct geographical boundaries. It runs north to south from the Euston Road to Oxford Street and west to east from Great Portland Street to Gower Street. Charlotte Street is its central artery. E.B. Chancellor, the first to chronicle the area, called it 'London's Latin Quarter.' Particularly authentic is the crooked-leg alley adjoining the Newman Arms which Michael Powell used to sinister effect in his film *Peeping Tom*. Less flatteringly, but more honestly, Fitzrovia has been shrugged off as 'North Soho', a sort of half-brother to its more favoured relation. However it wasn't until the late forties and early fifties that addicts of *la vie bohème* properly migrated south to escape the winter of post-war austerity.

Things were clearly edging in that direction by the mid-thirties. The Fitzroy Tavern on Charlotte Street had become too full of 'tourists', there to gawp at the likes of Augustus John in the same way that eighteenth century aristos visited Bedlam to look at the madmen, and been abandoned in favour of the less prepossessing Wheatsheaf on Rathbone Place. From there, when the Borough of Holborn's licensing laws called time at 10.30, forays would be made across

Oxford Street to the Highlander (now Nellie Dean's) on Dean Street where the Borough of Westminster remained drinking until 11.00. But the Wheatsheaf remained Fitzrovia's headquarters and two of its regulars set the lowbrow standards by which Fitzrovia came to be judged.

At the end of an evening's drinking, after a day's scriptwriting at Strand Films, Dylan Thomas turned to the short-story writer Julian MacLaren-Ross with; 'Fucking dandy. Flourishing that stick. Why don't you try to look more sordid? Sordidness, boy, that's the thing.' Sordidness amounted not just to prowling, bleary-eyed and red-nosed, around Fitzrovia's narrow enclave in shabby tweeds. Sordidness was the nearest thing Fitzrovia came to a collective aesthetic, whether in consciously aping Thomas's own bad boy behaviour or as a reaction against Audenesque intellectualism and the refined, sherry-sipping posturings of the 'Bloomsberries'. Fitzrovia lay gutter-side of Gower Street and those who rolled through it espoused unruly causes – the Spanish Republic, Surrealism – and mixed with dubious company. Spivs and tarts were fixtures in the Wheatsheaf and the Marquess long before they came to be thought of as 'poets' pubs'.

A more permanent fixture in the Wheatsheaf even than Dylan Thomas was Maclaren-Ross. With his dark glasses, camel overcoat and silver-topped cane (when it wasn't in hock) MacLaren-Ross was the forties equivalent of a *fin-de-siècle* decadent. One contemporary went so far as to describe him as 'a pistol-packing Oscar Wilde'. He would hold court at his self-appointed place at the bar – his court being anyone who cared to listen to monologue after opinionated monologue, delivered in his distinctive, high-pitched nasal drawl. Another contemporary, Dan Davin, recalled the man's 'working' day in his chosen kingdom:

> *Midday in the pub till closing time, a late lunch in the Scala restaurant in Charlotte Street, roast beef with as much fat as possible and lashings of horseradish sauce. A stroll to look at the bookshops in Charing Cross Road and to buy Royalty, his special jumbo-sized cigarettes. Opening time again at the Wheatsheaf till closing time. A hurried dash to the Highlander... Back to the Scala for supper and coffee. At midnight the tube home from Goodge Street...*

MacLaren-Ross's domain was a narrow one but it was one to which he clung tenaciously long into peacetime, long after everyone else had disappeared, died of drink or – worse – found regular employment at the BBC. Meanwhile MacLaren-Ross was stranded alone in the bar, wondering where everyone had gone. He is remembered today, if at all, as MacLaren-Ross the character rather than as a writer (none of his few published books remains in print), preserved as such by Anthony Powell who used him as the model for X. Trapnel in **Dance to the Music of Time**.

MacLaren-Ross's best work, *Memoirs of the Forties* (unfinished) was published after his death in 1964, in a decade hell-bent on freeing itself from the cares of the recent past, the forties especially.

In retrospect it is easy to endow those Fitzrovian nights with seedy glamour – sexual assignations involving sailors on leave, blackmarket booze, duffel-coated literary men crouched over pints of Younger's Scotch ale (price 6d). But what of the actual business of writing? Or the effect of war itself? Work was certainly completed and the proliferation of magazines and journals – among them John Lehmann's *Penguin New Writing* and Cyril Connolly's *Horizon* – attest to the flow of creative as well as alcoholic juices. But as the war progressed paper shortages and the scarcity of cash with which to pay authors, meant that authors were forced out of their pen-to-mouth lives into more lucrative work as lawyers, journalists and ad-men. Fitzrovia tried as best it could to keep the Blitz at bay. Dylan Thomas's *A Refusal to Mourn, the Death by Fire, of a Child in London,* with its assertion that, 'After the first death, there is no other', has a stronger grip on its own emotional rhetoric than on the reality it holds at arm's length. MacLaren-Ross's puzzlement over where his audience had gone once the war came to an end, also demonstrates that for bohemian London, fatally, real life was something that happened elsewhere.

The war had a seriously dislocating effect on this artistic and drink-fuelled illusion as it did on civilian life. But, war or no war, Fitzrovia would have fizzled out anyway, the victim of a disease of its own making. The highly idiosyncratic Ceylonese editor of *Poetry London,* Tambimuttu (who had once fished out a Dylan Thomas manuscript from his brimming chamber-pot) warned MacLaren-Ross of this disease in 1943:

> *"Only beware of Fitzrovia... It's a dangerous place, you must be careful."*
> *"Fights with knives?"*
> *"No, a worse danger. You might get Sohoitis, you know."*
> *"No, I don't. What is it?"*
> *"If you get Sohoitis," Tambi said very seriously, "you will stay there always day and night and get no work done ever."*

At cost to their personal health and respective literary legacies, if not to the personalities they cultivated, it was not a warning that MacLaren-Ross or Jeffrey Bernard, a later victim of the disease, paid much heed to.

## Fitzrovia – A Reading List

Accounts of Fitzrovia in its heyday are largely unavailable. However trawls through second-hand bookshops and out-of-print book searches may produce *The Fitzrovians* by Hugh David (Sceptre), *Under Siege* by Robert Hewison (Quartet), *Closing Times* by Dan Davin (Oxford UP), MacLaren-Ross's *Memoirs of the Forties* (in either Penguin or Cardinal editions) and *The Nine Men of Soho* (Wingate 1964). Chris Petit's 'Newman Passage or J. MacLaren-Ross and the Case of the Vanishing Writers' in *The Time Out Book of London Short Stories* (Penguin £6.99 0140230858) is a useful retrospective, perceptive and well-written. *Fitzrovia* by Nick Bailey (Historical Publications £4.99 0950365629) is a street by street survey. Bernard Bergonzi's *Wartime and Aftermath* (Oxford UP £7.99 0192892223) discusses the work of Thomas, MacLaren-Ross, Joyce Cary and Patrick Hamilton, among others. All three are in print. Also worth a look is Denise Hooker's biography of *Nina Hamnett* (Constable), artist, model and Fitzrovian par excellence who, referring to Gaudier-Brzeska's sculpture of her, boasted that she could be viewed in the V & A 'with me left tit knocked off.'

# London since 1945

The images in this chapter
are courtesy of the National
Museum of Photography,
Film and Television, Bradford
except opposite, courtesy
of Lene Bladbjerg, and
p158 and p184 courtesy
of Rob Andrews

# PETER ACKROYD (b. 1949)

London, both in its reality and in its metaphoric power, has been a notable presence in most of Peter Ackroyd's novels. Ackroyd was born and brought up in west London and the past and present of the city are skillfully interwoven in his books. In *Hawksmoor* a contemporary detective (the namesake of the 18th century architect) moves towards a mystical encounter with forces from the past as he investigates a series of murders in London churches. Part of the story is told in a prose which is an exceptionally skillful and convincing pastiche of eighteenth century language. In *The House of Doctor Dee* the contemporary and the archaic also clash and mesh when the central character inherits a house in Clerkenwell once owned by the Elizabethan magus Dr John Dee. *Dan Leno and the Limehouse Golem* evokes the world of late Victorian music-hall in a story centred once again (as in *Hawksmoor*) on a series of killings. Real individuals like Marx and Gissing interact with Ackroyd's inventions, fable and murder mystery mix with Gothic comedy, different narrative voices combine and contend in a characteristic blend. Ackroyd has also been acclaimed as a biographer (see entries on William Blake and Charles Dickens) and other novels, such as *The Last Testament of Oscar Wilde*, have demonstrated his skill in reconstructing and reinterpreting the lives of other figures in London's literary past.

It has sometimes been said of Ackroyd's books that they embody too easily achieved congruences between the present and the historical and that his reliance on the metaphysical and the mystical in his plots is too heavy. Certainly, in his less successful books (*First Light*, say) the parallels and recurrences can seem irritatingly predictable rather than originally conceived and his apparent endorsement of some kind of enduring, ahistorical 'Englishness' can appear facile. In his best books, *Hawksmoor* and *Chatterton* in particular, his ability to use fiction to illuminate society, the individual and the city in very different historical periods seems remarkable, as does his chameleon-like ability to inhabit different narrative voices from the past, and his status as a major novelist seems assured.

**Chatterton**
Penguin pbk £6.99 0140171142

**Dan Leno and the Limehouse Golem**
Minerva pbk £6.99 0749396598

**The Great Fire of London**
Penguin pbk £6.99 014017110X

**Hawksmoor**
Penguin pbk £6.99 0140171134

**The House of Doctor Dee**
Penguin pbk £6.99 0140171177

**The Last Will and Testament of Oscar Wilde**
Penguin pbk £6.99 0140171118

## MARTIN AMIS (b. 1949)

'If you are interested in ugliness and sleaze,' Martin Amis once remarked, 'London is the place to be.' The London that appears in Amis's fiction, most notably *Money* and *London Fields*, is at once the real city and an unreal city. Amis is careful to place his fiction in the genuine streets of W10 and W11 and any reader as bizarrely obsessive as some of his characters could, doubtless, trace the action across the pages of the A-Z. But Amis, writing his unique brand of apocalyptic comedy, depends on the imaginative power of exaggeration for many of his effects. His astonishing linguistic invention (a talent even his detractors are willing to allow him) is used to summon up for the reader a city that is also a fantastic conglomerate of all that Amis despises in contemporary culture. In *London Fields* the Black Cross is not just a thoroughly dodgy pub on the Portobello Road. It is an amalgam of all that is worst in all the dodgy pubs of West London, some kind of weird, platonic epitome of the dodgy pub. The crumbling streets and terraces of Ladbroke Grove are not just those Londoners know but part of an imaginative landscape created by Amis.

In the same way his characters have escaped the confines of traditional realism. Keith Talent, in *London Fields*, is not just a darts-playing slob; he is the darts-playing slob in his most purified, grotesque form.

> *The face itself was leonine, puffy with hungers, and as dry as soft fur. Keith's crowning glory, his hair, was thick and full-bodied; but it always had the look of being recently washed, imperfectly rinsed, and then, still slick with cheap shampoo, slow-dried in a huddled pub – the thermals of the booze, the sallowing fagsmoke.*

John Self, in *Money*, is not just a particular inhabitant of the urban jungle but a monstrous exemplar of those 'addicted to the twentieth century', a drink and drug fuelled devotee of instant gratification, living only for the present. 'The future's futures have never looked so rocky.' he says at one point, 'Don't put money on it. Take my advice and stick to the present. It's the real stuff, the only stuff.'

In the two books, *Money* and *London Fields*, Amis created a London that he could use for satiric purposes and peopled it with characters who embody the notion that, in the city, hell is other people. Without paying much heed to the demands of realism, he produced an unreal city which, nonetheless, was recognisable as a monstrous, comic distortion of the one Londoners inhabit.

**The Information**
Flamingo pbk £7.99 0006548830
**London Fields**
Penguin pbk £6.99 0140115714

**Money**
Penguin pbk £6.99 0140077154

# PAUL BAILEY

Paul Bailey has spent much of his life in London, is the editor of *The Oxford Book of London* and the city is an abiding presence in his fiction. Of none of his novels is this more true than his Booker-shortlisted *Gabriel's Lament*. The structure of the novel is a subtle one and three versions of the city appear in it. Firstly there is the contemporary London of the narrator, the eponymous Gabriel ('I live by the Thames these days at Chiswick') who has been the unlikely recipient of Hollywood money and looks back on his early life with his father, a sacred monster if ever there was one, Oswald Harvey. At Oswald's death at the age of 94, Gabriel inherits a strange bequest which leads him to America and to the grief that results in the lament that is the novel. Yet there are two other Londons which are of greater resonance in the book than the contemporary one. There is the poor London of terraced homes in which Gabriel grew up, the gaslit kitchen and the bar of the Prodigal's Return in which his father found the audience for his stories of a third London, that of the absurdly embellished tales of his deprived childhood with which he regales his son and others. The truths and lies behind all these Londons are revealed as the carefully executed narrative moves to its conclusion.

**Gabriel's Lament**
Fourth Estate pbk £6.99 1857025881

# J. G. BALLARD (b.1930)

After incidentally blitzing London in his first novel, *The Wind from Nowhere*, Ballard returned to the capital in the seventies with a remarkable trilogy which explored the disturbing pliability of the human psyche. Originating in one of his 'condensed novels' in the experimental collection *The Atrocity Exhibition*, **Crash** examines and re-examines the relationship between cars and sex in a series of encounters between a small group of professionals traumatised by past collisions, who seek an erotic transfiguration in those to come. The medical literature of wounds and the technical prose of automobile manuals fuse and give birth to breathtakingly erotic and lyrical passages that contain ideas both beautiful and profoundly disquieting. It is a work as dark and fine as any Ballard has ever written and its ability to sting and to provoke is unlikely to fade in the future, whatever changes occur in tastes and mores.

Where *Crash* roams over West London, **Concrete Island** restricts itself to the Westway and, in particular, one small traffic island alongside it. In a tale that updates Defoe by way of Beckett, Robert Maitland, an architect (ironically), crashes his car on this structure and then finds himself unable to leave or escape. Here the concrete landscape seen in *Crash* is rendered as elementally as any aspect of the natural world and the psychological transformation of Maitland, trapped on his urban island, is greater than that undergone by Crusoe.

In **High Rise** Ballard moves to the other side of town in the story of a deluxe Docklands tower block community descending into savagery. This more consciously mythic tale, with its greater range of characters and action, maybe lacks something of the impact of the other two novels. However it is a ferocious story by most standards – from its opening words ('Later, as he sat on his balcony eating the dog... ') onwards. In all three books the London that emerges is a bleak vision of flyovers, motorways and embankments, multistorey carparks, high-rises and the prospects of empty concrete spaces. It is also a singular and powerful vision, one which foregrounds aspects of the city more commonly overlooked, bringing them into prominence and focusing Ballard's characteristically surreal light on them.

*Mike Paine* Waterstone's, Hampstead

**Crash**
Vintage pbk £5.99 0099334917

**Concrete Island**
Vintage pbk£5.99 009933481X

**High Rise** and **The Wind from Nowhere** are currently out of print.

## NICOLA BARKER

Barker's first two prize-winning story collections established her as an adventurous explorer of all things urban and weird. In her second novel *Small Holdings* (1995) she confines her imagination to a single inner-city location. The setting is a North London park threatened with closure. The cast: the five people employed there. The mission: to implement a brilliant last-minute plan to save their sanctuary. The problem: every one of them is completely useless. As the story progresses, the characters struggle gamely to overcome their various, crippling eccentricities. Along the way, giant vegetables are slaughtered, poisonous herbs are administered, tractors run amok and love blossoms. Barker's view of North London is colourful, fresh and strange.

**Small Holdings**
Faber pbk £6.99 0571175880

## LYNNE REID BANKS (b. 1929)

Born in London, Lynne Reid Banks studied at RADA and worked as an actress for a number of years before joining the newly-create ITN in 1955, where she spent seven years as a reporter and scriptwriter. Her first novel, *The L-Shaped Room*, was published in 1960, made into a film by Brian Forbes three years later, and has never since been out of print. Since the publication of this novel Lynne Reid Banks has pursued a varied career as a writer for both adults and children. Her works include a couple of sequels to *The Shaped Room*, a novel (**Dark Quartet**) based on the lives of the Bror and a series of acclaimed children's books about *The Indian in the Cupboard*. Yet she is probably still best known for that first novel and it is not hard to see why. Very much of its time, filled with wha is now period detail, this story of Jane Graham who, unmarried ar pregnant, is turned out of the family home and forced to find a slightly squalid bedsit 'five flights up in one of those gone-to-seed houses in Fulham', remains a fine example of a particular kind of urban narrative. Like so many city-dwellers, Jane Graham, forced of the conventional family, is obliged to forge new relationships a new means of emotional support from friends and neighbours. H friendships with the Jewish writer Toby and the black jazz-player, v also live in the Fulham house, are the means by which she regains her self-esteem and her sense of identity amidst the city's anonym The London of *The L-Shaped Room* is one that has largely disappea but, even now, new Jane Grahams are undertaking the same journ in different ways.

**The L-Shaped Room**
Penguin pbk £5.99 0140019138

# The Freedom of the City: Writing Gay London

*by Neil Bartlett*

*The author of **Mr. Clive and Mr. Page**, a novel about gay London's past and present, looks at the writers who have shaped a specifically gay city.*

Gay London is a place which is necessarily as much fiction as fact, since it is always a place of desire, of private dreams, languages and landmarks. Sometimes the metropolis is, briefly, a dream come true; more often, it is a story in need of rewriting, a map in need of redrawing, a city whose freedom we have yet to be granted.

This London is at least as old as London publishing – Christopher Marlowe's poems (1598) glitter with the hothouse sensuality of the brothels and transvestite theatres of Elizabethan Southwark but it wasn't until the closing decades of the nineteenth century that the idea of a specifically gay city found its greatest chronicler, in our first and greatest London novel : Oscar Wilde's ***The Picture of Dorian Gray***. Dorian's damned nocturnal wanderings through the city, from hidden East End dens of debauchery to West End society salons ripe for the plucking, established our essential fictional geography.

In the wake of Wilde the dream of a city which our criminal desires might transform became fragmented, domesticated. E.M. Forster made Maurice's Bloomsbury (all cheap hotel rooms and the British Museum in the rain) somewhere to be escaped from, not revelled in. Gay pleasures could only ever be dreamed of in a Utopian future which was to be half Greenwood, half Arcadia. A decade later, Noel Coward created an entire fictional London – and even managed to sell it back to the city as the real thing – but his bitchy drawing rooms have nothing but phonecalls and the headache-inducing hum of traffic to remind us of the actual city, unless he was documenting the heterosexual miseries of his native lower middle-class Battersea and Teddington.

The bombing of the Second World War re-drew the map of London; and Mary Renault's pioneering *The Charioteer* re-drew the literary map by staking out its gay characters' places in genuinely best-selling fiction. It both captures the Blitz-lit realities of gay wartime romance and carves in stone the stereotypes of the next twenty years – the eternal dichotomy of tall dark man and bitchy, suicidal queen. Then the appalling fog of the nineteen fifties descended on London fiction; Terence Rattigan's fifties where the West End still glittered but where Dorian Gray's gothic attic had been transformed into a lonely mansion flat where the gas fire awaits the terminally depressed. However, out of the gloom shone flashpoints of invention, resistance and just plain debauchery (see James Gardiner's gorgeously illustrated *Who's A Pretty Boy Then?* for the real London behind the fictions and scandals). Rodney Garland's *The Heart in Exile* lovingly documents queer lives London-wide, from the House of Commons to the rough-trade slums of Islington; Quentin Crisp immortalised a very particular corner of the city, gay Fitzrovia, in *The Naked Civil Servant*. Robin Maugham in *The Servant* showed shabby postwar Chelsea poised on the edge of a sexual abyss – and, of course, on the edge of the King's Road (the same story was brilliantly updated for the swinging sixties and a malevolently queer Dirk Bogarde in Pinter's screenplay for the Joseph Losey film); Peter Burton's autobiography *Parallel Lives* details who took, wore, listened to and fucked what, when the nascent 'scene' moved to Soho.

After so much had been repressed the heady years of liberation themselves were perhaps simultaneously too stoned and too politically correct to need fiction but their real legacy – the marriage of politicised compassion with queenly naughtiness – is caught perfectly in Tom Wakefield's inimitable comic novels of North London snobbery, shabbiness and unlikely sex.

With a hundred years of writing behind us, contemporary gay London is now a site where authors use the past to re-imagine the present and the present to replay the past in a new light. Alan Hollinghurst's *The Swimming Pool Library* and my own *Mr Clive and Mr Page* share a passionate, disturbing reinvention of the past whose locations are as unexpected and hidden as anything in Wilde – a Mayfair mansion, an East End tower block, a Britten performance at Covent Garden, a lift in Selfridges. Ruth Rendell, on paper one of our unlikeliest chroniclers, has always been expert at including gay lives in her London and, in her latest Barbara Vine book *The Chimney Sweeper's Boy*, she leaves her beloved W11 to immortalise the steam-room of the late, lamented Mile End Baths with astonishing accuracy.

Meanwhile the consumerist, off-its-tits London of the shiny new gay *fin de siècle* has yet to find its up-to-date historian. Our main events – gay pride, a night at Trade, the gym, shopping – are still undescribed; our private triumphs – enduring love, death bravely faced – remain private. Oddly, given that gay London is getting both more and more public and more publicly influential on the styles of the city's daily life, the new gay Londoners are writing a city which barely has a geography at all. Aidan Shaw's *Brutal* and Mark Ravenhill's *Shopping and Fucking* happen in small rooms from which dangerous sex and fatal intoxicants provide the only vistas of escape. One hundred years on, we're having a fabulous time, but we're still in Dorian's attic.

*Oscar Wilde*
**The Picture of Dorian Gray**
Penguin pbk £2.50 014043187X

*Oscar Wilde*
**The Picture of Dorian Gray**
Oxford UP pbk £2.50 0192833650

*E.M. Forster*
**Maurice**
Penguin pbk £6.99 0140180826

*Mary Renault*
**The Charioteer**
Sceptre pbk £5.99 034040485X

*James Gardiner*
**Who's a Pretty Boy Then?**
Serpent's Tail pbk £25.00 185242513X

*Rodney Garland*
**The Heart in Exile**
Millivres Books pbk £8.50 1873741235

*Quentin Crisp*
**The Naked Civil Servant**
Flamingo pbk £6.99 0006540449

*Tom Wakefield*
**The Discus Throwers**
Gay Men's Press pbk £4.99 0907040799

*Tom Wakefield*
**Mates**
Gay Men's Press pbk £4.95 0907040241

*Tom Wakefield*
**The Variety Artistes**
Serpent's Tail pbk £7.99 185242138X

*Alan Hollinghurst*
**The Swimming Pool Library**
Penguin pbk £6.99 0140116109

*Neil Bartlett*
**Mr Clive and Mr Page**
Serpent's Tail pbk £9.99 1852423641

*Barbara Vine*
**The Chimney Sweeper's Boy**
Viking pbk £9.99 0670879371

*Aidan Shaw*
**Brutal**
Millivres Books pbk £8.50 1873741243

*Mark Ravenhill*
**Shopping & Fucking**
Methuen Drama pbk £6.99 0413712400

## JEFFREY BERNARD

Jeffrey Bernard arrived in Soho as a schoolboy during its heyday as a *louche* bohemia in the midst of a grey fifties Britain. Lucian Freud, John Deakin, Dan Farson, Frank Norman, John Minton, Henrietta Moraes were all regulars in the pubs and clubs. Francis Bacon held court at the French House, Muriel Belcher swore vigorously at her customers in the Colony Room. As the years and decades passed, Soho changed. The artists and the writers disappeared, succumbing to the varying demands of drink, fame and domesticity. Bernard, however, stayed, like a dutiful soldier, doggedly sticking to his post despite the widespread desertions of others. By the late seventies and eighties he seemed a relic of an earlier, more glorious era. The columns he was contributing to the Spectator, dispatches from the front-line of the Coach and Horses, were, in their reflections on drink, racing, smoking, the inexplicability of life in general and of women in particular, grim and funny affronts to what had not yet been designated 'political correctness.' They also constituted what one critic, an admiring one, described as 'a suicide note in installments.' Keith Waterhouse's 1989 play *Jeffrey Bernard Is Unwell* (the title comes from the line that so often explained the absence of Bernard's column) turned Bernard from Soho celebrity into, briefly, a national one. Yet Bernard's status in his last years, as an iconic example of the mis-spent life, disguises the fact that he was, when he could manage to put pen to paper for eight hundred words, a talented writer. The collections of his work that Duckworth

# PETER CAREY

**Jack Maggs**
Faber pbk £6.99 0571193773

*Jack Maggs* is one of the most inventive re-imaginings of Dickensian London in recent years. Carey, the Australian author of *Illywhacker* and *Oscar and Lucinda*, takes the basic storyline and a number of the central characters from *Great Expectations* and mixes them with elements of Dickens's life (his domestic circumstances, his interest in mesmerism) to produce a narrative that works both as historical reconstruction and as knowing examination of the power and limitations of fiction. Jack Maggs returns, after twenty years in the penal colony in Australia, to the London of 1837. Searching for a gentleman named Phipps, Maggs masquerades as footman in the household of Percy Buckle where he comes to the attention of Tobias Oates, rising young novelist and enthusiast for mesmerism. Fascinated by the enigmatic footman, Oates vows that he will be 'the archaeologist of this mystery... the surgeon of this soul.' In pursuit of the supposed truth about Maggs, Oates enters territory, moral and actual, where his normal self-assuredness and confidence in his own judgement desert him. As Maggs's secrets are slowly revealed, Carey succeeds brilliantly in combining historical fiction with reflections on the ambivalence of the creative process.

published often show how he skillfully transformed the flotsam and jetsam of his life into witty, opinionated, unself-pitying columns. Soho was, unquestionably, the death of Bernard. In its bars and clubs he drank himself, literally, legless. It was also his life and that is reflected in the best of his brief, apparently ephemeral pieces.

**Low Life**
Duckworth pbk £6.99
0715624458

**Reach for the Ground: The Downhill Struggle of Jeffrey Bernard**
Duckworth pbk £8.99
0715627260

*Keith Waterhouse*
**Jeffrey Bernard is Unwell**
Samuel French pbk £5.50
0573018049

## ANGELA CARTER (1940–1992)

At the time of her death in 1992, Angela Carter was recognised as a major English author. Her writings included poetry, essays and children's books but she will be best remembered for her novels, most of which are, essentially, fairy tales for grown-ups. A striking feature of all Carter's fiction is her enjoyment of the melodramatic moment when different worlds meet. The virgin faces sexual knowledge. The poor confront the rich. The hum-drum can become, at any moment, the fantastic. London, a city of extremes, is the perfect backdrop for several of her finest novels. In *The Magic Toyshop* (1967) spoiled country girl Melanie is sent to live with poor relations in Brixton. A mad puppeteer uncle, a downtrodden aunt and two brutish cousins set the scene for a classic riches-to-rags tale. Confusion and appalled fascination characterise the teenager's plight as she struggles through her new, strange city life. In *Nights at the Circus* (1984) Carter takes us to Victorian England. Here the author fully lives up to the 'magic realist' tag she was often given. Her heroine is Fevvers, a circus performer who can fly. With real wings on her back, Fevvers is a beautiful freak, and for a while London adores her. But then comes the inevitable fall. Perhaps the symbolism is sometimes a little heavy-handed but this is a wonderful novel, which brings acutely to life both the glamour and poverty of its imagined history.

However it is in her last novel that Carter really uses London as a character in its own right. *Wise Children* (1991) begins by describing London as 'two cities divided by a river.' The book opens as elderly twins Dora and Nora Chance prepare to cross that river, travelling northward to visit the famous father who abandoned them at birth. What follows is a tragi-comic family chronicle but the family, spanning generations of British show business, is a more colourful one than most. The narrator, Dora, vividly describes her grandmother's 'barely respectable' life as a vaudevillian artiste and is equally entertaining on the humiliations of her nephew Tristram, a slick TV gameshow host. Between these two stories the reader learns about Dora herself, the ex-chorus girl, and her own frustrated longing for recognition. Earthy, vivacious and richly evocative of time and place, this book is Angela Carter at her best, a writer who was quintessentially English yet uniquely herself.

*Tracy Reed* Waterstone's, Hampstead

**The Magic Toyshop**
Virago pbk £6.99 0860681904

**Nights at the Circus**
Vintage pbk £6.99 0099388618

**Wise Children**
Vintage pbk £5.99 0099981106

# JUSTIN CARTWRIGHT

*Look At It This Way* has been described as doing for London what *Bonfire of the Vanities* did for New York. The novel begins with a newspaper account of the killing of an unemployed City dealer by an escaped lion in Regent's Park. The piling up of events and coincidences which lead to this unlikely encounter draws together characters from a slick advertising agency, ruthless City banks, the forgotten world of music-hall and the criminal demi-monde of the East End. The result might have been bewildering and contrived but is, instead, a superb satire on Thatcherite London of the late eighties. Perhaps the most striking aspect of the novel is its incisive portrayal of London as 'a primitive and toxic growth', with 'its lamenting brickwork, its vomit-strewn streets, its dribbling skies, and its inexplicable smugness.' Property developments vie with each other for riverside views, like trees in a jungle competing for light, but the Thames itself is 'old, bored and cold.' By its sheer size and history London is unknowable, a city indifferent to its citizens. In his acknowledgments Justin Cartwright admits an urge to thank London for providing the material for the novel and it is hard to think of another modern novel which so generously allows the city to be the setting, the subject and its most compelling character.

**Look At It This Way**
Picador pbk £5.99 0330317695

## MAUREEN DUFFY (b.1933)

In a foreword to a catalogue of London fiction produced in the mid-eighties Maureen Duffy wrote of the city:

> *We both love her and hate her because she gives us, both as writers and people, freedom and variety but also loneliness and squalor. She is alternately Hierusalem the golden, with milk and honey blessed, and Hades, city of night and the dead.*

Duffy herself has written in a number of forms – poetry, plays, a biography of Aphra Behn – but she is primarily a novelist and the city, whether Hierusalem or Hades, has been a presence in much of her fiction. Most obviously this is true of the three novels which form a kind of 'London tryptych'. *Wounds* (1969), *Capital* (1975) and *Londoners* (1983) range in space from Clapham to Whitehall, from Regent Street to Earl's Court bedsitterland and, in time, from London past to London present. Taken together the books create a powerful sense of a city in which the real and the mythical intertwine, in which history can be drawn upon to help make sense of the present. Duffy's London is one which deserves to return to print so that readers can visit it as readily as they can the Londons of male writers like Iain Sinclair and Peter Ackroyd.

Maureen Duffy's trilogy is currently unavailable.

## NELL DUNN (b. 1936)

The two books for which Nell Dunn remains best known are the two novels of working class life in South London published in the sixties. Both were made into films, one by Ken Loach, and both are characteristic of the period. *Up the Junction* (1963), a series of sketches of Battersea life seen through the eyes of three female friends, was controversial at the time for its candour and the unsentimental, unillusioned attitudes to sex and men expressed by its central characters. *Poor Cow* (1967) was a further story of the tribulations and snatched pleasures of a working class woman caught between lawbreaking husband and new lover, mistreated by both. Dunn's talent is for convincing and unpatronising evocation of the South London working class, particularly through dialogue, and, in a decade which set about celebrating working class style and culture, she provides an interesting, female perspective. She has continued to write, producing both novels and plays, including *Steaming*, but has never repeated the success of her earlier books.

**Poor Cow**
Virago 0860689905 pbk £5.99
**Up the Junction**
Virago 0860689891 pbk £5.99

## BUCHI EMECHETA
### (b.1944)

Born in Nigeria, Emecheta came to London in the sixties where she struggled to come to terms with the alien environment in which, as a young, black mother of four small children, she found herself. She has published a number of novels, such as *The Bride Price* and *The Slave Girl*, which examine Nigerian society and, particularly, the position of women in that society. In 1983 she was named one of the Best of Young British Novelists. She returned to Nigeria in the eighties as an academic and has continued to write fiction, children's books and television drama. Her first two novels, *In the Ditch* and *Second Class Citizen* were later published in one volume as *Adah's Story*. These books draw on her own experiences of the city as unwelcoming, unfriendly and threatening, a place in which she had to fight to retain her identity and sense of worth, to describe powerfully the life of Adah and her children in North London, pressurised by racism and hardship on a council estate.

**In The Ditch**
Heinemann ILT 0435909940
pbk £5.99

**Second Class Citizen**
Heinemann ILT 0435909916
pbk£5.99

## ANTHONY FREWIN

One recent London crime novel that stands taller than its contemporaries is Anthony Frewin's excellent *London Blues* (1997). Set in the twilight world of Soho porn films in the early sixties, the novel is a tautly written account of Tim Purdom, blue movie director who disappeared around 1964, melting into the grey limbo of pre-swinging London. Within its Kennedy conspiracy theory-style plot, pornography, the Profumo scandal, the newly successful (and potentially vulnerable) Labour govern-ment, volatile race relations (many of the movies featured black men and white women), all merge together to form a gripping story that unfolds with a tenacity which only the recent past can possess. A companion piece to Chris Petit's *Robinson*, *London Blues* pays rueful homage to an age erroneously referred to as innocent, and is a distinctive addition to urban thrillers.

**London Blues**
No Exit Press pbk £6.99
1874061734

## JOHN HEALY

Healy's poignant autobiography, *The Grass Arena*, moves between a brutal childhood and a part-redemption through chess, focusing memorably on the abyssal life of London's down-and-outs amidst the streets, parks and doorways of the capital. Its rich and dark humour does battle with the straitened and diminished life of the streets; its characters endure a graceless spiral downwards or a violent, unexpected end. In an alcoholic fugue or in the army, in prison or in the gutter, a life is evoked as pungent as a tramp's fug – a London life that, however marginalised, is glimpsed and guessed at by every inhabitant of the city and one that has rarely been so well described. A less successful novel, *Streets Above Us*, partly set in the underground, appeared two years after the publication of *The Grass Arena*. Both books are currently unavailable and a second novel and a sequel to the auto-biography, rumoured to be written, remain unpublished.

# STEWART HOME (b.1962)

'Stewart Home – quick, clean and efficient since 1962.' This self-description in the addenda to *Red London*, together with the cover photo of the author with No. 1 crop and Harrington jacket, present Home's writing as a brand, the boot boy's reliable literary accessory. The homage to Richard Allen and the tastier elements of the New English Library is intentional. As Iain Sinclair has written, 'It's an exercise in futility to complain that Home's novels lack depth, characterisation or complex plots: that is the whole point.' Whether celebrating the hardcore pulp genre or ironically subverting it, the products of Home's 'heroically rancid imagination' are not for those averse to the depiction of casual violence, mechanistic sex and, it has to be said, to formulaic and repetitive prose. Home is, nonetheless, a self-consciously London writer. The characters in his novels view the city as a political patchwork, segregated by class and wealth. 'London is a microcosm of the world,' claims a member of Class Justice in *Blow Job*. 'The South is poor, the East heavily industrialised and the West affluent.' In *Red London* Fellatio Jones leads the Skinhead Squad, trained on the wastelands of Stratford, in a brutal assault on Hampstead which involves the slaughter of the audience watching a Fellini film at the Everyman cinema. The housing co-ops and anarchist groups of Stoke Newington and Hackney have no more dedicated a chronicler or satirist than Stewart Home. As a writer on the weirder psycho-geography of the capital, he has few equals. The narrator of *Come Before Christ and Murder Love* criss-crosses London remorselessly, using sex magick to tap into the occult current set up by Elizabeth I and John Dee between Mortlake and Greenwich. This current provided the genesis of the British Empire but required a human sacrifice. Bad news for Christopher Marlowe. To learn of the alleged occult activities of the present royal family, Home's anonymous contributions to the newsletter of the London Psycho-geographical Association are required reading. The best of these are collected in *Mind Invaders*, an anthology of resistance culture, edited by Stewart Home.

**Blow Job**
Serpent's Tail pbk £7.99 1852425482

**Come Before Christ and Murder Love**
Serpent's Tail pbk £8.99 185242575X

**Red London**
AK Press pbk £5.95 1873176120

## NICK HORNBY (b.1957)

North London middle class males found their spokesman in the nineties in Nick Hornby. His 1992 memoir *Fever Pitch* described a life shaped by an obsessional support of Arsenal F.C. It became a bestseller and enabled a whole generation of football-mad, middle-class men, hitherto slightly apologetic fans of the beautiful game, to come out of the closet and flaunt their newly fashionable zealotry. His first novel, *High Fidelity*, centred on Rob, a thirtysomething record-store owner, caught between a life of pubs and gigs and a world in which people own flats in the Holloway Road, give dinner parties and talk about subjects other than the Top 5 Soul Tracks of All Time. Once again Hornby, in his light and unpretentious prose, seemed to have hit on something. Rob's dysfunctional emotional life and his desire to hide himself behind lists, facts and a superbly organised record collection made him an archetypal example of one kind of nineties man and *High Fidelity*, too, was a bestseller. *About a Boy*, his most recent book, is also set convincingly in the middle-class ghettos of North London. Again the hero is a thirty-something male who shies neurotically away from any kind of commitment and again the book chronicles his journey, through a friendship with a terminally unhip twelve-year old, towards maturity. The book was, unsurprisingly, a commercial success and sold to Hollywood for an unfeasibly large sum of money but there is a sense that Hornby needs to move on from the subject of male emotional immaturity and widen his horizons, to look beyond Islington and its satellite manors for his fictional territory. Whether or not he will do so remains to be seen.

**Fever Pitch**
Indigo pbk £5.99 0575400153
**High Fidelity**
Indigo pbk £5.99 0575400188

## B. S. JOHNSON (1933–1973)

In his restless experimentation and his disdain for the naturalistic and realist novel, B. S. Johnson, who committed suicide in 1973, might seem a curious choice for inclusion in a guide to writing about a particular city, a particular place. Yet Johnson was born in London, lived most of his life there and the technical innovations and trickery in his fiction sit alongside the more specific. In *Christie Malry's Own Double Entry* (1973) Johnson himself may put in an appearance to argue with his own character but the accounting firm for which Christie works is undeniably located in Hammersmith. *Albert Angelo* (1964) contains a page with a hole in it through which the future can be read but the hole is also revealed to represent the knife-thrust which killed Christopher Marlowe in a peculiarly resonant London murder at a Deptford tavern in 1593. Johnson also co-edited, with Margaret Drabble, a curious collaborative novel, *London Consequences* (1972), in which different writers wrote different chapters. With a biography of B.S. Johnson in the offing and reprints of his novels appearing, a renewal of interest in this enigmatic writer is likely.

**Christie Malry's Own Double Entry**
W. W. Norton pbk £4.95 0811209547

# HANIF KUREISHI

'Englishman I am (though not proud of it), from the South London suburbs and going somewhere. Perhaps it is the odd mixture of continents and blood, of here and there, of belonging and not, that makes me restless and easily bored. Or perhaps it was being brought up in the suburbs that did it. Anyway, why search the inner room when it's enough to say that I was looking for trouble, any kind of movement, action and sexual interest I could find, because things were so gloomy, so slow and heavy, in our family.'

Thus the narrator Karim Amir introduces himself in Kureishi's 1990 novel *The Buddha of Suburbia*. Immediately the book is placed in a tradition of fiction in which the city, representing vitality, energy and sexual freedom, is set against stultifying suburbia. Karim Amir believes himself shaped, not so much by his ethnic background, as by the popular culture which has surrounded him, which gives him a shared generational language with others from very different social groups. (The novel's action shows this to be true, to a point, yet politically naive.) The city is to be the stage on which Amir's new social and personal identity, free from the confines of suburbia, can be performed. In the course of this witty and ironically detached novel we see how far the city lives up to its promises and how far a suburban background which includes a father who retires from the civil service to become a freelance guru and who plays Land of Hope and Glory on his stomach by slapping it, can be deemed dull and ordinary.

Kureishi himself was born in Bromley of Pakistani parents and, after a career in fringe theatre, first came to prominence with his screenplay for the 1985 film *My Beautiful Laundrette*. He has since written other screenplays including one for his own film, **London Kills Me** (1991). His love of pop, clear throughout *The Buddha of Suburbia*, is also reflected in his co-editorship of **The Faber Book of Pop**. He has published a short-story collection and two other novels, **The Black Album** and **Intimacy**, the last of which gained particular notoriety when his ex-partner alleged that the book was not so much fiction as a spiteful, self-justifying account of the ending of their affair. Kureishi's reputation as a writer might be in a slight trough as a result of this but there is no doubt that *The Buddha of Suburbia* is a skillful and immensely enjoyable reworking of an old theme in London fiction.

**The Buddha of Suburbia**
Faber pbk £6.99 0571142745

# Writers and the Jewish East End

*Ken Worpole, critic and cultural historian, looks at a rich tradition of London storytelling.*

'Nothing can happen nowhere,' the writer Elizabeth Bowen once said. Setting is often as important as character in fiction. Indeed, in a handful of the most successful novels about London, the city itself seems to be the main character. Few parts of the world have been as endlessly re-imagined as London's East End. Its richness as a source of fictional representation, most notably in the work of Dickens, and later in the ghost and seafaring stories of W. W. Jacobs and H. M. Tomlinson, might be attributed to two things: a brooding, riparian architecture encroached upon by a maze of ethnic ghettos, markets and tenements, and a demotic, hybridised speech. With the arrival of a distinctive East End Jewish novel-writing culture in the nineteen thirties (although there were earlier precedents), the locus of the writing, understandably, moved away from the river and towards the tenement blocks, sweat shops, synagogues, public baths, public libraries and Jewish meeting places close to Whitechapel.

This powerful set of institutions provided a milieu for writing and for artistic activity of all kinds. There was a Yiddish Theatre in Mile End Road already established by the nineteen twenties, and a number of workers' clubs where debates were held, music could be heard, poems read or declaimed, and plays or short sketches rehearsed. There was also the enormous popularity of the Whitechapel Public Library, where writers and painters such as Isaac Rosenberg, Mark Gertler, David Bomberg, Simon Blumenfeld, Willy Goldman and Julius Lipton met, talked, studied and socialised. Israel Zangwill's ***Children of the Ghetto*** was the founding text of this indigenous Jewish literary tradition, a set of fictional sketches of Jewish Whitechapel and Stepney – what Zangwill described in his introduction as a *terra incognita* as far as mainstream literary sensibilities were concerned. Later editions even came complete with a glossary of Jewish words, after complaints about the first edition's occasional linguistic obscurity.

But it was in the nineteen thirties that a whole school of writers developed, many of them active in the Communist Party, keen to use the novel as a way of airing strongly held political views and of asserting a defiant cultural identity. Simon Blumenfeld's novel *Jew Boy* (1935) took a conventional term of abuse and flaunted it as a title, creating a lively account of family, politics, sex and ambition amongst a group of young Stepney Jews who were already feeling distant from the religious and claustrophobic family life of the traditional ghetto. A subsequent novel ***Phineas Kahn*** (Lawrence & Wishart pbk £6.99 0853156956), first published in 1937, took the longer view of the Jewish experience, from the nineteenth century Russian *shtetl* to the (then) present day, employing a more conventional 'family saga' narrative.

Willy Goldman's *East End My Cradle* (Robson Books hbk £10.95 0860514919), originally published in 1940, grew out of a series of pieces for John Lehmann's magazine *New Writing*, and is an anguished, obviously autobiographical account of a young Jewish school-leaver, reluctant to go into the rag trade on account of his literary aspirations, but whose family regard him as 'lowlife', a lazy, self-indulgent dreamer and drifter. *Jew Boy* and *East End My Cradle* were well received at the time and both Blumenfeld and Goldman published a number of novels. They were joined by other autobiographers and fictionalists such as Ashley Smith (*Children with Fire*, 1934, and *A City Stirs*, 1939), Ralph Finn and Wolf Mankowitz (*A Kid for Two Farthings*, 1953). Other works include Bernard Kops's marvellous *The World Is a Wedding* (Vallentine Mitchell hbk £12.50 0853031797), published in 1963, the rich and exhilarating early plays by Arnold Wesker, *The Wesker Trilogy* (Penguin pbk £8.99 014048048X), as well as the novels and stories of Emmanuel Litvinoff, still writing today. Litvinoff called his wonderful evocation of Jewish Whitechapel in the nineteen thirties, published in 1972, *A Journey Through a Small Planet* (Robin Clark pbk £6.00 0860721558), a tiny district of London where 'people spoke of Warsaw, Kishinev, Kiev, Kharkov, Odessa as if they were neighbouring suburbs.' His trilogy about political violence (*A Death Out of Season*, *Blood on the Snow* and *The Face of Terror*) is highly regarded; he is also the editor of *The Penguin Book of Jewish Short Stories* (Penguin pbk £7.99 014004728X).

Cosmopolitanism, a hallmark of the modern London novel, had already been signalled and responded to in the East End Jewish novel for nearly a hundred years. This culture has also been rich in political histories and autobiographies, notably Bill Fishman's *East End Jewish Radicals 1875–1914* (Duckworth pbk £15.99 0715610775), Joe Jacobs's *Out of the Ghetto* (Phoenix Press, London pbk £9.00 094898418X) and, recently, Fermin Rocker's delightful memoirs of Jewish and secular anarchist circles in Stepney before the First World War, *The East End Years* (Freedom Press pbk £7.99 0900384921). The poet Denise Levertov, although her Russian Jewish father converted to Anglicanism early in his life, nevertheless grew up in a left-wing, Communist Party milieu in Ilford between the wars, before moving to America in her twenties and establishing her reputation there. A recent memoir, *Tesserae* (Bloodaxe pbk £8.99 185224383X) is particularly fine. Levertov died in 1997.

The two playwrights Bernard Kops and Arnold Wesker, who were amongst the first to celebrate the energetic world of East End street life and politics, have been increasingly overshadowed by Harold Pinter who has achieved a universal resonance for a language and sensibility that were almost wholly formed in the streets and utility interiors of post-war Hackney, according to his recent biographer Michael Billington. Pinter's early stage name was David Baron, an unconscious allusion, we must assume, to a contemporary, Alexander Baron, the young novelist who lived only a couple of streets away from Pinter. Baron's most successful novel, *From the City, From the Plough* (1948) sold more than a quarter of a million copies and remains one of the most striking novels of the Second World War. As a result of the success of *From the City, From the Plough* Baron became internationally famous, another Jew who, like Pinter later, had espoused atheism and bohemian and political dissent, and who carried on writing novels, some of which, such as the marvellous **Lowlife** (1961), were still set in Hackney. *Lowlife* has become something of a cult novel for more recent chroniclers and 'psychogeographers' of the East End, yet though Baron was at the height of his fame when Pinter was still living in Hackney, he sadly gets no mention in Billington's book **The Life and Work of Harold Pinter** (Faber pbk £12.99 0571190650).

However the book does provide biographical information which genuinely illuminates Pinter's strong relationship between topography and *mentalité*, between place-names and their immediate evocation of distinct sensibility and aura – another characteristic of much East End writing. One of Pinter's fondest – and therefore formative – memories is of regular outings with his then English teacher at Hackney Downs School, Joe Brearley. 'We embarked on a series of long walks, which continued for years, starting from Hackney Downs, up to Springfield Park, along the River Lea, back up Lea Bridge Road, past Clapton Pond, through Mare Street to Bethnal Green.' On their walks they would 'declaim passages from Webster into the wind or at passing trolley buses.'

The perambulatory mode is one of the distinguishing features of a certain kind of male writing about this part of London. This is a different kind of writing entirely from that of the strolling *flaneur*. The twentieth century East End fabulist strides the streets, parks, underpasses, towpaths, buffeted on all sides by the wind, indifferent to the sun or rain. Iain Sinclair has, on several occasions, claimed that most of his fictional divination is done on long night-walks through the gloomier parts of the East End, and in a recent review of Peter Ackroyd's book on **William Blake** described how he'd set about testing the veracity of Ackroyd's topographical knowledge by walking the streets late at night for several weeks in the distant hope of bumping into Ackroyd doing the same. 'Bowling along' the streets of Hackney seems to have been one of Pinter's favourite pastimes. The city of dreadful night has become rather more benign these days, one hopes. However the Jewish writers of East London have left a permanent and rich legacy of writing about this teeming and vital area of the city.

All titles currently in print have bibliographical details attached.

# ROSE MACAULAY
## (1881–1958)

Best known for her travel writing and for idiosyncratic novels like *The Towers of Trebizond* – its first sentence ('"Take my camel, dear," said my aunt Dot, as she climbed down from this animal on her return from High Mass.') must be one of the more arresting opening sentences in English fiction – Rose Macaulay deserves inclusion in any London writing guide for her 1950 novel *The World My Wilderness*. Few other books have described so well, and in such painstaking detail, the strange wasteland of the City in the immediate aftermath of the war. The story of Barbary, a young French girl living with her father and stepmother in the Adelphi, who explores the ruined landscape of the bombed areas, where nature is quietly reasserting itself, is a record of a London which existed briefly and has now disappeared beneath the new high rise offices.

**The World My Wilderness**
Virago pbk £6.99 0860683400

**The children stood still, gazing down on a wilderness of little streets, caves and cellars, the foundations of a wrecked merchant city, grown over by green and golden fennel and ragwort, coltsfoot, purple loosestrife, rosebay willow herb, bracken, bramble and tall nettles, among which rabbits burrowed and wild cats crept and hens laid eggs.**
**Rose Macaulay – The World My Wilderness**

## COLIN MACINNES (1914–1976)

To many people the title *Absolute Beginners* refers to the overblown, self-regarding musical film made by Julien Temple in the eighties. This is a pity. The original novel on which Temple's film was based, although clearly a product of its time (the fifties), is no period piece and its story of the developing Bohemian milieu of Notting Hill, with its multi-racial mix and its easy access to drink, drugs, sex and early rock and roll, retains its vitality, not least in the language in which its narrator describes his life. The book ends with a vivid recreation of the Notting Hill riots. The author was Colin Macinnes, a writer aptly characterised by his biographer as an 'Inside Outsider'. Macinnes was the son of the popular novelist Angela Thirkell and, related as he was to Kipling, could claim to come from the heart of English middle and upper middle class culture. Yet he was born and grew up in Australia and, when he returned to this country to pursue a career as writer and journalist, his homosexuality and his fondness for the *louche* side of London meant that he was always on the edges of cultural life. In many ways this placed him in the ideal position to observe and respond to the early evolution of youth culture in the capital. The other books in his so-called 'London trilogy' are *City of Spades*, an examination of the growing West Indian community in London, which some critics prefer to *Absolute Beginners*, and *Mr Love and Justice*, a slightly clumsy fable built around the relationship between a pimp and a policeman. Macinnes was also a pioneer of a particular kind of cultural essay, turning his attention to phenomena not, at the time, often subject to literary appraisal, in work published in magazines such as *New Society*. A collection of these appeared under the title *England, Half English*, which is now out of print.

The novels of Colin Macinnes are currently out of print.

# PATRICK MCGRATH

**Spider**
Penguin pbk £5.99 0140146423

*'Spider'* is the nickname and alter ego of Dennis Clegg, an increasingly ill schizophrenic who, beset by delusional fantasies in a dilapidated East End boarding house, describes his childhood in the area and the apparent murder of his mother by his father. As flashback sequences make Clegg's mental history clearer, growing awareness of his insanity undermines the reader's confidence in the reliability of the narrative. The result is a beautifully written study of the morbid unravelling of a human mind. The setting of London in 1957 is on a microcosmic scale. Much of the action of the novel takes place within the confines of few streets, 'a clotted web of dark compartments and narrow passageways.' Even when the landmarks of the larger city are briefly seen they are diminished. Tower Bridge is a 'dim grey structure of pencils and string.' There is an air of muted violence and decay. The names of Kitchener Street and Omdurman Close recall faded imperial glories but also echo Spider's urge to avenge his mother's death. When he finally finds the courage to revisit the home of his childhood, he discovers only a pile of dusty bricks and cables. The house was destroyed in the Blitz. Patrick McGrath combines his unnerving insights into the anguish of mental illness with a vivid portrayal of the austerity of East End life in the thirties and fifties. When *Spider* was first published he rightly received praise for 'his London', what one critic described as 'a vague, smoky, downtrodden place, redolent of the rich, seamy smells of the pre-plastic age.'

***Andy Walker*** *Waterstone's, Charing Cross Road*

## MARTIN MILLAR (b. 1959)

Millar was born in Glasgow but, since the late eighties, has carved out a niche for himself as the writer of cultish novels set amongst the giro generation of Brixton. His particular skill is that he can successfully combine a witty, ironic and uncondescending presentation of the buskers, squatters and dreamers who populate his novels with elements of fantasy and what can almost be described as magic realism. In *Lux the Poet* (1988) the would-be poet stumbles in and out of danger, pursued through a Brixton riot by gangs and the police. Supported by his own optimism and by a friendly spirit who has been suspended from Heaven, he continues his search for an audience responsive to his work. In *Milk, Sulphate and Alby Starvation* a paranoid drugs-dealer and comic-collector is on the run from the Kung-Fu mafia in low-life south London. The Milk Marketing Board has also taken out a contract on him because his well-publicised allergy to their product has hit sales. One critic has pointed out the bedrock of observational truth beneath Millar's fantasies. 'While we may admire the artifice and dazzling stylistics of Martin Amis, and while his descriptions of Ladbroke Grove's cavernous pubs and crumbling terraces may ring true, characters like Keith Talent, the grotesque darts-playing slob from London Fields, seem, by comparison (with Millar's creations) to derive from a very detached and literary concept of low-life.'

**Lux the Poet**
Fourth Estate pbk £5.99 0947795626
**Milk, Sulphate and Alby Starvation**
Fourth Estate pbk £5.99 1857022149

## TIMOTHY MO

Timothy Mo was one of the most acclaimed young British novelists of the eighties and has been twice nominated for the Booker prize. *Sour Sweet* was his second novel. Hong Kong immigrant Chen is a humble family man who wishes for little more than regular work and a future for his misshapen baby boy Man Kee. However, when his father needs hospital treatment back in the homeland the dutiful son needs to get hold of lots of money, fast. A failed attempt at gambling leads to an introduction to the London underworld of the Hung 'family' Drug trafficking and protection rackets are a stark contrast to Chen's happy family life but, once he is linked to one of the Triad clans, there is little chance of escape in the insular London Chinese community. Set in what is usually considered London's most fashionable decade this century, Mo's book nonetheless recreates a sixties Soho that is, in many ways, very down-to-earth Seen through the eyes of the Chens, the idiosyncrasies of both East and West are amusingly highlighted and the relentless energy of London's Chinese population shines out against the often dull background of a Britain emerging only slowly from the grey fifties.

**Sour Sweet**
Vintage pbk £5.99 0099962004

*Michelle Jenkins, Waterstone's*

# London Lit-Pop

*John Grindrod of Waterstone's, looks at some books which chronicle London's youth culture and music scene from the fifties to the nineties.*

Since the teenager was invented in the fifties writers have felt the urge to reveal to a wider public the hours and times of London's youth cultures and music clubs. Colin Macinnes's *Absolute Beginners* was one of the first to make the attempt. Set in Notting Hill in the run-up to the 1958 race riots, and with a cast of Teds, aspiring pop stars and teen consumers, this book set the tone for many to come, mixing the political, the personal and the fashionable in a distinctive style. The London-based mods and rockers in Macinnes's book were soon to be stigmatised by the media as the kind of 'devils' examined by Stanley Cohen in *Folk Devils and Moral Panics*, his classic account of press reactions to riots on the Brighton seafront.

More measured responses to London's emerging pop culture than press hysteria can be found in Hanif Kureishi's and Jon Savage's splendid, panoramic and fascinating *Faber Book of Pop* (Faber pbk £14.99 0571179800). Here you'll find snippets on fifties gay, mod and jazz clubs, as well as groovy Soho penthouse parties in the early sixties. This was when London famously started to swing, becoming the mythical place that drew teenagers from all over the country in pursuit of a good time. It was the place Billy Liar's girlfriend Liz escaped to, swinging down Carnaby Street in her mini-skirt, mingling with characters from a newly scandalous and sexually liberated London. *The Orton Diaries* (Minerva pbk £8.99 0749390050), Joe Orton's account of his tragically brief but heady Sixties fame, like so many memoirs of the period, both gay and straight, reveal a place full of strangers and possibilities, miles away from the straitjacket of suburbia.

The next decade was obliged to search anew for self-definition. Hanif Kureishi's excellent satire *The Buddha of Suburbia* (Faber pbk £6.99 0571142745) plays with many of the conventions and stereotypes of suburban teenage rebellion, and provides a neat dose of social history as well, in its story of a young man's reaction against his hippy parents and his embracing of the harder edges of glam and punk. The scenario is played for real in Jon Savage's landmark tome *England's Dreaming* (Faber pbk £11.99 0571167918). Ostensibly the story of the Sex Pistols, this book is the finest pop cultural history of seventies London and arguably the best book ever on pop music. Savage manages both to articulate sharp social and political observations and to communicate the passion and exuberance of punk London at its most anarchic.

*Nightfever* (Boxtree pbk £9.99 0752222147), the collection of Face magazine club writing, contains some vivid snapshots of hedonistic eighties hotspots, many of them London-based. Whether masquerading as a dandy highwayman at Blitz in Soho or grooving at a Soul II Soul warehouse party in King's Cross, Thatcher's children are seen at play in ways of which the nanny state would most certainly not approve. Michael Bracewell's *England Is Mine* (Flamingo pbk £6.99 0006550150) expands the *Billy Liar* theme of London as the escapee's paradise into an idiosyncratic cultural history of England in the last hundred years. London becomes somewhere for artists as diverse as Oscar Wilde and Morrissey to escape to, creating mythical selves along the way. An outsider to London himself, Bracewell is fascinated by the lure of the city and the ways in which its vastness and cultural diversity affect its provincial colonisers. The colonisation of London by ecstasy is examined by Matthew Collin in *Altered States* (Serpent's Tail pbk £10.99 1852423773). The book follows the setting up of ever bigger clubs until the acid house boom really took off and Londoners invaded the shires for huge weekend raves, creating a moral panic unrivalled since Londoners invaded the seaside for riots in the fifties. *Altered States* is an excellent book, every bit as culturally canny as *England's Dreaming*, documenting the lives of Hampstead intellectuals on one page and Hackney junglists on the next.

Inevitably, as the image of 'Cool Britannia' has developed, London writing has become very 'swinging' again. However it may be that two relatively mainstream novels give as good an idea as any other, more self-consciously hip fiction of where London pop culture has really reached. *Don't Step on the Lines* (Headline pbk £6.99 0747252807) by Ben Richards offers a recognisably unhip, unpretentious version of London youth, grown up and directionless, the fallout of generation E dodging in and out of employment, franchised bars, university and relationships. *High Fidelity* (Indigo pbk £5.99 0575400188) by Nick Hornby identifies the ghost from a previous generation, the seventies suburban rebel Jon Savage once documented, now comfortably ensconced in dad-rock heaven, forever harking back to his vinyl, v-necked youth. As a coda to all those sweaty, hormonal, ecstatic documents of London nightlife, Ben Richards and Nick Hornby show us a London that is diverse, funny, nostalgic and exciting, much as you'll find it for real on any Saturday night.

## MICHAEL MOORCOCK (b. 1939)

Few greater celebrations of the city – and of its post-war mythology – have appeared in recent years than Moorcock's *Mother London*. A moral tale, in part a search for a *modus vivendi* within the city, it moves gracefully back and forth across the capital from the Blitz to the present following its protagonists, patients blessed with the ability to hear the thoughts of others. Employing his telepathic device, Moorcock marshals his fictional voices – numinous, choral and anonymous – and balances the physical plenitude of the city with a psychic one, richly encompassing the lives of David Mummery, an 'urban anthropologist', Josef Kiss, a music-hall artiste, and Mary Gasalee, a sleeper woken from a decades-long coma. Moving and encyclopedic, *Mother London* is a great achievement, revealing and revelling in the full riches of the city without losing sight of the characters who inhabit it.

Twenty years before the publication of *Mother London*, Moorcock had first taken on London's mythology in the *Cornelius* stories. Jerry Cornelius, an archetypal figure of sixties counter-culture, made Derry and Toms's roof garden the stuff of legends and Notting Hill became a swinging anarchy. The books had an easy glamour and style and, among the *Cornelius* tales, Moorcock produced two novels, *The English Assassin* and *The Condition of Muzak* which had genuine bravura. They were hybrid works which yoked together popular and avant-garde forms to provide a snapshot of London and an adroit exploration of urban life in the second half of the century. Although he received a Whitbread nomination and the Guardian Fiction Prize (for *Mother London* and *The Condition of Muzak* respectively) Moorcock continues to be perhaps the most undervalued British novelist of his generation. His prodigious fluency (able to turn out over fifteen thousand words a day at one point) his easy commercial success in the fantasy genre and his rigorous self-identification as a 'popular' novelist – all have not helped his more ambitious work gain the wider audience it has often deserved.

*Mike Paine* *Waterstone's, Hampstead*

**Mother London** is currently out of print.

# GEOFF NICHOLSON

**Bleeding London**
Indigo pbk 0575400560

Mick Wilton, 'hardman with a conscience', arrives from Sheffield with a job to do – to visit his revenge on a group of well-to-do London friends who have supposedly gang-raped his stripper girlfriend at a stag night. His search for this revenge in an alien city allows the reader an outsider's view of London as Mick dispatches rough justice to each of his targets, in increasingly entertaining ways. He begins his odyssey with a visit to an imaginary London bookshop which ought really to exist – The London Particular – and there he meets Judy Tanaka, a complex person with her own agenda and her own particular methods for seeking absolution in London. Through their awkward friendship Mick learns more about the city, more about what he needs to know in his quest for vengeance and, in the end, more than he bargained for.

If this were all there was to this convoluted tale of revenge, it would lie on file as a kind of reverse version of *Get Carter*. What makes Nicholson's novel a stand-out 'London book' is the third major character. Stuart London is a Walking Tours operator who once employed and bedded Judy Tanaka. Stuart, having exhausted the possibilities of his normal life, now spends his time contentedly walking down the streets of the city. He intends to walk down all of them and, as he goes, he crosses them out in his A-Z, obliterating them with a big black marker pen. At the same time he is keeping a diary of the walks, recording for posterity the snippets of city life that he observes, and the throwaway events of anybody's and everybody's lives in the capital are delicately and superbly observed. Stuart's journal chimes with every reader's experience of London – the pubs and cafes visited, the conversations overheard, the collisions of coincidence, the frequent bleakness and loneliness of the city. Nicholson succeeds in portraying a London we all know, one that sits broodingly in the background of all our lives and yet holds us all in its thrall. And he does this in a concise and pared-down narrative that is both engrossing and entertaining.

*Andy Smedley*

# FRANK NORMAN

*Nick Robinson of publishers Random House writes about the legendary Soho writer, drinker and wide boy, Frank Norman, whose autobiography* Stand on Me *is a forgotten London classic.*

Frank Norman's memoir **Stand on Me** is a devastatingly authentic portrayal of life in Soho in the late forties and early fifties, a murky underworld of cheap cafés, seedy drinking clubs, prostitutes and dope addicts written by a man who lived and flourished in it. Like so many others, before and since, Frank Norman drifted into Soho without really knowing how he got there. He found himself immediately at home amongst the layabouts, no-hopers, has-beens and might-have-beens of the Frith Street Café – 'The 86' – which became his home. He writes in his own version of the vernacular – a combination of rhyming slang and hardened prison-speak which gives him a unique voice.

Norman is totally frank and unashamed – his commitment to the lowlife is complete. His addictions, both criminal and chemical, are described not so much with a sense of relish as a sense of inevitability. These things just happen. His life is largely spent leaning over a formica table at The 86, surrounded by empty teacups and half-smoked Woodbines. This drudgery (although Norman doesn't think of it as such) is punctuated by episodes of what can only be called low adventure. The 86 is populated, in Norman's own words, by 'ponces, tealeaves, con-men, jump-up merchants and lay-down merchants' together with poets and 'tortured intellectuals'. This is the Soho that survives as myth.

> *"Write or paint?" asked a geezer who was also sitting at the table.*
> *"Do wot?" I asked him back.*
> *"Are you a writer or a painter?" he asked again, giving me a dodgy look.*
> *I just shrugged and copped a deaf un, to tell you the truth I just put him down as a crank, or a nutter.*

The nickname is king in Soho – largely because, in the crime-ridden world Norman inhabits, nobody is willing to reveal his true identity. The characters are fantastic enough to stretch the reader's willingness to believe in their reality – 'Dirty Dan the Lavatory Man' who sleeps and performs in public toilets, 'Diabolical Liberty', a con-man who manages to stage a party in a Mayfair flat and steal a Picasso and a Modigliani, 'Snowball', a Jamaican who plants cannabis in the glasshouses at Kew Gardens and supplies the Soho market, and 'The Peach', an outrageously camp transvestite.

Norman's place in the lowlife hierarchy is assured when he gets his 'stripe' – a six inch razor scar from ear to chin he receives when working for an Italian sex-club owner who owes money to the wrong kind of people. Norman is singled out for treatment and ends up in hospital with multiple injuries after being dumped over railings onto a concrete floor fifteen feet below. His stripe earns him respect. He gets nods of approval and he gets bought drinks. He gets the best-looking women. He's wide.

One of the most popular highs at the time was gained by chewing the contents of benzedrine inhalers. This, combined with the effect of scrumpy, was Norman's preferred mental state and one which was to prove his undoing. From nicking books from Foyles ('Charlies') he progressed through housebreaking to cheque fraud ('flying kites'), arrest and prison. *Stand on Me* – candid, funny and brilliant – is a deserved classic of Soho literature. The world Frank Norman knew has changed but parts of it still exist in places like the Colony Room and Jerry's in Great Windmill Street and at Madam Jo-Jo's. Frank Norman also wrote **Banged to Rights** about his time in prison and **Fings Ain't Wot They Used t'Be**, a play which Joan Littlewood staged at. but it is *Stand on Me* which offers a perfect literary snapshot of a particular London world.

**Fings Aint Wot They Used t'Be** is available as a playscript from Samuel French (0573080453 pbk £5.50). The work of Frank Norman is otherwise out of print.

## CHARLES PALLISER
### The Quincunx
Penguin pbk £9.99 0140177620

A number of contemporary writers have felt a need to re-imagine historical London through a re-interpretation and re-working of the great eighteenth and nineteenth century fiction which reflected the city. Probably the most successful of such writers in the last decade has been Peter Carey in *Jack Maggs*, his powerful and imaginative version of *Great Expectations*. Nearly ten years before Carey's book appeared Charles Palliser published **The Quincunx**, a massively erudite facsimile of an early nineteenth century novel. Subtitled **The Inheritance of John Huffam** (Huffam is a knowing reference to one of Dickens's middle names), the book has the same ambition as its models, the same cast of thousands, the same fascinated gaze upon the turmoil, vitality and squalor of the city. Yet *The Quincunx* manages to be more than just pastiche. The intricate plot, with its slowly unwinding revelations of destinies shaped by the past and by the mysterious Quincunx, is intensely gripping and the world Palliser conjures up has a vigour which pastiche alone cannot supply. At the time of first publication Palliser was an academic with a special interest in the kind of fiction he recreated in *The Quincunx*. He has since published further fictions but none have had the impact of his huge, energetic recreation of late Regency London.

# Soho in the Fifties

*by Chris Rodden, Waterstone's Earl's Court*

Soho has always seemed to be the London setting for meetings between the indigenous and the exotic. Etymologically its origins are quintessentially English – 'Soho!' was a hunting call to proclaim the discovery of a hare - yet the dazzling variety of nationalities which have crossed its boundaries has created, over the decades, an area which is both multicultural melting-pot and a haven for the artistic, the musical and the literary. Evidence of the stimulus Soho has offered to writers is not hard to find. From a heartbreaking scene in De Quincey's ***Confessions of an English Opium Eater***, through episodes in ***A Tale of Two Cities***, ***Dr Jekyll and Mr. Hyde*** and ***The Secret Agent***, to encounters in ***The French Lieutenant's Woman*** and Timothy Mo's ***Sour Sweet***, Soho has provided an exotic, cosmopolitan background against which to play out the dramas of everyday life.

Before the Swinging Sixties, England retained a blinkered attitude to diverse sexuality, barely tolerated any divergence from the norm and frowned on lives of excess. In the stifled atmosphere of the fifties, Soho provided the breathing space for like-minded bohemians to meet together and the freedom in which their work could, theoretically, flourish. The pre-eminent chronicler of Soho throughout this era must surely be the recently-departed Daniel Farson who has detailed his love-hate relationship with the area in a number of lively books. ***Soho in the Fifties*** is a wonderfully evocative, if slightly bleary-eyed, recreation of a time when an exceptional collection of characters raged against the grey uniformity of an austere Britain. Farson uses the device of a hypothetical 'Day in Soho' to introduce the reader to the dens he caroused in and the people he encountered. One soon senses the Soho ethos. The ultimate crime is to be boring, yet the ultimate fear seems to be that of constructive accomplishment. There is a Peter Pan mentality in evidence, perhaps encouraged by spending all day in the half light of pubs and clubs, that is assumed to absolve all concerned from any deeper responsibility. Farson's recent autobiography, ***Never a Normal Man***, is a touchingly forthright account in which the author outlines his homosexuality, excessive drinking and dilettantism in an unsparing manner. The book invites the reader's disapproval and yet, paradoxically, the result is that one is drawn more firmly into the dizzy Soho world of booze and badinage. Professions and careers are picked up and lost with the same frequency as the young men and alcohol, the liquid fuel of the fifties Soho-ite, begins to take insidious effect. Yet this is no convert to a staider morality preaching to the populace about past sins and present repentance. Farson remains an unregenerate devotee of Soho pleasures. A life spent photographing, interviewing and socialising with the likes of Coward, Behan, Dali and Francis Bacon could never be humdrum and Farson creates authentic and evocative character sketches of the famous and infamous people he has known.

As the fifties progressed social expenditure began more and more to be dominated by the previously unheard-of phenomenon known as the 'teenager.' *Absolute Beginners*, *City of Spades* and *Mr. Love and Justice*, the trilogy of London novels by Colin Macinnes, all delve into the world of teenagers, crooks, policemen, immigrant blacks and prostitutes. Escalating racial tension is detailed over a period of four months, with Soho, where 'all the things they say happen, do', as the appropriately seedy background for it all. It was his warts-and-all portrayal of the booze-fuelled antics of the area which made Macinnes a literary Hogarth for the fifties, with his characters living, as Francis Wyndham put it, with 'one foot in the ephemeral world of fact, and another in the timeless realm of literary fancy.'

Another perspective on fifties Soho was provided by the young 'genius' Colin Wilson, who shot to overnight fame in 1956 with the publication of the philosophical/literary study *The Outsider*. Many books have followed on issues ranging from the occult to violent crime yet his early work, *Adrift in Soho*, remains one of his best, a successful evocation of the innocence of a newcomer to the Soho scene. The self-consciously intellectual, slightly earnest young existentialist would seem unlikely to thrive amongst the more superficial and devil-may-care denizens of Soho but Wilson's fictional account is as touching and revealing in its own way as Farson's autobiography. Characters drift in and out of the acquaintance of Harry Preston, Wilson's alter ego, as he dips his toes into the waters of bohemianism. Incidents and personalities seem to cross the border of fact and fiction as they bounce back and forth between Farson's and Wilson's accounts, both of which retain their own validity when set against the neon rainbow of night time Soho.

One of those personalities was Jeffrey Bernard whose death in 1997 severed one of the last links with the most legendary period of Soho's past. Perhaps the weekly Spectator columns of Soho's infamous barstool philosopher – 'a suicide note in weekly installments' as it was once described – demonstrated a self-loathing exacerbated by booze, fags, women and a steadfast refusal to work. Perhaps they displayed the skills of a diarist who ventured where others dared not, one whose honesty, humanity and romanticism exposed the hypocrisy of those, great and small, in the wide world beyond the doors of the Coach and Horses. Whatever the arguments, there is no doubt that Jeffrey Bernard's scribblings, as collected in volumes like *Low Life* and *Reach for the Ground*, are endlessly entertaining. Regrets, for health debilitated or life squandered, do not enter into the equation. Bernard's chosen *modus vivendi* necessitated a blithe disregard for trivialities like health, security and money. It may be that this is the final bequest of fifties Soho. Its stars shone bright and faded fast or, like Bernard, they lingered on in an increasingly changed environment, surrounded by a rising tide of commercial exploitation of Soho's past and worn down by the inexorable toll taken of their bodies by their preferred way of life.

# CHRIS PETIT

Known for his talents as a journalist (he was Time Out's film editor from 1973 to 1978) and renegade film maker (*Radio On*, 1979, *An Unsuitable Job for a Woman*, 1981, *Flight to Berlin*, 1983, *Chinese Boxes*, 1984), Chris Petit has also written one of the most interesting London novels since the war. *Robinson* (1993) is a flawed piece of magic, a half-remembered spell that fellow-sorcerer Iain Sinclair described as 'an unmatched (and largely unnoticed) exercise in literary and cinematic archaeology... where lost fiction converges with lost cinema.' Laconically narrated by a nameless character, the novel is set in a hallucinogenic demi-monde of Soho pubs, dingy Cecil Court bookshops and even dingier editing rooms. In its pages lurks a rogue's' gallery of London types, most notably Robinson himself, a sinister figure, part Harry Lime, part Golem. Even the title echoes with portent, evoking images of Celine's *Guignol's Band*, Kafka's *Amerika*, Defoe's *Robinson Crusoe* and, most importantly, Patrick Keiller's film *London*, whose own nameless (and unseen) narrator wanders through the city searching for his lover Robinson, and for the ghostly presences of Defoe and Edgar Allan Poe. Petit's other take on the city is his piece *Newman Passage or J. Maclaren-Ross and the Case of the Vanishing Writers*, an engrossing miniature biography of one of literary London's most fascinating failures (and the basis for the character X. Trapnel in Anthony Powell's *A Dance to the Music of Time*). Part memoir, part critique, this little jewel, like the best of Petit's work, has the power to dazzle.

**Robinson** is currently out of print

## Reading List

*Soho in the Fifties* is, sadly, out of print. *Never a Normal Man* is published by Harper Collins (pbk £8.99 0006383262). Other books by Farson which are worth looking out for are *The Gilded Gutter Life of Francis Bacon* (Vintage pbk £6.99 0099307812), an idiosyncratic but interesting biography of another famous bohemian, and *Sacred Monsters*, a collection of portraits of larger than life characters he knew, including Brendan Behan, Salvador Dali and Trevor Howard. *The Outsider* (pbk £8.99 0575400056) is published by Gollancz and *Adrift in Soho* (pbk £6.99 1874057028) by Brainiac Books. *Low Life* (pbk £7.99 0715624458) and *Reach for the Ground* (pbk £8.99 0715627260) are available from Duckworth. Graham Lord's biography of Jeffrey Bernard, *Just the One* (Headline pbk £7.99 0747260044), is a riveting account of a life easier to read about than live.

## DEREK RAYMOND (1931–1994)

Derek Raymond was a legendary and unique figure among British crime writers and in the pubs and clubs of Soho. He first came to notice as the author of a handful of lowlife London novels written under his real name (Robin Cook), including his first novel, *The Crust on Its Uppers*, published in 1962, which was a vivid portrait of a city full of spivs, bent coppers and crooked public-school men. After a fallow period he started writing crime fiction. With an irony he no doubt found hilarious, he was then asked to change his name after the arrival of another Robin Cook, author of several successful medical thrillers. Perhaps this change of identity was just what he needed because Raymond, under his new name, published three excellent detective novels, all set in the seedy environs of the London underworld and all featuring a nameless policeman known only as the Detective Sergeant, Soho's answer to the Continental Op. Specialising in casual displays of horrific violence, their pages littered with garish characters, the 'Factory' novels, as they're called, are superb, chilling examples of a particularly English hard-boiled crime fiction. Revered in France, where he lived for eighteen years and where his work has been filmed, Raymond returned to London to write *I Was Dora Suarez*, his last novel and a candidate for the title of the most gruesome book ever published. He died in 1994 following the completion of an auto-biographical work *The Hidden Files*. Always a disturbing talent, he deserves to be read by all who admire writers with a fierce personal vision.

**The Crust on its Uppers**
Serpent's Tail pbk £7.99 1852422688

**I was Dora Suarez** is currently unavailable

# NICHOLAS ROYLE

**The Matter of the Heart**
Abacus pbk £6.99 0349110026

Royle, book reviewer for *Time Out* and other newspapers and magazines, anthologist and short-story writer, has published three novels. The latest, **The Matter of the Heart**, is an intriguing and well-executed venture into the same psychogeographical territory as Iain Sinclair and Peter Ackroyd. The book may move to Australia and reach its conclusion on Dartmoor but at its centre, indeed its heart, is a room in a luxury London hotel. The hotel was once a Victorian hospital and the room was once the scene of a deranged nineteenth century surgeon's attempt to pre-empt the medical advances of this century and perform the first heart transplant. The room and its power reach out across the years to entwine the central characters in strange webs of deceit, desire and obsession. Royle places half his story in a very clearly defined, and almost obsessively catalogued, London streetscape, the other half in an Australian outback described with equal precision. His theme of London past and London present interacting within certain parameters is borrowed from other writers but the way in which he teases it out is entirely his own.

# ANDREW SALKEY
## (b. 1928)

One of the earliest of writers to explore West Indian experience in English society, Salkey lived in London for more than twenty years before moving to the States in 1976. He has published children's novels, poetry and travel books and has edited several influential anthologies of Caribbean writing. **Escape to an Autumn Pavement** (1959) is a novel rooted in the time it was written but its portrait of the bleak inhospitability of a bedsitter London is worth revisiting. So too is **Come Home, Malcolm Heartland** (1976), a more formally adventurous novel in which Salkey explores the feelings of a character about to return to Jamaica after years of 'meaningless drift' in London. Although much of the novel reflects the interior monologue of the character the sense of a real London, of the streets of Notting Hill for instance, is strong.

# WILL SELF (b. 1962)

Will Self's career as the bad boy of contemporary fiction reached some kind of apogee in the public's mind during the run-up to the 1997 election when he was accused of snorting heroin in the lavatory of John Major's campaign plane. This, and his subsequent sacking as an Observer journalist, meant that, for a few days, he was a household name in other than literary households. All the notoriety tends to obscure two truths about Self. Firstly, he is not some urban warrior from the wrong side of the tracks but a middle-class, Oxford-educated professional writer, although, admittedly, one who seems to have sampled an interesting cocktail of drugs in his time. Secondly, he is a very good writer, a skilled satirist whom Martin Amis once described as 'thrillingly heartless, terrifyingly brainy.' Like most satirists, a lot of Self's *saeva indignatio* is directed at the corruptions and hypocrisies of urban living. The London Self describes (perhaps unsurprisingly given the quantities of prohibited substances he is alleged to have consumed) is an hallucinatory city. Nothing is as it seems and the fantastic lurks beneath surface reality, ready to emerge at the first opportunity. In his novel *Great Apes* the artist Simon Dykes awakes after a night of dissipation to find that the human city has slipped away from him while he slept. His girlfriend has turned into a chimpanzee and so too have all the other inhabitants of London. In *The North London Book of the Dead,* one of the great short London fictions of recent years, the narrator's mother appears, dead but talking, in the streets of Crouch End. In another story in the same early collection, *The Quantity Theory of Insanity*, those strange Ariels of the city, motorcycle messengers, mystically intuit the traffic flow. Few contemporary writers need the city more for their subject matter than Self. Few seem to doubt the permanence and substantiality of urban life more than he does.

**Great Apes**
Penguin pbk £6.99 0140268006

**The Quantity Theory of Insanity**
Bloomsbury pbk £5.99 074751013X

## SAMUEL SELVON (1923–1994)

Born in Trinidad, Selvon emigrated to Britain in 1950 and, thirty years later, moved to Canada. He began to publish fiction in the early fifties and, throughout the rest of his career, he wrote prolifically as novelist, short-story writer and dramatist. Selvon undoubtedly deserves to be better known than he is and his originality as a writer acknowledged. He wrote convincingly and vividly of his birthplace and of Indian immigrants to the West Indies coming to terms with the ambivalences of their dual heritages. As an immigrant himself to Britain he was also able to turn a sharp eye on the Afro-Caribbean experience in this country and on the burgeoning black community. In his language he showed for, perhaps, the first time, that Caribbean dialect was flexible enough to encompass a range of tones beyond the merely comic. In *The Lonely Londoners* (1956) a form of Trinidadian dialect is used by the narrator, Moses, as he tells the story of the group of immigrants, including the naively optimistic 'Sir' Galahad, to whom he is mentor.

**The Lonely Londoners**
Longman Caribbean Writers
pbk £6.99 0582642647

## ANDREW SINCLAIR

Born in Oxford, educated at Eton, Harvard and Cambridge (where he became a don), Sinclair wrote his first novel *The Breaking of Bumbo* in 1959, an amusing account of a guardsman and his military and amatory exploits. Set in an incisively-depicted 1950s London, the novel follows Bumbo's erratic course as he marches away from the Suez Crisis into the arms of various debutantes, before heading towards alcoholic oblivion and the achievement of a destiny of sorts. Sinclair's best-known work is the epic *Albion Tryptych*, a sweeping and surreal study of British and London history, beginning with the building of Stonehenge in *Gog* (1967), continuing through *Magog* (1972), a political satire on corrupt governments, and concluding with *King Lud* (1988), which opens in pre-war Cambridge and moves to contemporary London. Similar to the psychogeographical looks at the city and English (and Celtic) mythology of his namesake Iain Sinclair, this is a fascinating and ambitious trilogy which deserves to return to print. Among Sinclair's other books are a biography of *Francis Bacon* (1993), *The Facts in the Case of E. A. Poe* (1979), an intriguing mixture of fact and fiction and *War Like a Wasp: The Lost Decade of the Forties* (1989), a study of Fitzrovia during the Second World War.

The novels of Andrew Sinclair are currently unavailable.

# IAIN SINCLAIR

*Mike Paine of Waterstone's in Hampstead looks at Iain Sinclair's twenty-year London Project.*

> *that was the beginning of a London Project… I realised that what I was going to do for some time was cope with the mythology and the matter of London, incorporating diary material from my everyday life and essay-type explanatory and exploratory journeys and so on.*
>
> Iain Sinclair interviewed in Entropy Summer 1997

Discovering the headwaters of that London project, the operations out of a samizdat underworld, would require the services of Sinclair's own characters, a Dryfeld or a Nicholas Lane – 'a great bookman' – to pick over the 'most leprous and flaky dogs' haphazardly stacked in the condemned, secondhand book emporia of urban backstreets. No mere 'scuffler' could do the job. Sinclair's early poetry collections, published by his own Albion Village Press, are elusive enough to figure rarely in even the most exclusive of catalogues from the shops of Museum Street and Pied Bull Yard. Glimpses of what has become an all-conquering vision of the city appear in these verses, the initial stages in the coalescence of an underground dream that, more than twenty years later, has effaced the politer, establishment fictions of London of that time.

After the trial run of **Red Eye** in 1974 (unpublished) the following year saw the first appearance of **Lud Heat**, a chronicle of a period spent as a parks gardener and brewery worker in the East End. Diary entries and poems are interspersed with prose reflections on the works of Stan Brakhage, Brian Catling – a long-standing friend and collaborator – and, most famously, Nicholas Hawksmoor. Sinclair's explication of the latter's churches, their role as reservoirs of psychic power, their construction upon 'lines of force', their charged use of Egyptian symbolism renders Hawksmoor less architect than hierophant. It is an idea that would later prove to be particularly fruitful in Peter Ackroyd's novel *Hawksmoor*. In *Lud Heat* Sinclair is marshalling all forms and forces at his disposal to investigate our relationship with place – the personal and poetic, the documentary, the mythic and historic. This great, invisible confluence flows over a bedrock formed by a metaphoric use of the occult, a tool found in all his fictions from this point on. Likenesses of act or image (the Whitechapel and Ratcliff Highway murders, the recurrent obelisk) reinforce an invisible city of the author's apprehension, a city that seems curiously immanent in its real counterpart. This marked a sea-change both in the literature of the capital and of its author. His future work on London, his psychogeographical investigations stem from it, becoming greater, more open-ended and progressively more complex portrayals of a city.

*Lud Heat* became the first part of a trilogy. Its successor, in 1979, was **Suicide Bridge**, an altogether denser and darker piece. Celtic and Egyptian religions blend with Sixties gangland in an attempt to construct a new mythology for London and the South and East of Britain. The early influence of the Beats wanes to be replaced by that of Blake, of David Jones. One can even detect echoes of the Eliot of *Four Quartets*. In places **Suicide Bridge** contains some of the most powerful passages of Sinclair's early writings and yet, as a whole, it fails to match the success of its predecessor. As a development of themes from **Lud Heat** it resembles, perhaps, an evolutionary dead-end, spectacular and hallucinogenic though it is.

For most of the next decade Sinclair's role was that of a book-dealer specialising in the Beats, noir fiction and those peripheral figures that richly litter his later books, writers who have become the 'reforgotten'. David Gascoyne, Jones, W.S. Graham, Nicholas Moore, Alexander Trocchi, William Hope Hodgson and others populate an unwritten history of British literature, an alternative tradition, if such a word can be used, of which Sinclair feels himself to be a part. His own writing over this period surfaced in poetry collections from his own Hoarse Comerz Press, editions that rarely reached print-runs in double figures. He appeared occasionally before a wider audience in anthologies such as Carcanet's *A Various Art*, as a figure on the periphery of the 'Cambridge School' of poets. A representative sample of the poetry from 1970 to 1989 appeared from Paladin entitled **Flesh Eggs & Scalp Metal**, of which a smaller selection remains available in the tenth **Penguin Modern Poets** anthology.

1987 saw, finally, the end of the trilogy in the form of Sinclair's first novel, **White Chappell Scarlet Tracings**. A work of extraordinary vitality, it brought the poetry, the vision of his earlier work together with a supple, noirish prose style. The tale of Jack the Ripper unfolds alongside a modern story of those desperate and heroic, thinly-fictionalised book dealers, Dryfeld and Nicholas Lane. There is a breathtaking assurance to this beautifully written novel, which was impeccably published by Mike Goldmark's eponymous imprint.

The critical success of White Chappell was followed by what is undoubtedly his greatest work to date, **Downriver**. Ostensibly a tale of the Thames, it draws the reader into an unparalleled depiction of London. Of twentieth century literary realisations of the city in the English language, only the Dublin of *Ulysses* clearly surpasses it. Multitudes are contained within it: a city of the living and of the dead, Londons past, present and possible. *Downriver* is the antithesis of neat, English fiction. It is an out-of-control sensory overload in which Victorian boatmen, aboriginal cricketers, nuclear-waste train drivers, sixties' casualties, murderers, dancers, television directors, all have roles to play. As Sinclair tellingly reveals, 'these inventions are versions of my own history.

After such an ecstatic, revelatory novel, *Radon Daughters* suffers by proximity. The grail-like search for a manuscript purporting to be a sequel to William Hope Hodgson's *The House on the Borderlands* is at the heart of the novel, a search pursued by Todd Sileen, an X-ray addict and police informer 'living in a spectacularly wasted East London borough.' The dark imagination that fills the book captures something of Hodgson's profoundly unsettling work. *Lights Out for the Territory* – a series of excursions in the Secret History of London – proved to be a very different work. Developed mainly from shorter pieces that had appeared in the *London Review of Books*, it shows Sinclair at his most open, displaying his enormous knowledge of the city, commenting wryly and perceptively on the capital and its culture. It is in some ways a non-fiction companion piece to *Downriver*, without the latter's feverishness. The Krays, the East End, London's current crop of artists and writers of underground tendencies, the old, 'reforgotten writers', Lord Archer, Rachel Whiteread's *House* are all there in a vastly entertaining read which also proved a commercial success.

With the publication of *Slow Chocolate Autopsy*, a combination of short stories and graphic works done in collaboration with the artist Dave McKean, it seemed as if Sinclair's grand London endeavour was reaching an end. His much-anticipated new novel, *Landor's Tower*, appears some distance from publication and looks likely to be set in the West Country and Wales. Yet Sinclair is, surely, unlikely to abandon his adopted city for long. Outside of literature his recent exhibition at the Jago Gallery and his film with Chris Petit, *The Falconer*, add to his urban lore, as, in their own way, do his monthly appearances under his own name as a Victorian occult detective in an American comic strip written by Michael Moorcock. The greatest literatures of London build among a city of the common imagination, uncovering new historic discourses and subsuming others. Sinclair's contributions are the richest of our era.

**Lud Heat**
Granta 1862072078

**White Chappell, Scarlet Tracings**
Granta 186207206X

**Downriver**
Vintage pbk £5.99 0099576414

**Radon Daughters**
Granta 1862072086

**Lights Out for the Territory**
Granta 186207092X

**Slow Chocolate Autopsy**
Phoenix 0753801523

**Significant Wreckage**
Words Press 1871299004

**The Ebbing of the Kraft**
Equipage 1900968509

Other important Sinclair works such as **The Shamanism of Intent**, **Flesh Eggs and Scalp Metal** and **The Kodak Mantra Diaries** are currently out of print.

# Excavating the Unburied: Some London Writers

*by Iain Sinclair*

Buildings vanish. Whole blocks can disappear. Sly Street, a minor tributary off the east side of Cannon Street Road, on my favourite walk down through Whitechapel towards the river, was converted to rubble in the space between two visits. I felt responsible. The name was deleted from the map. Had it ever been there in anything beyond my imagination? I hoped that its obscurity, even in a period of the most breathtakingly optimistic development scams, was inviolate: which is why I chose the site for a house that existed, out of time and between worlds, in my novel *Radon Daughters*. I was wrong.

Paul Smith (the impresario of *King Mob/Disobey*) tried, without success, to buy the Sly Street nameplate for his library. The city as a great metal book filled with references to forgotten novels. A library that could be hung around the walls like a Waterstone's window display. A London of signs and hints and mysterious journeys. Men who become streets who become books. Real addresses can have their literary stock gazumped: London Fields being upgraded from John Milne's proletarian fable of 1983, set where it belonged in E8, to Martin Amis's customised bestiary of 1989, which wasn't. Then there are fictional addresses that should be found a place in any true mapping of the city: gravy-coloured afternoons fighting a migraine in Patrick Hamilton's *Hangover Square* (1941) or, early evenings, collar turned up, shades on, to avoid being recognised by any of *The Tenants of Dirt Street* (1971), as depicted by Robin Cook. A last of last drinks at Gerald Kersh's *Fowler's End* (1957).

But it's not just the streets that can be banished into the theatre of memory; books and the people who write them are doomed to go the same way. If fame is oblivion postponed, there is also the privileged anonymity of the antiquarian bookdealer's catalogue. A poignant fate in which a book's value (its purchase price) climbs vertiginously in relation to its occulted status. (If the plebs haven't heard of you, you must be hot). Writers can be reinvented, their scandalous lives talked up, to create a market for a couple of wearied thrillers knocked off to pay the rent on a coldwater burrow. One collector, expressing mild interest, can send the stock of some vanished journeyman soaring. A decent, lively, book-a-year man, like John Lodwick, is suddenly – for about half a dozen people – flavour of the month. If he can also be tagged a 'London novelist', so much the better. That increases the catchment area. And Lodwick's book, *Peal of Ordnance* (1947), does have a London setting: the newsreel backdrop – grey faces, hats at all times – to a postwar thriller. Austerity plus Neo-Romanticism. Like Carol Reed's Belfast or Vienna. A traumatised fisherman who blows up the Albert Memorial and wrecks a BBC studio. The book exploits a certain amount of Soho picaresque and fits into a genre of London fiction that sees the city as labyrinth.

The London novelists I admire shift between dystopian visions of the city as an enclosed system, complex and treacherous, and open-field narratives that try to invent ways of escaping the pull of this gravitational centre. Drift or fissure. The treadmill of Gerald Kersh's **Night and the City** (1938) or the Mass-Observationist travelling shots of David Gascoyne's **Opening Day** (1933). Harry Fabian, the speedy grifter of *Night and the City*, 'saw London as a kind of Inferno – a series of concentric circles with Piccadilly Circus as the ultimate centre.' By his futile pursuit of the ultimate con that will relieve the pressure, translate him to domesticity and the suburbs, he drives himself deeper and deeper into the dark heart of things.

*Opening Day*, published when he was seventeen, was the poet David Gascoyne's only novel. It's a book of the riverine suburbs, of Twickenham. (Kersh, curiously, was born in the adjacent manor of Teddington). *Opening Day* is a catalogue of movement, skillfully annotated drifts through the reverie of London's outer limits, and a diary of petty frustrations: a writer and a potential bohemian trapped within the gothic prison that is the middle-class home. Gascoyne was a premature European. He understood that the most memorable takes on London, particularly the suburbs had been achieved by exiles, aliens passing through. 'Dostoevsky, Rimbaud and Verlaine,' he wrote in his journals, 'Strindberg, Alain-Fournier – they were all in London at one time or another... and all have left some sort of record of their impressions, which are naturally strange, only half-recognisable, like a dream of a place one knows. I particularly like Alain-Fournier's appreciation of the suburban villas of Chiswick and Kew, and of the atmosphere of London summer Sunday afternoons at the beginning of the century, and his saying that of all towns, he would prefer London to be unhappy in.'

Louis-Ferdinand Céline was a master, with his deranged hyper-energised prose, of the twin modes, drift and fissure. Helter-skelter bus trips to the honkytonk of the Piccadilly and Soho netherworlds, dream quests through smoky De Quincey nocturnes, then the slow convalescence of a fantastic Willesden. 'Now that we were on our way, escaping from that Willesden prison, I felt perky... I shouted out to the passersby... in a burst of joy.' There are no London novels I relish more than **Guignol's Band** (1954) in its lurid pink dustwrapper and **London Bridge** with its moody riverscape and yellow lettering.

But manic possession doesn't only occur at the centre. It's possible to argue a case for J. G. Ballard's **Crash** (1973), the most pathological of his books, as a London novel. Ballard can be seen operating a poetic that shares a base with

Gascoyne in surrealism. But he embraces the weirdness at the rim of things, where the heat of the city gives way to a landscape of alienation. 'Rather than fearing alienation,' Ballard told me, 'people should embrace it. It may be more interesting. That's always been the message of my fiction.'

Nicholas Royle in *Counterparts* (1993) and *The Matter of the Heart* (1997) takes on, with a necessary sense of pain and tenderness, Ballardian alienation. Specific areas of London have their own peculiar narratives. An unwary narrator can be swallowed by stepping into the wrong story.

Probably the most implicated successor to the *Crash* template was Christopher Petit's 1993 Soho novel, *Robinson. Robinson* made the difficult transition from non-fiction to fiction, from scholarly study (detached) to the momentum of a night-marish pseudo-autobiography from which there was no escape. Ghostly avatars, undying, from the literature of the reforgotten copulated with their shadowy fetches. Ballard taught Petit that the list, the weather chart, the polaroid and the questionnaire, can stand in for all the ethical apparatus of the over-hyped novel of manners and society.

But two of my favourite London novels made a fruitful treaty with their Victorian and Edwardian ancestors. Angela Carter's *Wise Children* (1991) celebrates the city through character, not through a taxonomy of place: gin-soaked madeleines of dusty Brixton parlours, humour, bloody-mindedness and an improper relish for human mess. Michael Moorcock's *Mother London* (1988) seemed to be the last of its kind, magnificent but somehow redundant. Too true to itself to be appreciated. It's a great-hearted monument of a book, in which the author takes on the damaged dreaming of the city, its subterranea and its suburban foothills. The narrator divides the story, his own and London's, between the living and the dead, male and female, the river and our collective memories of fire and blitz. For me, this book is the best of all guides to London fiction, steering us through branching narrative streams with a prescient sense of all the previous hacks and temporary geniuses, Gerald Kersh and Jack Trevor Story, Pett Ridge and Arthur Morrison, Conrad and Machen, Dickens and De Quincey. Start there and grow your own London like a viral culture.

Iain Sinclair is the author of *Downriver, Radon Daughters* and *Lights Out for the Territory,* among other works.

## MURIEL SPARK (b. 1918)

Novelist, short-story writer and biographer, Muriel Spark is one of the post-war era's most respected literary figures. She has the elegance and wit of Jane Austen and, at her best, the satirical bite of Evelyn Waugh, who was a vocal supporter of her early work. She is best known as the author of the Edinburgh-based *The Prime of Miss Jean Brodie* (1961) which may come to stand as the 'crème de la crème' of her fictional achievement. Two of her London fictions are, perhaps, less well known but are immaculate examples of fine prose and resonant documents of city-dwelling in the fifties. *A Far Cry from Kensington* (1988) is written as the memoir of the self-styled 'Mrs Hawkins' who reflects on her life in the mid-fifties as both resident of a shabby-genteel boarding-house in South Kensington and editor with various small publishers. She casts an affectionate eye on the oddball inhabitants of 14 Church End Villas (of whom Wanda Podolak, the hysterical, preyed-upon Polish dressmaker is the best-realised) and coolly shares her insights into the eccentrically run houses of Ullswater and York and Mackintosh and Tooley. The book is redolent with period detail – A-line dresses, radionics (a peculiar cure-treatment of the time), the Third Programme, pennies and shillings for the gas meter – and noisy with literary politics. Hector Bartlett, 'pisseur de copie' or urinator of hack journalism is consistently despised by Mrs Hawkins and probably stands for a breed of literary fake that his creator has no time for herself.

One of the best passages in the novel is when Mrs Hawkins, between editorial jobs, talks of days spent taking bus rides across London to its forgotten suburbs – 'Stanmore, Edgware, Bushey, Chingford, Romford, Harrow, Wanstead, Dagenham, Barking'. We are given a picture of a London still stricken by the after effects of war, its reconstruction as the city it now is not yet begun:

> *There were few streets intact although the war had been over ten years. Victorian houses, shops, churches, were separated by large areas of bomb-gap. The rubble had been cleared away, but strange grasses and wild herbs had sprung up where the war-demolished houses had been. While it was still light I rode past the docks and the railway sidings, and the dark pubs not yet open...*

Peckham is an entirely different milieu to SW7 but Spark, in an earlier work, displays an equal and entirely unself-conscious concern for period accuracy. Set in the late fifties *The Ballad of Peckham Rye* (1960) depicts a claustrophobic, village world of pubs, coffee bars and dance-halls. It is peopled largely by the employees of Meadows, Meade and Grindley, a local firm infiltrated by the devilish figure of Dougal Douglas, who charms his way into the parochial community before making a hasty exit once his anarchic spell has caused mayhem and murder.

More particular in its locale than *A Far Cry from Kensington* – the action rarely strays from Peckham – *The Ballad of Peckham Rye* is a more substantial work, not simply a snapshot of a lost era but a comment on marginalised lives and the damage that can occur when the grip on them is forced loose. Spark's sympathies are neither with the destructive outsider nor with the innocent Peckhamites whose 'inner lives' Dougal 'researches' so ruthlessly. Rather she maps out a narrow terrain and allows her characters to speak and act within it as if their small-town lives depended on never leaving. Her eye for detail is matched by her knowledge of Peckham's geography and history ('Mendelssohn wrote his Spring Song in Ruskin Park. Ruskin lived on Denmark Hill. Mrs Fitzherbert lived in Camberwell Grove. Boadicea committed suicide on Peckham Rye, probably where the bowling green is now, I should imagine.') Her ear for dialogue recalls Patrick Hamilton's expertise as a chronicler of saloon-bar speak:

> *"Hullo, Trevor,"* Dixie said.
> *"Hi, Dixie,"* Trevor replied severely.
> *"Hi,"* Collie Gould said.
> *Beauty, who was on her fourth martini, bowed graciously, and had some difficulty in regaining her upright posture.*
> *The barmaid said, "Are you ordering, sir?"*
> *Trevor said over his shoulder, "Two pints of bitter".*
> *He lit a cigarette and blew out the smoke very very slowly.*
> *"Trev,"* Collie said in a low voice, *"Trev, don't muck it up."*
> *"I'm being patient,"* Trevor said through half-closed lips.
> *"I'm being very very patient… "*

*The Ballad of Peckham Rye* is a far cry from the Peckham popularly associated with John Sullivan's *Only Fools and Horses* but, as a dark situation comedy of manners, it manages both to immortalise and transcend the borough it takes for its inspiration.

**Simon Roberts** *Waterstone's, Notting Hill Gate*

**The Ballad of Peckham Rye**
Penguin pbk £5.99 014001909X

**A Far Cry from Kensington**
Penguin pbk £5.99 0140108742

# BARBARA VINE

Ruth Rendell is known for her Inspector Wexford detective
novels, set in the country town of Kingsmarkham, although
this prolific author has also written of crime and mystery in
the city. However it is in some of the novels published under
her pseudonym of Barbara Vine that she has produced her
most resonant investigations of the darkness hidden beneath
the surface of London life. *Asta's Book* mingles past with
present in its story of a woman unearthing the truth about her
grandmother, a turn of the century emigrant from Denmark
to London, and her diaries which may hold the key to a long-
forgotten murder. In *The House of Stairs* the narrative again
moves between the present, in which a middle-aged writer
regains contact with an old friend, and the past (in this book,
the late sixties and early seventies), in which the reasons why
the two have lost contact are slowly revealed. The book's
portraits of the waifs, outcasts and con-artists of Swinging
London who gather in the house of the title and of the
beautiful, amoral egotist who is one of the central characters
are vivid and compelling. Most striking of all Barbara Vine's
London fiction is *King Solomon's Carpet*, described by one critic
as 'by far the most sustained and serious attempt to probe the
mysteries of the London underground rail network and put
them to artistic use.' The central character Jarvis lives in a
strange crumbling house with a view of the Jubilee Line,
nursing his obsession with the Tube and its secrets, its hidden
tunnels and its deserted stations. The house, once a school,
he lets out to a collection of misfits drawn together by their
connections with the Tube. The sense of mystery and dread that
we all feel sometimes in the Tube is brilliantly evoked in a novel
that weaves together its characters' lives and destinies to create
a very particular, and very chilling, vision of the city.

**Asta's Book**
Penguin pbk £6.99 0140176616

**The House of Stairs**
Penguin pbk £6.99 0140114467

**King Solomon's Carpet**
Penguin pbk £6.99 0140156917

# PAUL WEST

### The Women of Whitechapel

Published in 1991, *The Women of Whitechapel* novel remains American author West's finest book, a new and entirely convincing addition to the overcrowded field of Jack the Ripper narratives, both fact and fiction. Ranging from the Royal family and the aristocracy to the prostitutes and drunks of the poverty-infested East End, West unfolds his tale with chilling precision. From his cast of thousands, he focuses on two central characters – the painter Walter Sickert and his friend 'Eddy'. Eddy is Prince Albert Victor Christian Edward, the heir to the throne, who possesses an honorary degree from Cambridge but can neither read nor write, who is as happy in the male brothel at Cleveland Street as he is in the arms of Sickert's model Annie Crook, a Catholic shopgirl whom he impregnates. Once news of the pregnancy leaks out, a conspiracy emerges to silence those aware of it. After the royal bastard is born, the sinister surgeon William Withey Gull lobotomises Annie and, with the reluctant help of Sickert, hunts down her friend, streetwalker Marie Kelly, who shares her secret. Skillfully wielding his scalpel, Gull haunts the sordid streets of Whitechapel, butchering Kelly's sisters of the night, in his attempt to erase the drunken and garrulous whore. As a retelling of the Ripper myth (in his brief introduction, West notes that, although he based the novel on facts, he 'based it on few enough of them, having discovered that one Ripper specialist's fact is another's fiction') this is a powerful and original novel and a protean piece of London fiction.

**The Women of Whitechapel** is currently unavailable.

## NIGEL WILLIAMS

Just as the Grossmiths immortalised Charles Pooter, anxious suburbanite of eighteen nineties Holloway, so Nigel Williams has immortalised Henry Farr, anxious suburbanite of nineteen nineties Wimbledon. Farr first appeared in *The Wimbledon Poisoner*, a man driven to the brink of doing away with his wife whose wildly unsuccessful attempts to dispose of her led him further into disaster. He has since also appeared in a collection of short stories, *Scenes From a Poisoner's Life,* an ordinary suburban male (despite nearly poisoning his wife), trying to make his way as best he can through a world that seems set on thwarting and humiliating him. Williams, who is often described as Britain's best comic novelist, has also established Wimbledon even more firmly on the literary map by publishing two more novels set in the neighbourhood, *East of Wimbledon* and *They Came From SW19.*

**East of Wimbledon**
Faber pbk £5.99 0571171516

**Scenes From a Poisoner's Life**
Faber pbk £5.99 0571174981

**They Came from SW19**
Faber pbk £5.99 0571168361

**The Wimbledon Poisoner**
Faber pbk £5.99 0571161316

## ANGUS WILSON
### (1913–1991)

After education at Westminster and Oxford, Angus Wilson worked at the Foreign Office and the British Museum before making a second career as novelist and university lecturer. His novels include *Anglo-Saxon Attitudes*, *The Old Men at the Zoo,* a strange fable of England in the near-future, and *No Laughin Matter*, a large and ambitious saga of a family which spans some fifty years. However it was as a short-story writer that he first made his name and it is in the short stories, notably those collected in his first book *The Wrong Set* (1949), that he pinpointed, and elegantly satirised, a particular class of Londoner, caught in a particula environment at a particular moment in history. His upper-middle class characters, living ir Kensington and Knightsbridge, cling to their gentility and their snobbery amid the changes being wrought in the social make-up of the city.

**The Collected Stories of Angus Wilson**
Penguin pbk £8.99 0140159649

## Anthologies

*Dominic Kennerk of Waterstone's makes a selection of anthologies which reflect the diversity of the capital.*

London is many things to many people, making the diversity inherent in an anthology the perfect means of capturing the variety of experience the capital offers. An excellent illustration of this is Paul Bailey's *Oxford Book of London* (Oxford UP £7.99 0192832441) which begins with the 12th century monk, William Fitzstephen, eulogising the 'throne of the English Kingdom' and ends with Angela Carter lamenting the protean nature of a city where a Brief Encounter style farewell in the 1990s, would take place in '… a bloody nicker shop.' Between these two disparate scenes Bailey has used prose, poetry, memoirs and journalism to illustrate eight centuries of change. He provides a 'quotidian history', an account of the everyday – an under-ground journey, a walk by the Thames, a trip to a football match – which is as fascinating and insightful as any study of London through the great events of the ages.

   Written to mark the 25th anniversary of London's essential living guide *The Time Out Book of London Short Stories* (Edited Maria Lexton Penguin £6.99 0140230858) reflects the multifariousness of urban living. Where else could authors such as Clive Barker, Hilary Mantel and Ronan Bennett rub shoulders but in this provocative collection of tales from the bright and dark sides of the metropolis. Stories of sex-changing couples, gangland murders, cultists in the suburbs and lonely suicides are played out by the angst-ridden characters that populate the pages of an intense collection. Oscar Zarate's collection of extreme and perverse tales, *It's Dark In London* (Edited Alan Moore Serpent's Tail £9.99 1852425356), features some of today's most distinctive graphic illustrators combining with several fine writers to produce a series of short graphic stories immersed in the seedy and sinister aspects of the city. The dramatic combinations of Christopher Petit and Gary Marshall, Iain Sinclair and Dave McKean and Warren Pleece with Neil Gaiman generate a series of unsettling experiences in which the striking, cinematic imagery of the graphic novel style and the offbeat themes create disturbing and challenging narratives. More dark tales unfold in *London Noir* (Edited Maxim Jakubowski Serpent's Tail £8.99 1852423080), an excellent collection of crime stories, in which the city appears closer to the menacing streets of New York and L. A. than to any notion of London as a city of history, heritage and grand monuments. Maxim Jakubowski, experienced editor and owner of London's Murder One bookshop, has assembled fifteen stories from contemporary crime writers – Liza Cody, Mark Timlin, Christopher Fowler and many others – who imbue the London streets with the kind of gritty realism often found in the best of American crime fiction.

Prolific writer and anthologist A.N. Wilson takes a more conservative approach in *The Faber Book of London* (Edited A.N. Wilson Faber £12.99 0571171745), in which he has gathered over two hundred authors and arranged excerpts from their works in themed chapters. We have the London of great events in 'London at War' and 'Royal London' and a more intimate London in chapters entitled 'Love' and 'Hating It', providing a useful shortcut to pieces to suit the many different moods which the city inspires.